The Spirit and the Lake of Fire

The Spirit and the Lake of Fire

Pneumatology and Judgment

Rustin Umstattd

Foreword by Malcolm B. Yarnell III

WIPF & STOCK · Eugene, Oregon

THE SPIRIT AND THE LAKE OF FIRE
Pneumatology and Judgment

Wipf & Stock
An Imprint of Wipf and Stock Publishers
199 W. 8th Ave., Suite 3
Eugene, OR 97401

www.wipfandstock.com

PAPERBACK ISBN: 978-1-5326-1542-9
HARDCOVER ISBN: 978-1-5326-1544-3
EBOOK ISBN: 978-1-5326-1543-6

Manufactured in the U.S.A.   MAY 22, 2017

Contents

CONTENTS

Foreword

Comfort and Discomfort

WAIT! SURELY NOT! HAS the evangelical theological academy finally lost its mind with the publication of the innovative thesis of Rustin Umstattd? Is it really true that the Holy Spirit, "the Comforter" of the Gospel of John, is also the Discomforter? Can we say that the One who "sheds abroad the love of God in human hearts" is also the One who applies the condemnation of God? Is it theologically appropriate to assert that the Holy Spirit is the Executor, expending the wrath of the Father against his Son at the cross?

Umstattd, a respected professor of systematic theology at one of the largest evangelical seminaries in the world, originally discerned that an orthodox doctrine of the Trinity requires not only that the Holy Spirit must fully participate in the creative and redemptive work of the Trinity, but also in the Trinity's work of judgment. Bringing that supposition to the test of Scripture, he discovered the presence of a major lacuna in the discipline of systematic theology vis-à-vis the biblical witness. Through judicious exegesis, he highlights the ways that Scripture employs the symbols of "fire" and "breath" as well as the "finger," "hand," and "arm" of God. He then shows how the God who loves is the same God who punishes. Finally, he argues that a Trinitarian rather than Binitarian approach to the atonement is required.

This is a most enthralling book that will challenge theologians to consider revising long-established ways of thought. As a result, it will bring both discomfort and comfort. On the one hand, Umstattd's thesis will disconcert those who hold to the modern attitude that seeks to separate God, especially the Holy Spirit, from the work of applying divine wrath. On the other hand, it will encourage us not to allow cozy tradition or current culture to establish Christian teaching. With Umstattd as our teacher, we must learn to submit our systematic theology yet again to the authority of the biblical text. And there, in the midst of such respectful exposition of Scripture, we will find the greatest comfort of all, the presence of the living God who is Father, Son, and Holy Spirit as we encounter him in both love and judgment.

Umstattd's book comes with my highest recommendation due to its innovative thesis, its engaging style, and especially its pristine biblical orthodoxy.

Malcolm B. Yarnell III
Research Professor of Systematic Theology
Southwestern Baptist Theological Seminary
Fort Worth, Texas

Introduction

IN THE LAST ONE hundred years, the Holy Spirit received a much-needed revival in interest from theologians who delineated his role in such diverse areas as salvation, sanctification, ecology, ecclesiology, eschatology, and ethics. There is, however, a widely neglected aspect of the Spirit's work: judgment. Is this neglect due to a lack of interest in the doctrine of judgment, or perhaps to an unwillingness to discuss and debate the Spirit's condemnatorial work? While there has been an increased interest in final judgment among evangelicals recently, this interest has revolved around the narrow issues of annihilationism and universalism. There has not been a widespread discussion about the nature of God's judgment under either category; instead, both issues have focused their attention on the duration of punishment.

In conjunction with a lack of interest in the doctrine of judgment, many people picture the Spirit as the Comforter, with "comforter" conjuring up images of being reassured during hard times or consoled during distress. Unfortunately, the original meaning of the word comforter has been lost. The translation of *Paraclete* as Comforter derives originally from Wycliffe and was subsequently adopted by the KJV, thus bringing it into the use we see today. The meaning of comforter in the time of Wycliffe and King James, however, does not align well with the modern usage of the term. Comforter for most people denotes someone or something that makes the best out of a difficult situation or that offers consolation. A comforter is a warm blanket on a cold night used to make someone feel better. The derivation of the word comforter from its Latin root would imply someone who is strong (*forte*) with (*con*) someone.[1] The use of the word comforter to describe the Holy Spirit has contributed greatly to a perception of the Spirit as being uninvolved in the harsher aspects of God's nature. The misconception of the Holy Spirit as a security blanket needs correction, for while the Spirit most definitely offers security and comfort he also manifests God's awesome presence; a presence that caused Israel to tremble in fear at the base of Mount Sinai and Isaiah to tremble at the knowledge of his own sinfulness.

The Spirit is God's empowering presence within creation and his work is the "expression and execution of what the three of them (Father, Son, and Holy Spirit) have planned together."[2] Charles Hodge offers a telling description of the Spirit's work when he writes, "The Spirit is the executive of the Godhead. Whatever God does, He does by the Spirit."[3] Similarly, Wayne Grudem posits, "The work of the Holy Spirit is to manifest the active presence of God in the world, and especially in the church."[4] Stanley Grenz and Graham Cole adopt the Augustinian postulate that the Spirit is the reciprocal love between the Father and the Son, and from this postulate of the immanent Trinity, Grenz argues he is "the power of God at work in the world bringing to completion the divine program."[5] All of these theologians share the common deficiency of ascribing the actualizing of God's work to the Spirit, while failing to follow through consistently on this assertion by explicating his role in judgment.

Grenz comes close when he argues that hell is the "dark side" of God's love, but he never makes the explicit statement that the unredeemed encounter the "dark side" of God's love, his wrath, in the Spirit. He writes, "Those who reject God's reconciling love in this life must know that love as wrath in eternity."[6] He is, however, eager to relate that "eschatological judgment is the Spirit's radical perfecting of the community we now share."[7] The depersonalizing of God's love in reference to wrath is incompatible with the personalizing of his love in the Spirit regarding eschatological glorification.

1. Morris, *Gospel According to John*, 587.

2. Erickson, *Christian Theology*; Fee, *God's Empowering Presence*.

3. Hodge, *Systematic Theology*, 1:529.

4. Grudem, *Systematic Theology*, 634.

5. Grenz, *Theology for the Community of God*, 488; Cole, *He Who Gives Life*, 74–75.

6. Grenz, *Theology for the Community of God*, 839.

7. Ibid., 845.

As unfamiliar as it might be, we should neither depersonalize, nor neglect the "dark side" of the Spirit.

While it is widely accepted that the Holy Spirit actualizes the redemptive work of the Father through the Son, as Grenz and others have asserted, this acceptance does not readily extend to the Spirit's actualization of the Son's role as creation's judge. The Father has given all judgment to the Son, but an adequate delineation of the Spirit's work in relationship to the Son's role as judge, both presently and eschatologically, still needs to be offered.

Second Peter 3:10–13 relates that there is coming a day when God will judge both the living and the dead, a day that will test with fire the secrets of people's lives. In Noah's day, God destroyed the world with water, and likewise the world is currently awaiting its final judgment by fire. Throughout the Bible, fire serves as a symbol for both God's judgment and his presence. The pillar of cloud and fire revealed the glory of God to the ancient Israelites during their desert wanderings, serving many of the same functions as God's Spirit.[8] Fire is but one symbol that the Bible uses to describe both God's judgment and the Holy Spirit. Additionally, God's breath and his finger serve as images for the Spirit, with both also functioning as symbols for judgment. Since the Bible uses many of the same symbols for both the Holy Spirit and judgment, and furthermore, since the Spirit is the executor of the Godhead, the question arises, what role does the Spirit undertake in judgment?[9]

Some theologians have attempted to elucidate the Spirit's role in judgment; however, it is interesting to note that the ones who have mentioned this aspect of the Spirit's work tend to have universalistic leanings. Wolfhart Pannenberg argues the Spirit's role at the Final Judgment will involve both glorification and condemnation. The Spirit is not only the source of salvation, but also the "organ of judgment."[10] While Pannenberg only briefly mentions the negative aspect of the Spirit's judgment, he nevertheless

8. "Much like the activity of the *ruach*, the pillar serves to guide, protect, reveal, and even judge people to fulfill the work of Yahweh." Hildebrandt, *Old Testament Theology*, 72–76.

9. The term "executor" relates to one who actualizes the will of another. In the case of the Holy Spirit, he carries out and actualizes to creation the will of the Father given to the Son. The analogy of executor breaks down, as all analogies do in relation to God, due to God's triunity. The union of the three allows for one will, but for each person of the Trinity to have particular works for which he is the executor. Swete, *Holy Spirit in the New Testament*, 293–94.

10. Pannenberg, *Systematic Theology*, 3:622–26.

mentions it, and one reason for this might be his reluctance to rule out a universal salvation. He does not endorse universalism, owing to the multitude of biblical texts that speak against it, but he does hold out hope for universal redemption. This outlook might allow him to present the negative aspect of the Spirit's judgment in that he is not fully convinced the Spirit will in fact judge in this manner.

Jürgen Moltmann offers a scant two pages on the Spirit's role in judgment in *The Spirit of Life*. While his understanding of the Spirit is somewhat depersonalized and tends toward panentheism, he contends the Spirit's presence in the world accounts for the pain felt by those wronged, the guilty conscience of those who commit wrong, and in world history by the instability of unjust systems. The Spirit will not ultimately allow evil to succeed. The godless know no peace, and the reason for this is that the Spirit confronts them in their godlessness.[11]

For Norman Pittenger, the Spirit works in the world to conform humanity to the pattern of God. In this work, the Holy Spirit is operative in any group or individual who achieves truth, peace, and understanding. Pittenger nevertheless recognizes that human freedom entails some people choosing to use their freedom to bring harm to others. When this is the case, the "Spirit who normally works only in gentleness, persuasion, and mercy, may work in judgment."[12] The judgment envisioned is not condemnatory, but purifying, for the Spirit will not break people, but will bend them to God's will.

It is unfortunate that only those theologians who conceive of judgment in a purifying sense have ventured to elucidate the Spirit's work in judgment. This unwillingness on the part of conservative evangelical theologians to present the Spirit's work in judgment is perhaps predicated upon an unwillingness to ascribe God's condemnatorial work to the Spirit. It is clear there is a need to present the Spirit's role in judgment, which is the goal of this book.

There has been extensive research done on both the doctrines of the Holy Spirit and judgment, but not many works address the interconnection between the two, especially as regards condemnatory judgment. This work will focus its attention upon an evangelical orthodox understanding of both the Holy Spirit and judgment as a confining constraint upon research that could potentially become overwhelming. Additionally, I will highlight

11. Moltmann, *Spirit of Life*, 142–43.
12. Pittenger, *Holy Spirit*, 70.

several contemporary evangelical theologians who have produced major systematic works in an effort to demonstrate the logical necessity of the Spirit's role in judgment, even though they do not make the connection between the Spirit and judgment in their respective works.

As already mentioned, numerous theologians have portrayed the Holy Spirit as the executor of the Godhead. This portrayal will serve as a springboard from which to launch and carry their observations to their logical conclusion as regards the Spirit's work in judgment. While the Holy Spirit has enjoyed an upswing in interest in the last century, the doctrine of judgment has not fared quite as well.[13] Even though in this day judgment is a culturally taboo subject, we do a disservice to God's revelation by not addressing the issue. I will join the neglected doctrine of judgment with one of the currently popular doctrine of the Spirit in order to demonstrate the vital and inseparable link between them. The combination will establish the validity of God's judgment while at the same time expanding understanding of the Holy Spirit.

In order to explicate the Spirit's role in judgment, it will first be necessary to define judgment. With that in mind, the first chapter will attempt to make such a definition by establishing an understanding of the nature of judgment as presented in the Bible. This will involve both exegetical work on specific passages, as well as historical work to determine the prevailing concept of judgment within the biblical time frame. God subsumes to himself all the powers of sovereignty, in that the laws by which God judges humanity have been established by him. God also actively seeks out injustice in order to bring righteousness, with his seeking to establish justice on the earth of necessity involving the condemnation of those who act unjustly.

While God is a God of judgment, his judgment is predicated upon his love for creation. God is not dispassionate in his judgment, but quite the opposite; he is intimately involved with his creation, and his love for his creation causes the Father to send the Son in the power of the Spirit to make atonement for humanity's sins. God's love and his holiness are not at war in his nature, but are inseparably connected. His love will not allow him to abandon his creation to its rightful punishment, but his holiness will not allow him to overlook humanity's rebellion. Therefore, God offers himself as the atoning sacrifice and in so doing maintains the integrity of

---

13. Martin, *Last Judgment.*

both his love and his holiness. God is just and the justifier of those who call on his Son's name.[14]

Having established an understanding of judgment in the first chapter, I will give a theological and biblical grounding for the Holy Spirit's role in judgment in chapter 2. I will first present the necessity of the Spirit's work in judgment from within the framework of Trinitarian theology. I will then present those passages treating the Holy Spirit and judgment with the intent of biblically grounding the Spirit's role in judgment. With the presupposition in place that the New Testament unfolds and explicates the Old Testament, an investigation will be made into those passages in the Old Testament that relate the Holy Spirit to judgment. This will primarily involve work in the book of Isaiah. Once the work in the Old Testament is complete, I will unpack several passages in the New Testament.

In chapters 3–6 I will offer four motifs related to judgment and the Spirit. The four motifs are not the only ones under which the Bible presents God's judgment, but I chose them because of their intimate connection with the Holy Spirit. The first motif to be addressed is fire. Fire is one of the major judgmental motifs throughout the Bible, and it will be shown that fire is both purifying and destructive. It is both beneficial and harmful to humanity, depending upon a person's relationship to it. It will be shown that the Spirit functions in the same manner in judgment as the symbol of fire.

The second motif of judgment is God's breath. Like fire, the Bible presents God's breath both as bringing to life and as destructive. When God sends his breath into the world, it brings purification and purgation. God's breath both breathes life in the first man and withers the grass of the field, is a raging stream of fire and accomplishes judgment upon the earth. The Holy Spirit, as God's breath, works in both creating and judging.

The third motif is the hand and arm of God. As with the other motifs, his hand and arm are both protective and destructive. The same hand/arm that saves the oppressed destroys the oppressor. The Bible presents the arm/hand of the Lord in both a protective and a destructive manner. It can deliver the Israelites from Egypt, but also destroy the Egyptians in the process. I will accomplish the connection of the Holy Spirit with God's arm/hand by an investigation into Jesus' statement that he casts out demons by God's finger, which is nothing other than the Holy Spirit.

---

14. Rom 3:26.

The final motif under consideration is God's wrath. The nature of God's wrath will be presented and it will be shown that his wrath is intimately related to his love so that one does not get the wrong impression that he is a sadist who delights in torturing his creation.

In chapter 7 I will show that the crucifixion of Jesus was not an event from which the Spirit was absent. While the cross is often presented as a binitarian event between the Father and the Son, I will demonstrate that the Spirit is active in the atonement, as he actualizes the Father's wrath and as sin is condemned in Jesus' flesh. The Spirit pours out God's judgment upon the God-man on the cross, and in so doing, defeats the powers of darkness and opens up the way of salvation for all who come to Christ in faith. The chapter will conclude with a discussion of the Spirit's relationship to eschatological condemnation as symbolized by the Lake of Fire.

1

Biblical Judgment

The Dance of Love and Justice

To JUDGE OR NOT to judge, that is the question: whether 'tis nobler for God to enforce his justice or to embrace his love, and in so embracing it to relent from the punishment his justice requires. It would appear that God is trapped in a dilemma between his love and justice, at least according to modern society's predilection for a nonjudgmental God. If he is just then he must not love people, for how could a loving God punish anyone? However, if he loves people then there is no possible way that he would eternally punish them for their sins. The contradiction established by this description is of course false and needs to be overcome, not by eliminating or compromising either of the poles, but instead by clearly defining what is meant by justice and love, and how the two dance together in God.

In order to define the relationship between God's judgment and his love, I will seek to accomplish three goals. The first will be to offer five reasons why the topic of judgment has fallen out of favor with Western culture. This is necessary in order to establish the modern predilection for avoiding discussions about God's judgment and to unmask some false ideas that exist regarding it. Having briefly examined the reasons for the neglect of the doctrine of judgment it will be possible to accomplish the second goal by examining God's nature in relationship to judgment. God's role as the judge of the universe will be explicated under the titles of his role as legislator, the creator of law, as executive, the enforcer of law, and finally in his judicial role as he determines the guilt or innocence of individuals as well as the punishment to which they are sentenced if found guilty.

I chose the United States' governmental system with its separation of powers as the paradigm under which to explicate God's relationship to judgment, not because the United States' system finds a biblical mandate, but instead because I am writing this book in the context of those who are familiar with the US arrangement. You should recognize that this is not the only possible scheme with which to explicate God and judgment, but I chose it more for illustrative purposes than for theological ones.[1] The final goal will be to present the theological implications of judgment in order to offer a well-grounded definition of what exactly is meant when it is argued that the Spirit actualizes the Father's judgment given to the Son.

Neglect of the Doctrine of Judgment

"Let justice roll down like waters, and righteousness like an ever-flowing stream."[2] Amos' words resonate with the deep-seated cry for justice in the world, the cry for the vindication of those who suffer, who have been abused, abandoned, and neglected: for the child forced to labor countless hours in a sweat shop, for the family whose loved one is taken away from them by a murderer, for the heartbroken spouse whose partner has walked away. There is a sense of outrage when the guilty walk free, when the "least of these" have no hope and no help. The soul cries out that the world must be changed in order to eliminate the injustice that pervades humanity, and yet talk of justice is often reduced to exactly that—talk. Behind the cry for justice lies the reality that there are the oppressed and the oppressors, the afflicted and the afflicters, and for justice to roll down like waters the oppressors and afflicters must be brought to judgment.[3]

Judgment is, unfortunately, a concept seldom discussed in the modern church. While justice rings out as a battle cry, its necessary corollary of judgment is quietly removed from the dialogue. Too often, talk of justice and righteousness becomes merely a word game in which those who participate create for themselves a feeling of striving for justice, but in which

1. For an example of judgment treated under a different governmental paradigm see O'Donovan, *Desire of the Nations*.

2. Amos 5:24. All quotations taken from the English Standard Version unless otherwise noted.

3. Travis correctly states, "Many people think that if you remove the idea of judgment you set men free from fears and taboos. Far from it, what you do is make men less than men." Travis, *Jesus Hope*, 58. For a general overview of judgment in Judaism, Christianity and other religions see Brandon, *Judgment of the Dead*. See also Griffiths, *Divine Verdict*.

they often, either consciously or unconsciously, reject the means whereby God has determined to establish justice and righteousness. All talk of responsibility and justice is merely idle chatter apart from the reality of God's judgment upon the world.[4]

Why is there reluctance to discuss a theme that runs throughout the Bible, weaving itself into discourses on God's love, Israel's historical narratives, Jesus' teachings, and Paul's epistles? Why is judgment taboo in our modern, enlightened society?[5] Though not exhaustive, five reasons will be presented for the neglect of the doctrine of judgment in the church: (1) misunderstanding of the nature of judgment; (2) a postmodern mindset that wishes to avoid absolutes; (3) a rejection of the divine; (4) a belief in evolutionary progression in which sin is conceived of as a vestige of man's earlier existence that will eventually disappear; and finally, (5) a misrepresentation of the outcome of judgment.

A fundamental misunderstanding of the nature of judgment has contributed greatly to its neglect. The image that often rises up is of God poised over the earth eagerly waiting to strike down fiery vengeance upon anyone who dares to challenge his authority. This image owes more to Zeus than to the Bible, yet it remains nevertheless. God is a sadist who takes delight in inflicting suffering on his creation, like a malicious child burning ants with a magnifying glass. If this were indeed a true picture, it would be a good idea not to discuss him. If the Creator delights in inflicting suffering, the best thing to do would be to try to ignore him and hope that he does not turn his glass upon you. This misconstrual of God's role as judge maintains itself beyond the grave as well, so that discussions of hell revolve around God as the master torturer. The preceding image causes many to remain silent about judgment, and rightly so, because it is difficult, if not impossible, to reconcile this image with that of a loving God presented throughout the biblical text.[6]

The misconstrual of God as a sadist is not the only one restraining people from discussing judgment. For many, the subject is politically incorrect; it does not make for polite conversation in today's enlightened milieu. In a postmodern world, who has the right to cast judgment? What arrogance one must have to judge another! Did not Jesus himself warn people

---

4. Brunner, *Eternal Hope*, 179.

5. For a concise overview of some reasons for the neglect of judgment see Lischer, "Embarrassed by God's Wrath," 259–62.

6. Williams, "Speaking Judgment," 206–11; Robinson, "Judgment of God," 136–47.

not to judge?[7] No, it is not a faulty understanding of what the Bible means when it speaks of judgment that is the problem, but an unwillingness to judge at all. If one accepts that God judges people, then it follows naturally that those people must be in conflict with him. While this desire not to judge may cause some to avoid the doctrine of judgment, it often functions on a superficial level, for while it is easy to embrace a pluralism that wishes to be open and inclusive, it is much more difficult to live consistently within that worldview.[8] When the issue under discussion is religion, people argue for inclusiveness and tolerance, but what if the issue becomes pedophilia or genocide? Is pluralism ready to open wide its arms to include these activities as valid expressions of humanity, or would the cry for justice lead to the action of judgment?

Yet a third reason for the rejection of divine judgment is the rejection of the divine itself. Atheism is not an issue within a believing community, but the secular society that surrounds and often penetrates the believing community has in many ways thoroughly embraced this view intellectually, if not practically.[9] In *The Gay Science*, Nietzsche presents the character of the fool who comes to proclaim that God is dead. The fool realizes that the people are not ready for the message and that he has come too early. They want God dead, but they also still want to live as if he is alive.[10] Nietzsche had great contempt for the atheists of his day who intellectually assented to atheism, but were still living under a moral code undergirded by theism. The same is still true today. Most atheists are intellectual atheists, but have not gone all the way to embrace the absolute relativism that atheism demands.

The influence of the surrounding culture can subtly affect the thoughts and actions of the church, both explicitly and implicitly. If society rejects that there is a God, then there cannot be a basis for ultimate judgment. At best, society itself becomes the basis, but in that case, judgment is no longer absolute, but fluid, able to change with the changes in society. The individual is no longer under an uncompromising authority, but under one that is malleable. In modern society, one is labeled as a fundamentalist or a radical if he subscribes to an ultimate judgment awaiting people beyond the grave, and even more so if he believes in a God that dispenses temporal

---

7. Matt 7:1. The naive proof texting involved in this claim is patently obvious. Morris, *Gospel According to Matthew*, 164–65.

8. Phillips, "Religious Pluralism," 254–66.

9. Garrett, *Systematic Theology*, 1:214–18.

10. Nietzsche, *Gay Science*, 181–82.

judgment in conjunction with a final judgment. The idea of divine judgment is too archaic to retain intellectually in a world that has come of age.[11]

Arising from the Enlightenment and carried forward within liberal Protestantism, a new view of humanity gained ascendancy in which people are not fallen, but, quite the opposite, are progressing ever closer to God. Based on a Darwinian evolutionary model, humanity never experienced a fall from a state of wholeness, but has instead been evolving both physically and morally. Sin is analogous to the human appendix: nothing but a leftover relic from a former time, a part of a person's animal nature that needs overcoming. Tennant quotes Archdeacon Wilson as saying, "Man fell, according to science, when he first became conscious of the conflict of freedom and conscience. To the evolutionist sin is not an innovation, but is the survival or misuse of habits and tendencies that were incidental to an earlier stage in development, whether of the individual or the race, and were not originally sinful, but were actually useful."[12]

With sin reduced to instinct and instinct overcome by evolution, there is no need of judgment, at least not of a future one. The most that can be judged is the past and that part of humanity that has yet to fully evolve. Humanity no longer stands in estrangement from God, but is moving ever closer to him.[13] Of course, social Darwinism works off the flawed idea that evolution means progress. Biological Darwinism does not see evolution as progress, only change. There is no goal to reach in evolution. There is no good and evil, there is only adaptation. Social Darwinism, on the other hand, sees social evolution as moral progress, as moving ever closer to some ideal state. In the absence of God, however, there is no ideal state to achieve, and hence all behavior becomes relativized to its current potential for survival.

The final reason offered for the neglect of the doctrine of judgment is the often one-sided presentation of the doctrine itself, in which judgment is synonymous with guilt. If a person comes under judgment, then by default he is punished. In this reductionist understanding, judgment is always condemning, never vindicatory. When God judges, he does indeed punish, but the Bible does not confine judgment to such a one-dimensional conclusion.

---

11. Niebuhr, *Kingdom of God*, 191–96.

12. Tennant, *Origin and Propagation*, 82.

13. Garrett, *Systematic Theology*, 1:523–25; Erickson, *Christian Theology*, 601–5. Martin presents a comprehensive overview of the rejection of eschatological judgment within liberal Protestantism. Martin, *Last Judgment*.

When he judges, there are two outcomes: salvation or condemnation.[14] With an understanding of judgment that encompasses both results, people might be willing to discuss the doctrine more openly.

The reluctance to discuss condemnation is not removed by recognizing that judgment can also be vindicatory, for what is likely to happen is a neglect of the negative side of judgment, while the positive outcome becomes the only one discussed. Universalism at its core is a doctrine of judgment that has eliminated condemnation.[15] Rob Bell is a modern advocate of this position. In his book *Love Wins*, he argues strongly for a God of judgment in light of the atrocities that he sees around the world. He also, however, argues that God's love will ultimately outlast every resistance to it from those in hell. In the end, hell is emptied of all its rebels as God's love wins.[16] Within the universalistic framework, one longs for judgment because judgment always and everywhere leads to redemption.[17] If, however, one rejects universalism, he must then embark upon the difficult discussion of condemnatory judgment.[18]

The neglect of the doctrine of judgment effectively creates a distorted understanding of God. I hope to demonstrate the intimate relationship between the Holy Spirit and judgment to reclaim judgment for Trinitarian theology, and in the process show the natural connection between judgment and God's nature. Therefore, it is to that discussion that we must proceed.

First, I will look at the language the Bible uses to describe God's judgment. I will then establish God's role as judge by comparing it with the United States' doctrine of the separation of powers and its three branches of government. I will further argue that God encompasses all three branches, thus doing away with the checks and balances in the United States' system, since there is no need for God to be either checked or balanced. Finally, by way of conclusion, I will highlight some theological implications of the nature of judgment.

14. Aulén, *Faith of the Christian Church*, 148.

15. Garrett, *Systematic Theology*, 2:793–99.

16. Bell, *Love Wins*.

17. Origen was one of the earliest exponents of universalism or *apokatastasis panton*. Origen, *On First Principles*, 1.6.1–4, 3.5.6–3.6.9. See also Schwarz, *Eschatology*, 337–51.

18. Buis, *Doctrine of Eternal Punishment*, 112–23. See also Davis, "Universalism," 173–86.

The Language of Judgment

As we seek to undercover exactly what is meant by judgment, the first place to start is the language of Scripture. What words are used to convey the idea of judgment and what are the detonations and connotations of those words? As we move from the Old to the New Testament we will uncover the language of judgment and how it is related to God.

The primary word in the Old Testament employed in relation to God's judgment is *shaphat* and its derivative *mishpat*.[19] The precise meaning of *shaphat* is difficult to ascertain, but it encompasses at least three ideas: custom, to rule, and to judge.[20] Some have tried to encapsulate all three meanings of *shaphat* in an umbrella term such as discrimination. While trying to combine the various nuances of the word is commendable, it results in a catch-all word that does not fully catch all that the original word conveys. It is therefore best to allow the word to remain partially ambiguous, letting the context of the passage drive the choice between the various options.

As judge, God is not beholden to an exterior law to which he refers when administering judgment, for he himself is the law. The laws that people create should be based upon the outworking of God's nature in the world.[21] This reliance upon God's law encompasses the first major understanding of *shaphat*: custom or established law. The people are to judge based upon God's customs/laws. It is not, however, a call to defend the status quo, to concretize the people's actions that have been established over time, but is instead a radical call for the people to constantly seek to align their actions with God. If the nation has abandoned God's customs and established other customs, or adopted the customs of other countries, then judgment will involve a realigning of its perspective and focus. The established custom of the people is only valid and binding insofar as it accords with God's customs.[22]

The second major understanding of *shaphat* is rulership. It is clear from passages in the book of Judges and elsewhere that judgment and rulership are intimately related.[23] The ruler is empowered to judge the people

19. Meador has a helpful appendix in his dissertation where he lists all the occurrences of the Old Testament words relating to judgment. Meador, "Motif of God". Morris, *Biblical Doctrine of Judgment*, 26–43; Baird, *Justice of God*, 42–44.

20. Morris, *Biblical Doctrine of Judgment*, 7–25; Meador, "Motif of God," 23–40; Mafico, "Judge, Judging," 3:1104–7.

21. Barth, *Doctrine of Reconciliation*, 528–33.

22. Morris, *Biblical Doctrine of Judgment*, 12–13.

23. Meador, "Motif of God as Judge," 27–31.

because of his position, but this power to judge does not allow him to judge arbitrarily or capriciously, for God's law acts as a restraint. Judgment must be in accord with the relationship established between God and his people.[24] Judgment, as illustrated in the Old Testament, is linked to fidelity to the covenant relationship; in the New Testament, it is linked to one's relationship to Jesus Christ.[25]

The pervasive reformational power of God's judgment vis-à-vis Israel's ability to break free from its false customs leads to the third and most comprehensive of the semantic uses of *shaphat*: judgment. When God judges, or when a human judge executes God's judgment, he is fundamentally discriminating between the parties involved. The Bible does not present God as a passive judge who waits for a case to come before him, but as an active one who seeks out the oppressor and the oppressed in order to establish justice. God judges, and in that action both salvation and condemnation are delivered with the oppressor being condemned and the oppressed being liberated. God not only establishes right and wrong, but also actively involves himself in the triumph of right over wrong. In the vindication of the innocent, the guilty are exposed and punished.

The Greek word *krino* is used in the Septuagint to translate the Hebrew word *shaphat*.[26] It is therefore clear that *krino* encapsulates more than a strictly legal understanding of judgment. It can carry a meaning as simple as forming an opinion; however, it most often refers to the passing of a sentence or a verdict, frequently with the emphasis upon the negative outcome. While the noun *krites*, "judge," appears in Jesus' parables, Jesus never directly relates it to God in his dialogues.[27] That is not to say, however, that Jesus does not place a strong emphasis upon judgment in his message. There are numerous parables that are about judgment, such as the wedding of the king's son, the wicked tenants, and the wise and foolish virgins.[28]

According to John 5:22 the Father is the ultimate judge, but he has given all judgment into the Son's hand. John 5:30 further reveals that Jesus

---

24. Herntrich, "Κρίνω," 924–26.

25. Grenz, *Theology for the Community of God*, 816–19.

26. Rissi, "Κρίνω," 2:317–21; Schneider, "Judgment, Judge," 362–67; Baird, *Justice of God*, 58–62.

27. Travis, "Judgment," 625.

28. Matt 22:1–14, 21:33–46; Mark 12:1–12; Luke 20:9–19; Matt 25:1–13. Capon, *Parables of Judgment*.

does not judge on his own, but only as the Father directs him.[29] As given to him by the Father, the Son bases the judgment of the world on its relationship to him.[30] Faith in Christ is the deciding factor under which all other judgments are subsumed. Augustine correctly stated that the sin of unbelief affects all other sins for "while this one remains, the others are retained, and when this one departs, the others are remitted."[31] While a person's work is the basis for judgment, the works are filtered through his relationship with Jesus Christ. Paul declares in 1 Cor 3:10–17 that self-righteous works will not survive the final judgment, but only those works built upon the solid foundation of Christ.

The New Testament maintains present judgment, but the overall thrust aligns itself with the prophetic tradition of the Old Testament in which there is coming a great day of judgment of the living and the dead. The eschatological emphasis in the New Testament causes one to live in either hope or fear of the future: hope for those who will be purified and fear for those who will be punished.[32]

Now that we have established the semantic range of judgment in the Bible, we can turn our attention to understanding how the Bible presents God as a judge. We will accomplish this by using the analogy of the United States government as a grid through which to understand the various aspects of God's role as judge.

The Checks and Balances of Judgment: God as Legislator, President, and Judge

Under the paradigm of the United States' legal system, the judge is ideally a dispassionate observer who resists all temptation to allow his personal opinion to influence the verdict, judging strictly upon the law as it stands. It

29. Pannenberg astutely notes that the Bible is not univocal in its declaration of who is the Judge. Jesus is given the role of judge in passages such as 1 Cor 4:5 and 2 Cor 5:10, while God the Father is given the role of judge in such passages as Matt 6:4, 1 Pet 4:5, and Rom 2:3–6. Also, Paul writes in 1 Cor 6:2 that the saints will judge the world. The saints' judgeship is intimately tied to the judgeship of Christ, which is in turn intimately tied to the judgeship of God the Father. Pannenberg, *Systematic Theology*, 3:613–14.

30. Travis, *Christ and the Judgment of God*, 168.

31. Augustine, *Tractates on the Gospel of John 55–111*, 187–88.

32. Brunner states that the Final Judgment is the ultimate discrimination where all inconclusiveness is removed, and it is therefore a basis for both fear and hope. Brunner, *Eternal Hope*, 170.

would be entirely inappropriate for the judge to also be the arresting officer, the prosecuting attorney, the defense attorney, and the jury all at the same time.[33] The United States' legal system is not constructed upon a model in which the above situation could, or should, ever take place. The reason for this stems from the Founding Fathers' absorption of the biblical understanding of humanity's flawed nature. Lord Acton's statement that "absolute power corrupts absolutely" is evidently clear in human actions, and therefore the United States has strictly prohibited the accretion of the powers to make laws, to enforce laws, and to sentence those accused of breaking laws to one person or group. Yet, within the Bible, God accomplishes these various roles within himself. There are no checks and balances within him, for he is not only the judge and jury, but also the prosecuting attorney, the defense attorney, the legislator, the executioner, and even the accused who takes upon himself the punishment of the guilty.

The threefold meaning of judgment in the Bible has an interesting parallel with the United States and its division between the legislative, executive, and judicial branches of government. As already mentioned, the Bible reveals God as the one from whom all law gains its ultimate source, who seeks out injustice in order to correct it, and who passes sentence both upon those people who are found to be in violation of his law and those who have suffered the effects of injustice. In what follows, I will investigate the doctrine of divine judgment in relation to God as legislator in the creation of laws, as executive in relation to his role in law enforcement, and as judge in his role in passing sentence upon those brought before him.

One must not portray God arbitrarily dispensing punishment upon the world, for he is neither capricious nor sadistic in his relationship to humanity.[34] In Rom 1:18, Paul stated that humanity had willfully suppressed the truth about God that is self-evident in creation. From the beginning, God has revealed his will for people's proper response to him. God created Adam and Eve with the one restriction not to eat the fruit from the tree in the center of the garden. This restriction established the dependent nature of the first couple, for they were to look to God for their provision and guidance. He was the legislator; they were the faithful citizenry.

The list was indeed short for them to follow, and yet they, like all humanity save one, refused to accept God on his own terms and under his

---

33. For a study of God as prosecutor and judge as developed in the Old Testament prophetic lawsuit see Nielsen, *Yahweh as Prosecutor and Judge*.

34. Eichrodt, *Theology of the Old Testament*, 1:265.

law. Instead, they sought to become like God, and in eating the forbidden fruit found themselves under judgment. Their expulsion from the garden was neither arbitrary nor capricious. It was instead the first sign of God's graciousness in that he did not immediately consign them to death, but allowed them, and humanity as a whole, room to return. Of course, humanity cannot return the way it came, for the gate to the garden was barred forever. Instead, God made a way forward for his rebellious creatures, for he did not impose the full extent of his judgment immediately.[35]

One could argue that from Adam until Moses the divine legislator took an extended recess while the judge continued to punish people for the violation of laws of which they were not aware.[36] Fortunately, God did not do that between Adam and the Mosaic Law, for Rom 2:12–16 makes it clear that those who have never heard the Law have it instinctively written on their hearts. Furthermore, when God did not accept Cain's sacrifice he was told that sin was crouching at his door. Cain's anger was displeasing to God, and God informed him of the danger that sin posed.[37] The fact that God expressly gave his commandments to Israel in the Covenant does not absolve the rest of humanity from responsibility to the divine legislator.[38] God's laws are universal, but they come to sharp focus first in Israel and the Covenant that was established between it and God and then, in the incarnation, they are focused most clearly in Jesus Christ.

Upon entering into a discussion of the Mosaic Covenant, it must be reasserted that God's law is not external to him. Unlike a Supreme Court Justice who is bound to a controlling document in his decisions, God is his own controlling document, and hence all the laws prescribed by him directly relate to himself and his relationship with his people. Therefore, God's law is not cold and impersonal, detached from his being, as if it was something decided in a Senate subcommittee, but comes directly from his nature.[39]

The personal nature of God's judgment is evident in that other nations served their gods according to their own customs. In 2 Kgs 17:24–33, the king of Babylon relocated people from other nations into the land of Israel,

---

35. Matthews, *Genesis 1—11:26*, 248–55.

36. There is some support for this view when in Rom 5:12–14 Paul relates that from Adam until Moses sin was in the world, and that death reigned over those who sinned, even though their sin was not in the likeness of Adam, for where there is no law sin is not imputed. Moo, *Epistle to the Romans*, 316–30.

37. Gen 4:1–7.

38. Moo, *Epistle to the Romans*, 145–57.

39. Herntrich, "Κρίνω," 940.

and they were subsequently attacked by lions because they did not "know the custom of the God of the land." Therefore, the king dispatched a priest to the area to teach them how to fear the Lord, but the people "served their own gods, after the manner of the nations from among whom they had been carried away." While the Bible recognizes that other nations have different customs or laws regulating how they are to relate to their god(s), it clearly shows that God's people should reject these customs since the God of Israel is the one true God and all other gods are mere creations of their people.[40] The Bible affirms, in all cases except the God of Israel, Feuerbach's thesis that god is nothing more than humanity's view of itself writ large.[41]

The relational nature of God's law can be summed up by Lev 26:12, in which Moses writes that God "will also walk among you and be your God, and you shall be My people." Abstract morality is not the primary issue when God's law is under discussion, but it does assume an ethical quality in that judgment must have a criterion of judgment. In order to judge Israel, Solomon asked God to give him the ability to judge between good and evil.[42] Judgment, while based upon the relationship between God and humanity, is established upon humanity's obedience to concrete statutes, such as the prohibition of murder and stealing, which flow from God's nature. He requires humanity to act in a certain manner both in relation to himself and to each other because his nature prescribes such behavior.[43] In Jer 9:23–24 God says, "Let not a wise man boast of his wisdom, and let not the mighty man boast of his might, let not a rich man boast of his riches; but let him who boasts boast of this, that he understands and knows Me, that I am the LORD who exercises lovingkindness, justice, and righteousness on earth; for I delight in these things." In knowing God, a person comes to know God's love for justice and righteousness, which is intimately linked to how people act toward him and each other.

As Moses ascended Mount Sinai to receive God's law for the people of Israel, so too did Jesus ascend a mountain to pronounce God's law. After affirming the validity of the Old Testament commands, Jesus proceeded with divine authority to expand those commands from outward obedience to inward disposition. Murder is no longer understood as the physical act of taking a life, but as the inward act of anger toward one's brother.

40. Brueggemann, *1 & 2 Kings*, 482–85.

41. Feuerbach, *Essence of Christianity*, 12–13.

42. 1 Kgs 3:9.

43. Mark 12:29–31.

This internalizing of the law was not new to Jesus, for he was following in the tradition of the prophets who had castigated Israel for its outward observance of the Covenant without a corresponding inward relational commitment to the God of the covenant.[44] The prophets, likewise, were not the first to recognize the internal nature of the relationship between God and his law. The tenth commandment forbids the internal act of coveting a neighbor's possession.

In John 12:48, Jesus said that the words that he has spoken would be what judges people at the last day. He is the supreme legislator, and one's response to his words becomes the basis for judgment. Once again, God is not capricious in his judgment, but quite the opposite, for repeatedly and in numerous ways he has revealed to humanity the criterion of judgment. He has placed his law within the conscience of humanity, he gave his law to Israel in the covenant, and he has extended the covenant to the entire world in Jesus Christ. Judgment is based upon God's revelation, both general and special, and thus people are without excuse regarding his judgment upon them.[45]

God's judgment is dynamic![46] It is not a static activity of intellectual assessment regarding the innocence or guilt of a person or peoples, but is such that when the decision is reached regarding guilt or innocence, action ensues to bring about the outcome of the decision: vindication for the innocent and punishment for the guilty. In the relationship between God and judgment, he subsumes to himself not only the place of establishing laws, but also of enforcing those laws. God actively seeks out the guilty and the innocent, to punish the former and vindicate the latter.[47] He does not remain trapped behind either his legislative pen or his judicial bench. That is, in the case of the former, he does not pass laws that will never be enforced, and in the case of the latter, he does not wait for others to bring cases before him on which he can then rule. Instead, he rises from his bench in search of injustice.[48] This search does not confine itself to strictly public matters, but reaches into the most private of relationships, for God is concerned with the righteousness of the community.[49] Biblical righteousness entails

44. Matt 5–7; Isa 29:13–14.

45. Rom 1:20.

46. Jenson, *Works of God*, 325; Morris, *Biblical Doctrine of Judgment*, 17–20.

47. 1 Sam 24:12.

48. Ps 34.

49. The personal nature of God's involvement is demonstrated in Sarah's request for God to intervene on her behalf in Gen 16:5. Jenson, *Works of God*, 324. Likewise, the

living up to the requirements of a relationship.[50] Whenever someone does not live up to the requirements of a relationship as established by God it is unrighteousness. The community is disrupted, and the disruption must be mended for relationships to be restored and for justice to be done.[51]

Unlike human courts, in which the oppressed are often oppressed more, within God's court the oppressed receive special status as he actively seeks them out to release them from oppression. He does not overlook the needy, the outcast, and the downtrodden, but reaches out to them to establish righteousness and justice. One of the hallmarks of Jesus' ministry is that he went to those who were outcasts, offering healing and restoration.[52] For the victims of injustice, judgment carries with it the ring of freedom, redemption, and healing, while for the perpetrators of injustice judgment is the bringing to account of their actions and the end of their domination over those they have injured. Judgment and justice walk hand in hand, but even for the condemned God offers mercy and grace.

The classic example in the Old Testament that relates to God seeking out the guilty to punish is the Flood in Gen 6. God looked down upon the earth and it grieved him that he created humanity, for its thoughts were only evil all the time. In his displeasure, he decided to wipe humanity off the face of the earth, except Noah and his family, who had found favor in his eyes. God, seeing the injustice in the world, took action to remove the evil from his creation. Once again, though, judgment is not all-pervasive, but is conditioned by Noah's deliverance. God judges with the intention of salvation. He is not a dispassionate judge who seeks only the impersonal fulfillment of the law, but is passionately involved in his judgment, and furthermore his lovingkindness, mercy, and grace condition his judgment.[53]

The prophets stand in a unique relationship to the law as those who eschatologically pronounce God's intentions concerning people's present behavior and the expected outcome including the themes of judgment, restoration, righteousness, and covenant. Amos 1:3–4 will serve as an example

---

recounting in Acts 5 of the death of Ananias and Sapphira highlights God's concern with the inner motivation of people's actions and their impact upon the community.

50. Kelly, "Righteousness," 192–95. See also Snaith, *Distinctive Ideas of the Old Testament*, 51–78.

51. Schneider, "Judgment, Judge," 363.

52. Matt 9:10–13 and Luke 4:16–21 are but two examples that could be multiplied.

53. Hanson, *Attractiveness of God*, 146–54; Heschel, *Prophets*, 285–96.

that is repeated often in the other prophets.[54] "Thus says the LORD, 'for three transgressions of Damascus, and for four, I will not revoke the punishment, because they threshed Gilead with threshing sledges of iron. So I will send a fire upon the house of Hazael, and it will devour the strongholds of Ben-hadad.'" While Amos presents God as a destroyer, he is markedly different from the deities of the surrounding nations. Amos presents God reacting to the sins of the people, while the deities of the surrounding nations operate more capriciously.

First Peter 3:12, quoting Ps 34:15, reiterates that the eyes of God are upon the righteous, but he sets his face against those who do evil. God's primary concern in judgment is to vindicate the innocent and the oppressed, with the destruction of the wicked being an inevitable corollary to the salvation of his people.[55]

Jesus' encounter in John 9 with the man born blind presents a paradigmatic example of God seeking out a person to liberate from oppression and the subsequent judgment that comes upon those who stand in opposition to that liberation. As the disciples encounter a man born blind, they debate whose sin caused this situation. Jesus interjects that it was neither the man's sin nor that of his parents that caused the blindness, but it was so that God could be glorified through him. Jesus proceeds to heal the man, who is then brought before the rulers who seek to discover who healed him. After an interrogation, the man finds himself in conflict with the Pharisees and in league with Jesus. After the man proclaims his belief in Jesus, Jesus tells him that it was for judgment that he came into the world, "So that those who do not see may see, and those who see may become blind."[56] The Pharisees cannot share in the blind man's newfound sight because they fail to perceive that they are themselves blind.[57] As long as they maintain their own righteousness apart from Christ, they will never be able to participate in the freedom that he brings as he seeks and saves "that which was lost."[58]

God actively seeks out the wicked to punish, but he does so in the context of seeking out the oppressed and victimized to vindicate. It is not within the power of a human judge to restore the one who has suffered at the hands

---

54. Kapelrud, "God as Destroyer," 33–38.

55. Grenz, *Theology for the Community of God*, 822–24; Pannenberg, *Systematic Theology*, 3:580–86.

56. John 9:39.

57. Carson, *Gospel According to John*, 359–79.

58. Luke 19:10.

of another. The most a human judge can do is punish the offender in an attempt to honor justice, but the punishing of the offender is not a guarantee of the restoration of the offended. It is beyond the power of a human judge to reconcile the rift in the community; at best, he can remove the offending party. God, on the other hand, seeks not only to remove the offending party, but also to reestablish righteousness within the community.[59]

It is indeed difficult to understand how God can heal the deep rift of injustice in this world. Dostoevsky poignantly portrays the moral struggle of how suffering and injustice can be justified in his novel *The Brothers Karamazov*.[60] Ivan Karamazov argues that if one little child suffers then there is no means whereby God can undo that suffering. There is no greater good that could overcome that evil. Aloysha, a monk and Ivan's brother, is speechless after the exchange. He does not have a response for his brother's accusations. The reader finds himself in a similar state. How can God go back and bring justice to a past event? How can he undo that which has been done? The answer to that question is a mystery, but faith will receive an answer to it one day. Until that time, we can rest in the knowledge that our God is not immune to the suffering in the world, but entered into it and encountered it by the incarnation. The cross is evidence that God does not sit aloof from our pain, but has endured it himself.

As already demonstrated, God encompasses both legislative and executive power within himself, and he bases humanity's judgment on its relationship to him, and correlatively on its fulfillment of the law that he has established. The issue of judgment according to deeds and justification by faith is not to be understood in such a way as to pit one against the other. Justification by faith does not preclude God's judgment based upon a person's deeds, but instead conditions it.[61]

There is ample evidence throughout the Bible to demonstrate that a person's actions are the basis upon which God makes his judgment.[62] A person's actions are indicative of who he is as a person. What one does can in no way be disconnected from one's being. The tendency to disconnect the action from the person, at least concerning morally reprehensible behavior, is not aligned with a biblical anthropology, in which the mind, will,

---

59. Grenz, *Theology for the Community of God*, 823–26.

60. Dostoevsky, *Brothers Karamazov*, 245–55.

61. Yinger, *Paul, Judaism, and Judgment*, 290–91.

62. Ibid., 283; Garrett, *Systematic Theology*, 2:781; Hoekema, *Bible and the Future*, 258–61.

emotions, spirit, and actions constitute the whole person.[63] Jesus remarked that you would know a person by the fruit he produces.[64] So then, how can one relate justification by faith to judgment according to deeds?

It is not through deeds that a person is justified, but as Calvin stated, "the faith which justifies is not alone."[65] The tension often created between justification and deeds is based upon a misunderstanding of justification. James and Paul are not in dispute on this issue, as some have claimed, but are speaking of the same event from two separate perspectives. One comes to Christ by grace through faith alone, but once in Christ, the person's deeds attest to his transformed life. A faith that has no deeds, when ample time has been given for deeds to sprout, is a questionable faith, one that might not be faith at all.[66]

Having established that judgment is according to a person's deeds, it will be beneficial to understand how God carries out his judgment. Does judgment take place temporally, eschatologically, or both? If judgment is temporal, how is it related to the offense? Are we to understand judgment under C. H. Dodd's conception of impersonal cause and effect, or does God take a more active role?[67] Is judgment carried out by means of supernatural events or is it imposed under the guise of natural catastrophes? What is the relationship between God's execution of judgment and Jesus Christ? What is the relationship between temporal and eschatological judgment? One must answer these questions in order to present a complete picture of how God executes judgment.

Beginning with the writing prophets, it became common stock that there was coming a time, a great day, the revolution of the ages, in which

63. Garrett, *Systematic Theology*, 2:497–519.

64. Luke 6:43–44.

65. Calvin, *Acts of the Council of Trent*, 3:152.

66. Jas 2:20. The classic example of a person justified with no apparent deeds beyond the initial act of belief is found in the repentant brigand's request of Jesus to remember him when he comes into his kingdom. Luke 23:39–43. Richardson, *James*, 136–37.

67. Dodd, *Epistle of Paul to the Romans*, 45–50. Miller rejects the idea that God is not directly involved in judgment when he writes, "One cannot fully express the relationship between sin and judgment as one of the fate-effecting deed under the guidance of God. While a number of passages do not clarify the issue one way or another, there are several which emphasize the idea of correspondence and suggest that while there is always a casual effect in the relationship between someone or some people's actions and the judgment they receive, that relationship is not necessarily internal but is perceived as resting in the divine decision and not happening apart from that decision or decree." Miller, *Sin and Judgment in the Prophets*, 134.

God would execute judgment in order to vindicate his people and establish peace in the land.[68] The Day of the Lord was not univocally perceived to be a day of deliverance for Israel, but was also understood to be a dark day for the nation, a day in which God would inflict punishment on his own people.[69] Isaiah vividly portrayed how God would purge away the sin in Israel to establish peace. The Day of the Lord will settle all accounts and put down all resistance to God. The created order will cease to be in bondage as lions and lambs will lie down together and children will be able to play fearlessly with an asp.[70]

While the Old Testament refers to the Day of the Lord, the New Testament speaks of the Day of Judgment. Jesus and his disciples steeped themselves in the Jewish story of God's call, exile, and eventual deliverance of his people, and it was from within this story that they spoke of the Final Judgment as the time in which God is going to set his creation free from bondage. Creation expectantly waits for the revealing of the sons of God so as to be released from its bondage. Likewise, those who are the sons of God have the Spirit of God within them, who also groans for the redemption from the Fall.[71]

The final judgment will accomplish three things. First, it will display the sovereignty and glory of God. In the end, all things will be put under the feet of Jesus and he will then hand all things over to the Father.[72] The final judgment will display for all to see that the God revealed in Jesus Christ is indeed the supreme ruler of the universe. Second, it will reveal the degrees of reward and punishment that people are to receive.[73] It is only at the end that we can completely evaluate a person's life story. As long as it is called "today" there is hope that a person can be redeemed. It is only after the individual's death, and then only at the end of the present age, that the full extent of a person's deeds can be disclosed, for his influence will ripple through time long after he is gone. Therefore, it becomes necessary for judgment to occur at the end of the present age in order for those

---

68. Eichrodt, *Old Testament Theology,* 1:457–71; Carroll, Crowder, and Cranfill, *Day of the Lord.*

69. Amos 5:18–20; Eichrodt, *Old Testament Theology,* 1:462–67.

70. Isa 11.

71. Rom 8:19–28; Wright, *Crown and the Cross,* 81–94.

72. 1 Cor 15:24–28.

73. Garrett, *Systematic Theology,* 2:784; Hoekema, *Reformed Dogmatics,* 849–61; Grenz, *Theology for the Community of God,* 816–26.

ripples to reach the farthest shore. In the words of Pannenberg, "Eternity is judgment."[74] The third and final purpose of the final judgment is for God to impose his judgment upon each person, for it is both the reading of the verdict and the imposition of the sentence. The verdict read, however, is nothing other than the sum total of each person's entire life.[75]

It is clear from the foregoing discussion of judgment that there is a strong sense of eschatological expectation in judgment, but is that the only sense in which God executes judgment? Must the righteous wait for their vindication while the guilty roam free in their transgression until the end? The answer is a resounding "no," for while the final judgment will settle all accounts, finally bringing complete judgment to humanity, there are temporal judgments that anticipate that great day. In the course of time, in the warp and woof of daily life, God executes his judgment upon people, bringing both deliverance and condemnation. The Gospel of John starkly portrays the reality that judgment is executed in the present moment in one's relationship to Christ.[76] Yet, one should not make the mistake of separating God's temporal and eschatological judgment. For it is from the eschatological judgment that the temporal judgment gains its bearing and power.[77] What God will accomplish ultimately in the eschaton he brings to pass partially in the present. The "now" but "not yet" of eschatology relates also to judgment.

Additionally, one must reject a Bultmannian over-realized eschatology in which there is no room for God's future work. This rejection is predicated upon a complete reading of the scriptural evidence, not one in which those passages that seem to contradict an already established worldview are excised from the text as the work of a later redactor who did not understand the nuanced view of the original author.[78] Conversely, one must also reject an exclusively future eschatology. In the life, death, and resurrection of Jesus and in the subsequent sending of the Holy Spirit, the life of the age to come has broken into this age, not symbolically, but ontologically.[79] The Holy Spirit is the down payment of the future that God has planned for his creation; his presence brings the future that God has in store for his

---

74. Pannenberg, *Systematic Theology*, 3:610.

75. Hoekema, *Reformed Dogmatics*, 254.

76. John 3:18; Bultmann, *Gospel of John*, 154–56.

77. Pannenberg, *Systematic Theology*, 3:580–607.

78. Bultmann, *Gospel of John*, 258–62.

79. Pannenberg, *Systematic Theology*, 3:604–7.

creation into the present, and in so doing the present gets a foretaste of the glory that is to come.

Since God does execute temporal judgment, the question arises: What are the methods employed for this judgment? The above examples offer two of God's methods. The first is that a natural event takes place, but it is ascribed to a supernatural cause. The floodwaters were a part of nature, with nothing in the flood defying the laws of nature, but the text is clear that God used the natural order to execute his judgment. Similar examples include when God withholds rain from the land or sends a plague among the people.[80]

God also uses various "rods" that can be either corrective or condemning. War is one such natural event that God uses. It is meant to bring repentance, but will proceed to condemnation contingent on human response. The nation of Israel is repeatedly defeated in war and the explanation given is that God is passing judgment upon its idolatry. Eventually, however, the nation is exiled by the military power of Nebuchadnezzar. The prophets refer to wars and battles repeatedly as God's means of judgment. Isaiah declares that Assyria is the rod of God's anger and that he uses that nation to execute his judgment upon his chosen people.[81] The book of Revelation speaks of the final great war, Armageddon, in which God will be victorious over all his enemies.

In addition to natural events with an underlying natural execution, the second method God employs are natural events that have a decidedly supernatural execution. The earthquake that consumes Korah is natural, but the timing and placement of it is such that there is little doubt that supernatural intervention had occurred.[82] Likewise, in the case of Ananias and Sapphira, while the text only states that they fell over and breathed their last, not indicating a supernatural means of expiration, it is clear that the timing of both deaths is related to a supernatural execution.

At other times, God's judgment is outside the bounds of nature. This is the case in Moses' final plague upon Egypt, the parting of the Red Sea, in which God redeemed Israel and punished Egypt, and in the healings of Jesus, in which he set people free from sickness. God acts to bring judgment in a manner that vividly portrays his direct intervention in the affairs of the world. While God often works through natural processes to execute

---

80. 1 Kgs 8:35–38; Harrelson, "Famine in the Perspective," 84–99.

81. Isa 10:1–7; Miller, *Divine Warrior in Early Israel*; Lind, *Yahweh is a Warrior*.

82. Num 16:32.

his judgment, the law of cause and effect in no way binds him. God is free to send down fire from heaven on Mt. Carmel in a display of his judgment on both the prophets of Baal and Elijah.[83] A deistic scheme in which judgment is a natural process of a moral universe is not congruent with the God of the Bible.[84]

Theological Conclusions

Having established the nature of biblical judgment, it is now necessary to move into a theological reflection on judgment. First, judgment is revelatory of God's nature by highlighting his justice and holiness. It is furthermore vindicatory of both God and those who are his. While judgment vindicates both God's way with man and man's way with him, it also purifies those who have entered into a faith relationship with him. While judgment is experienced as purifying by some, it is also experienced as condemning by others who choose to stand outside of God's love and forgiveness. In this regard, judgment is universal in that it affects all people, but it goes further in that it affects all of the created order.

As already shown, God's judgment is a present reality, but it is also an eschatological event. It is from the eschatological judgment that all temporal judgments gain their bearing. Scripture is clear that a faith relationship with the Father through his Son in the power of the Spirit is the means whereby one can encounter judgment as purifying. It is equally clear that judgment is based upon the deeds that people perform while on this earth. Finally, God's judgment is one that is based upon and rooted in God's love. His love cannot be set aside in a discussion of his judgment.

God does not judge the world capriciously, but with a fixed purpose in mind, a purpose that is intimately connected to his nature, so that when he brings judgment upon the world, it functions to reveal his nature. Temporal judgments highlight his displeasure with humanity, but in the midst of a fallen world it is often difficult to separate out his judgment from his intent to use a person for his glorification. The blindness of the man in John 9 was not a judgment upon his sin, but was instead an opportunity for Jesus' glorification. Temporal judgments, such as the Exile, the Flood, and the deaths of Ananias and Sapphira, reveal God's reaction to disobedience, while at the same time showing his desire to protect those he loves.

83. 1 Kgs 18.

84. Morris, "Wrath of God," 142–45; Cranfield, "Romans 1.18," 330–35.

Temporal judgments are often ambiguous, but the final judgment will in no way suffer in this manner. The final judgment will fully reveal God's nature as it relates to rebellion. There will be no place to hide when he judges the world that has turned its back upon him, a world that has chosen to take upon itself those prerogatives that are only due God.

Yet God reveals his graciousness in judgment. He provides mercy in his judgment, seeking the restitution of the offender. He repeatedly judged Israel in order to bring her back from her wanderings. The Exile serves as the paradigm of remedial judgment in which he cast his people away in order to purify them so that they could return to him. As Hos 6:1 says, "Come, let us return to the LORD; for he has torn us, that he may heal us; he has struck us down, and He will bind us up." Pannenberg writes, "While his mercy is gracious and overflowing, there comes a time when he will no longer strive with man. At death, a person's destiny is finalized based upon the totality of his life. Death is the 'period' at the end of a person's life and thus seals his story, either with redemption or with condemnation."[85] There is always hope for change until a person breathes his last breath, and then comes final judgment.[86] Pinnock states it well when he writes, "Only when judgments fail to provoke repentance do they provoke eschatological wrath. Only when the final no is rendered does God close the books on the impenitent (Rom 2:5). Before that they remain open."[87]

Not only is God's judgment revelatory of his nature, but it is also a vindication of his ways with humanity.[88] At the final judgment, every knee will bow and every tongue will confess that Jesus is indeed Lord.[89] The goal of all theodicy is to vindicate the ways of God in a world that appears to be in contradiction to his nature and purpose. The writer of Job tackles this very problem, but with enough honesty to stop short of trying to solve the mystery intellectually. The mystery, however, will one day be solved; in fact, presently it is being solved by God's judgment. God has not abandoned his creation to its own self-destruction, but has entered—and is entering—into history to bring justice and righteousness to creation, on a limited scale in the present age, but completely in the age to come. All the questions

---

85. Pannenberg, *Systematic Theology,* 3:610–11. See also Pannenberg, *What is Man,* 68–81.

86. Rom 2:4; 2 Pet 3:9.

87. Pinnock and Brow, *Unbounded Love,* 70.

88. Hoeksema, *Reformed Dogmatics,* 849.

89. Phil 2:10.

that have been asked of God about suffering in the world will one day be answered, but in fact the answer has already been given in the death and resurrection of Jesus.

God judged and condemned the rebellion of humanity on the cross. The innocent man stood in the place of the guilty and took upon himself the judgment due them. On the cross, Jesus experienced the overwhelming anguish of the Father's judgment upon sin and cried out, "My God, my God, why have you forsaken me?"[90] He eventually died on that Roman execution device, and the ambiguity of the following days must have been torment for the disciples. Their leader, friend, and Messiah had been executed. Was the world indeed a place where justice is unattainable, where death reigns supreme and God is powerless?

It was, however, on the first Easter morning when Jesus rose from the grave, when the judgment of condemnation was swallowed up in the judgment of glorification, that Jesus' life and mission were vindicated. Jesus underwent the judgment of condemnation in order to open a way for the judgment of glorification. As a loving Father, God is calling his prodigal children home. It is out of his deep love for humanity that God takes upon himself condemning judgment so that his children will not have to experience it, but will instead experience the joy and freedom of redeeming judgment.

God's vindication of his purpose for humanity leads to the purifying aspect of judgment, both temporally and eschatologically. Hebrews 12:5–13 relates that all discipline at the time seems harsh, but that God disciplines those he loves with their well-being in mind. When he judges the sinful actions of his people, he does so with the intent and purpose of purifying them from those elements that hinder their full relationship with him. He seeks to remove all obstacles standing between himself and humanity. In the moment of purificatory judgment, God brings calamity upon a person, allowing his strong arm of discipline to do its work, in order for the person to reflect more fully his image and hence to accomplish more fully the purpose for which he was created.[91]

C. S. Lewis describes God as a master architect who is building his image in each believer out of an unformed house. The image is located in the house, but is obscured and hidden. As the architect builds new additions and takes down old wings, the image becomes more recognizable, until at last the perfect image of the architect is revealed. This process of building a

90. Matt 27:46; Mark 15:34.

91. Morris, *Biblical Doctrine of Judgment*, 45–53.

new house is God's judgment upon those parts of the believer's life that are incompatible with the image being created.[92] Purificatory judgment is not restricted to individuals, but is applicable to the church both universal and local, to institutions, to cultures, and to nations.

As painful as purificatory judgment might be, the result is the wholeness and completion of the one being judged. The same is not the case in condemnatory judgment. The Bible is clear that there will be people who reject God's love, who refuse to accept their appointed purpose in life, and who instead seek to build their lives upon something other than God.[93] When Christ's redeeming love is rejected, all that awaits a person is a fearful judgment, a judgment in which the dissonance of his entire life rings out in eternity.[94] Hell is the result of the ultimate rejection of God's love, but it is not the removal of God's love for the person.

God does not cease to love those who are in hell. This point is in direct contradiction to Crockett in which he argues that God's love and God's eschatological wrath are two separate entities, so that God ceases to love the unrepentant. He bases his conclusion upon an understanding of God's love as always leading to salvation. He does not allow for God to accept the rejection of his love. Crockett writes, "Moreover, *orgē* in Paul excludes any notion of divine love. When he speaks of wrath, and especially of eschatological wrath, he never hints that it is a manifestation of God's love leading to improvement and repentance."[95] In contradiction to Crockett, Brunner asserts, "The wrath of God under which the idolatrous, sinfully perverted man stands is simply the divine love, which has become a force opposed to him who has turned against God. The wrath of God is the love of God, in the form in which the man who has turned away from God and turned against God, experiences it, as indeed, thanks to the holiness of God, he must and ought experience it."[96]

God does not remove his presence from them, but just the opposite, he is still present with them. Their rejection of his love, however, transforms their experience of that love into suffering and torment. Millard Erickson

---

92. Lewis, *Mere Christianity*, 176.

93. Matt 7:26–27.

94. Grenz, *Theology for the Community of God*, 824.

95. Crockett, "Wrath that Endures Forever," 199. Pinnock offers a more satisfying understanding of God's love and wrath in his concept of creative love theism. Pinnock and Brow, *Unbounded Love*, 8–12.

96. Brunner, *Man in Revolt*, 187.

is mistaken in his reliance upon C. S. Lewis when he states that hell is God leaving man to himself. The reality is that God cannot leave man alone, for God's love will not allow that. Hell is man's experience of God outside of Christ.[97] The light of God's love is darkness to them who have rejected that self-same light.[98] Their rejection does not change God, but it does change their experience of him.

Having established that God's judgment can be either redeeming or condemning, it must be asked, what is the basis for judgment? Throughout the Bible, God reveals that people will be judged based upon their deeds.[99] The actions of the person, both internal and external, will constitute the evidence upon which God will base his judgment. As argued earlier, this understanding of judgment in no way conflicts with justification by grace through faith. The evil deeds of believers are not merely overlooked in the final judgment, but are in fact judged on the cross of Christ. The Son took upon himself the condemnation that was rightly due to the believer. Therefore, God does in fact judge the believer's sin, but the judgment is on Christ, not the believer. It is in this way that God is able to both be just and the justifier of those who believe in Jesus.[100] Furthermore, once a person is saved, God continues to judge the person's action so that those actions that are not congruous with the Kingdom will be burned up as so much wood, hay, and stubble.[101]

What is in a person's heart will be revealed by his actions, and hence it is those actions, both outwardly as a visible example of the heart and inwardly as the actual condition of the heart, that will be judged. In Matt 25, Jesus relates that in the final judgment the criteria for separating the sheep from the goats will be how they responded to the least of these. God's basis of judgment upon a person's action provides a safeguard against the ascription to him of arbitrariness in his judgment. He does not pull names out of a hat to determine who he will punish and who he will save, but instead bases his judgment upon a person's concrete actions in time as determined by that person's response to his call. Grenz captures this idea well when he writes, "In short, the judgment is not a capricious or arbitrary assigning of

---

97. Erickson, *Christian Theology,* 1240. Luther was correct when he stated that God is even in hell. Luther, *Lectures on the Minor Prophets,* 68.

98. Matt 6:23.

99. Garrett, *Systematic Theology,* 2:781; Hoekema, *Reformed Dogmatics,* 258.

100. Rom 3:26.

101. I Cor 3:12–15.

eternal fates to individuals; rather it is God's public revelation of the significance of all history. This cosmic disclosure will indicate the extent to which our individual histories reflect and incorporate the meaning of God's history. The judgment will indeed be a day of surprises."[102]

As a corollary of the redeeming and condemning nature of God's judgment, it will also be universal.[103] All people will be included in judgment, as well as the universe. Creation's organic nature necessitates that judgment encompass its entirety. It is not enough that God judges people on an individual basis; he must also judge transtemporally. One generation's sin leaves a burden upon subsequent ones and in the eschaton those injustices must be reconciled so that those who have been oppressed can be set free and those who have contributed to oppression, not just in their immediate context but through time and around the globe, can be forgiven and likewise set free.[104] It is for this reason that a final judgment upon creation is necessary in order to usher in the new age. It is not until the full extent of humanity's rebellion is complete that God can judge its consequences. At that time, he will purge the old from his creation and will usher in the new heavens and earth, in which his purpose for creation will be fully accomplished.

In relation to God's judgment, including the entirety of his created order, it is an obvious conclusion that all judgments in time gain their bearing from the final judgment.[105] The eschaton is the point to which the world is heading, the goal for which it was created, and thus naturally all judgments that are enacted in the present age are related to the new age that will supersede the current one. In the cross and resurrection and the subsequent bestowal of the Spirit at Pentecost, the age to come has proleptically broken into the present age.[106] On the cross, God's final condemning judgment on humanity was historically consummated, and yet there is coming a time when this judgment will be fully realized.

In like manner, in the resurrection, God's final redeeming judgment upon humanity has historically taken place, but it also awaits a future time

102. Grenz, *Theology for the Community of God*, 632.

103. Morris, *Biblical Doctrine of Judgment*, 62–65; Grenz, *Theology for the Community of God*, 811–46; Hoekema, *Reformed Dogmatics*, 257–59.

104. Jenson, *Work of God*, 325.

105. Moltmann, *Coming of God*; Grenz, *Theology for the Community of God*, 851–52; Pannenberg, *Systematic Theology*, 3:595–607; Berkhof, *Christian Faith*, 521–25. For a brief history of the Last Judgment in Christian tradition, see McGinn, "Last Judgment in Christian Tradition," 2:361–401.

106. Cullmann, *Christ and Time*, 139–43.

in which it will be fully revealed. Both of these aspects of judgment are being realized in the present time by the Spirit's power. It is the Spirit who makes available to the believer the resurrection life of Christ, and conversely, it is the Spirit who applies the Father's judgment given to the Son, both in purification for the redeemed and in condemnation to those who have refused the Son's invitation to the marriage feast.

Finally, God's judgment is a judgment of love.[107] Unlike a dispassionate courtroom judge who removes his emotions from the proceedings, God is passionately involved in all aspects of judgment. The motif of God as judge has to be conditioned by and derived from the motif of God as father, for God judges as a father. Gustav Aulén writes, "Our starting point is Jesus' disclosure of God as a father who cares for us even though we are sinners. From this we take our cue that the most fundamental image is one of the family, not of the law court. Of course there is a legal dimension in the picture, because God is Judge and because the situation between God and humanity is broken in a complex of ways."[108] When God inflicts punishment upon people, like the old saying goes, it does hurt him more than it hurts the person. As terrifying as the prospect of hell is, it is a prospect that God himself has encountered on the cross. John 3:16 poignantly states that God so loved the world that he gave his only son so that those who believe could be saved.

As Jesus approached Jerusalem for the last time, he lamented that he often wished to gather its inhabitants under his wing, but they would not allow him.[109] As he approached God's impending judgment upon Israel's rebellion, he wept over it. God is love and at no point can one dissociate his love from his actions. One must not seek to divorce his love from his holiness so that his aversion to sin is overcome by his love for the sinner to the end that he pardons the sinner in spite of his sin. The supreme seriousness of sin is self-evident in the lengths that he has gone in order to provide a means for humanity to be freed from its bondage. No, it is God's holy love with which humanity must reckon, a love that cannot abide sin, because sin by its very nature is antithetical to love.[110]

---

107. Aulén, *Faith of the Christian Church*, 146. See also Pinnock and Brow, *Unbounded Love*, 67–77.

108. Aulén, *Faith of the Christian Church*, 9.

109. Matt 23:37.

110. Berkhof, *Systematic Theology*, 118–33.

Sin is love's negation, the refusal to love. How can God overlook sin because of his love, when it is sin that denies that very love and refuses to allow love to hold sway over all a person's relationships? When a person closes himself off from others and from God, when he refuses love out of either hatred or fear, God will not force him to love. God created humanity for fellowship with himself and with each other. Moreover, for true fellowship to exist, freedom to choose must be present. As much as a father desires his child to love him, it is not within a father's power to make that love a reality. The child must freely choose to love his parent. The same holds true with God the Father. Like the father of the prodigal son, God waits for his children to return from the far country, to come home to his love; but unlike this parable, God the Father sent his own Son into the far country to take upon himself the suffering of humanity and to offer a means of return from exile.[111] The judgment of God is indeed a lament, a lament from the heart of God.

111. Barth, *Doctrine of Reconciliation*, 211–83.

2

The Spirit and Judgment

A Trinitarian and Biblical Basis

A FULLY ORBED TRINITARIAN theology necessitates that the Spirit have a role in judgment. Wayne Grudem writes, "In general, the work of the Holy Spirit seems to be to bring to completion the work that has been planned by God the Father and begun by God the Son."[1] While the church has embraced a Trinitarian understanding of God, it has not consistently explicated his work in relation to each person of the Trinity. In some areas, such as creation and redemption, it has shown how each person participates in the unified Trinitarian work, but in others, the three are in practice reduced to a monad and the unified work of the one God overshadows the economic work of each person. If each person is involved in all of God's works as maintained by Trinitarian doctrine, then by default, each member has a role in judgment. In what follows, we will seek to ground the idea that the Holy Spirit executes the Son's judgment given to him by the Father.

The grounding of the above idea will focus primarily upon the biblical evidence that links the Spirit to the Trinitarian work of judgment. Initially, the church's Trinitarian doctrine will serve as a point of entry into the defense of the Spirit's role in judgment. The placing of the systematic section first is not to imply that the systematic construction holds weight over the biblical evidence. Instead, it should be clear by the end of the chapter that the Bible is the basis for the grounding of the Spirit's work in judgment. The systematic section is offered first to establish the church's historical understanding of the Trinity, and to demonstrate how that understanding

1. Grudem, *Systematic Theology*, 246.

29

demands that the Spirit have a role in judgment. However, if the Bible cannot support the historical understanding, then the systematic formulation of the church will need to be modified. What we will find, however, is that the Bible does indeed support the Spirit's work in judgment as delineated by the systematic formulation.

The depth and breadth of Trinitarian theology is staggering and an attempt to give an exhaustive outline of it is beyond the scope of this book. Therefore, I will not explicate Trinitarian doctrine in detail, but will instead work from the presuppositions of a Trinitarian theology that fully affirms the orthodox position of one God in three persons. The doctrine of proper operations will serve as the fulcrum for lifting the Spirit's work in judgment to a position from which it can then be demonstrated that the Bible indeed affirms this work.[2] Additionally, it will be shown that the adoption of the Augustinian maxim that the Spirit is the outgoing love of the Father and Son necessitates his role in judgment.

Having established the Spirit's role in judgment from a systematic perspective, it will then fall to the bulk of the chapter to ground this systematic understanding in the biblical text. The biblical evidence does indeed support the systematic conclusions reached regarding the Trinity, even though most theologians have not followed through with the implications that this creates for our understanding of the Holy Spirit. Initially, those passages that make a direct narrative connection between the Holy Spirit and judgment will be investigated. This will include the accounts of several of Israel's judges and the Spirit's work in two narratives in the book of Acts: the death of Ananias and Sapphira and the blinding of Elymas.

The third section will address those areas where there is a correlation between the Holy Spirit and judgment. This will include prophecies in which the Messiah is able to establish justice on the earth due to the Spirit's resting upon him. In addition, Jesus' statement that the *Paraclete* will convict the world regarding sin, righteousness, and judgment will be highlighted. Finally, the opposition Paul established between the flesh and the Spirit highlights the Spirit's role in condemning humanity's sinful nature.

---

2. Yarnell, *God the Trinity*, 226. Yarnell prefers the term proper operations to refer to the economic work of each person of the Trinity as opposed to the more traditional term appropriated operations. His reasoning for this change is sound in that he demonstrates there is no place in Scripture that shows the persons of the Trinity agreeing to appropriate certain economic actions. Instead, what we read is that each person does that work that is proper to his personhood.

Trinitarian Grounding of the Spirit's Role in Judgment

Friedrich Schleiermacher treated the Trinity as an appendix to the church's doctrines, a relic of patristic speculation that has no use within modern theology.[3] Conversely, Karl Barth employed it as the lynchpin of his entire systematic enterprise. In this debate, Barth is clearly the winner in regards to the Bible's presentation of God's nature. While the Scriptures do not explicitly state the doctrine of the Trinity, they do lead toward this under-standing of God.[4] In the incarnation, Jewish monotheism was redefined as Jesus prayed to the Father and told his disciples that he would send the Holy Spirit to be with them once he returned to the Father. The New Testa-ment authors did not explicate in a systematic manner how God is three persons in one nature. Instead, they wrote with the intent of exhortation and proclamation that God was saving his people through his Son who was none other than God himself, and that furthermore, his Son had revealed that even after his ascension he was with his followers through the Spirit. While the Trinity is a mystery, it is a mystery to which believers have some access through God's revelation.[5]

God in three persons, blessed Trinity! The orthodox faith has affirmed that God is both one and three, but not in the same way. The church does not affirm three Gods that have come together to form one unified committee called deity, nor does it affirm one God that reveals himself consecutively in three modes.[6] Instead, the church has affirmed that God is one in es-sence or nature and three in person or mode of subsisting.[7] The entry point into this knowledge is not metaphysical speculation upon God's nature, but his self-revelation in history in Jesus Christ as recorded in Scripture. God's work in the world shows that he is Father, Son, and Holy Spirit, each equal

---

3. Schleiermacher, *Christian Faith*.

4. Yarnell, *God the Trinity*. Yarnell's entire book is a defense that while the Trinity is not explicitly affirmed in the Bible in a systematic manner, the doctrine is the implied idiom of the Bible.

5. Jenson, *Triune God*, 1–51.

6. Both views, tritheism and modalism, have been condemned as heretical. For an overview of the historical development of the doctrine of the Trinity see de Margerie, *Christian Trinity in History*; La Due, *Trinity Guide to the Trinity*; Letham, *Holy Trinity*; Fortman, *Triune God*; Welch, *In This Name*.

7. The debate over what exactly to call each member of the Trinity and the unified divinity is legion. The argument is beyond the scope of this book. For further insight see Cunningham, *These Three Are One*, 19–126.

in essence, but distinct in their relation to each other. These relations of opposition are what distinguish the persons within the unity of God.[8]

The Father is Father because of his relationship to the Son; and the Son is Son because of his relationship to the Father. The Spirit proceeds from the Father by means of *spiration*, as opposed to *generation*, and is, therefore, not a second Son. The Spirit is the love between the Father and the Son, and there is no inherent reason for the Spirit to be depersonalized by his description as love, any more than the Son is depersonalized by the relational description of being a son. Sonship does not describe the Son's nature, but the relation in which he stands to the Father. To call a person a son only says that he has a father. Likewise, to call a person a father only shows that he has a child. The description of the Spirit as the love between the Father and the Son does not reveal the Spirit's personal nature, nor does it preclude him from being a person, but instead reveals his opposed relationship to both Father and Son.[9]

God's work in creation reveals his Trinitarian nature, and in this revelation, it is God himself who is revealed. The Father is the source of the work in the world, the Son is the means of the work, and the Spirit is the agent that accomplishes the work. Since God is Trinity in unity, there is no economic work of one person that does not involve all three. This statement should not be taken to mean that any of the three could have done any work within the economy. The doctrine of proper operations affirms that all three persons are involved in each work of the Godhead, but that certain works are proper to each. Therefore, the Father could not have accomplished redemption on the cross. That work was proper to the Son.[10] Likewise, the Son cannot send the Father, for the Father sends and the Son is sent.[11] Each person is present in the work of the other because of the unity in Trinity.[12] Each fully penetrates and inhabits the others so that while there is distinction between the persons because of the opposed relations, there is still unity within God's nature.[13]

The doctrine of proper operations has allowed the church to ascribe certain works to each person of the Godhead. For example, in creation

---

8. Ibid., 55–65.

9. Jenson, *Triune God*, 90–114.

10. Rahner, *Trinity*, 24–30.

11. Ware, *Father, Son, and Holy Spirit*, 43–68.

12. Weber, *Foundations of Dogmatics*, 393–94.

13. Cunningham, *These Three Are One*, 58–65.

the Father creates through the Son in the Spirit's power. It is the Father who is the source of the work, the Son who is the effecting agent in the work, and the Spirit who is the power in which the Son executes the work. Grenz states, "The Father functions as the ground of the world and of the divine program for creation. The Son functions as the revealer of God, the exemplar and herald of the Father's will for creation and the redeemer of humankind. And the Spirit functions as the personal divine power active in the world, the completer of the divine will and program."[14] The doctrine of proper operations has most often been used in relation to creation and redemption, but the idea is applicable to all areas of God's work. If the pattern that Grenz formulated holds true, then the question is, what role does each person of the Trinity play in judgment? The answer could be that the Father is the source and ground of judgment, the Son functions as the revealer of judgment and the judge appointed by the Father, while the Spirit functions as the divine power that completes the Son's judgment given to him by the Father.

In each work of the Trinity, "the Father acts through the Son and by the agency of the Spirit."[15] There is, therefore, a necessity within God's nature for the Spirit to be involved in judgment. While many scholars have adequately delineated the Spirit's work in such areas as regeneration, conversion, sanctification, and glorification, they have neglected his work on the condemnatorial side of judgment, failing to apply consistently the premise that the Father works through the Son in the power of the Spirit. What is typically presented is that the Trinity is reduced to a Binity as regards condemnation, in that the Spirit's proper role in condemnation is never addressed. One reason for this might be that the bulk of the work done in the area of condemnation focuses on the nature of hell itself, specifically its duration and occupants, and not the various economic works of the Three. This is understandable since condemnation is not a pleasant subject, and the tendency has been to distance God from it. While conservative theologians vigorously defend God's condemnatorial action, they do not invest as much energy in explicating the specific work of each person in condemnation.

Not only does the economic ordering of the Trinity's work necessitate that the Spirit have a role in judgment, but the immanent Trinity reveals that the Spirit who proceeds from the Father through the Son must be involved

14. Grenz, *Theology for the Community of God*, 67.
15. Ibid., 68.

in judgment. First John 4:8 states, "God is love." It is not that God loves, but that he himself is love. The Spirit is the Father's outgoing love for the Son and the Son's outgoing love for the Father. Love and wrath are not separate attributes of God, but are intimately related and are in fact the same thing, being experienced differently depending upon a person's relationship to God. Chapter six will address the relationship between God's love as believers experience it in the Spirit and God's condemnation as experienced by those who reject and stand in opposition to his love.

Biblical Grounding of the Spirit's Role in Judgment

Having established a Trinitarian grounding for the Holy Spirit's role in judgment, it is now necessary to ground his role in the biblical text. As stated earlier, it is the Bible that holds authority over theological formulations, and therefore, even if theological formulations affirm the Spirit's role in judgment, if that affirmation cannot be grounded in Scripture then at best it holds a speculative position within theological inquiry. The following section will demonstrate that the Bible does indeed affirm the conclusion reached above. This will be accomplished by first highlighting narrative passages in which the Spirit is active in judgment. That will be followed by an investigation into passages that correlate the Spirit and judgment.

The Old Testament

Within the Old Testament, there are numerous examples of the Spirit, either directly or indirectly, involved in actions of a condemnatorial nature. The following section will highlight two areas that narrate the Spirit's involvement in such actions. The first part will investigate the Spirit's role in the actions of four of Israel's judges, in which he was the empowering presence that allowed them to successfully wage war against those nations that were oppressing God's people. In addition to the preceding passages that offer a narrative depiction of the Spirit's work in judgment, others tell of his work in a more didactic fashion. The next group of passages to address occurs in Isaiah and focuses upon the Messiah's work as he establishes justice and righteousness in the land. He is able to accomplish this work because the Spirit rests upon him. What is often neglected in the Spirit's role in this work is that, in order to establish justice, the Messiah must defeat those forces that are opposed to justice by purging them from the land.

The Spirit and Judgment in Judges

In some of the Bible's earliest narratives, the Spirit rushes upon or clothes a person in order for him to accomplish a specific task. This clothing of the person with the Spirit was in no way related to the person's holiness, in that men like Samson and Balaam, who were morally repugnant, and a man like David, who was a man after God's own heart, are equally used by the Spirit to accomplish his purposes.[16] In Judges, a series of men are empowered by the Spirit in order to gain liberation for captive Israel. Not only did they conduct wars against the enemy, but they also judged the nation in the Spirit's wisdom.[17] While this liberation can be viewed from a strictly secular perspective as due to the judge's strategic abilities, the Bible affirms that working behind the judge is the Spirit who is the actual power that enables him to perform his task.[18] The Spirit goes to war for Israel through the judges, for without the Spirit they would have been unable to accomplish God's intended liberation.

Eichrodt writes "Hence even in those figures who, to our way of thinking, are purely 'secular' it is the miraculous power of the spirit which is the real force behind those acts of redemption that preserve the life of the nation, since the judges are motivated and empowered by the Spirit to accomplish their task." Eichrodt further writes, "The result is that in many respects they're warrior heroes, who often exercised their power only within very restricted limits, who are able to furnish the colours for the portrait of the one great Redeemer who is to bring order out of life's chaos and set up Yahweh's rule over the sorely pressed land." Jesus, the great Redeemer, fills in the colors that the judges provide. Both the judges and Jesus are able to bring God's rule to the land because the Spirit rests upon them. In both cases, in order to establish peace and justice, the Spirit must condemn in order to liberate. Those elements in the land that are incongruous with the peace to be established must be removed.

Starting with Othniel, moving to Gideon, then on to Jephthah and finally arriving at Samson, the Spirit empowered each of these men to execute judgment upon Israel's enemies. Within Judges, there is a downward spiral exhibited as the nation moved further away from God, until at the end in Judg 21:25 the telling statement is made that "everyone did what

---

16. Fredricks, "Rethinking the Role of the Holy Spirit," 88.

17. Keil and Delitzsch, *Joshua, Judges, Ruth*, 292–94; Benson, *Spirit of God*, 71–74.

18. Eichrodt, *Theology of the Old Testament*, 1:308–09.

was right in his own eyes." In a similar fashion, the Spirit's work within the lives of Othniel, Gideon, Jephthah, and Samson follows a downward spiral. This downward spiral is not to be equated with the Spirit himself any more than the nation's decline is to be equated with God. Instead, each judge's immoral behavior must be laid squarely at his own feet.

Othniel is the paradigmatic judge, the one against which all other judges are to be measured.[19] In contrast, Gideon repeatedly seeks a sign from God to confirm what he has been told, Jephthah makes a rash pledge that God did not require and eventually sacrifices his own daughter, while Samson is a man driven by his emotions, often entangled in activities that are in direct violation of God's will.[20] The Spirit works, nevertheless, through these men to execute God's condemnation upon the surrounding nations that are oppressing his chosen people.

In Judg 3:7–11, Israel found itself in the midst of hostile nations and tested in its faithfulness to God. Eventually, Israel broke fellowship with God by worshipping Baal, and for this offense God gave them into the hands of the king of Mesopotamia. When the Israelites cried out to God, he raised up for them a deliverer by the name of Othniel, the younger brother of Caleb. In 3:10, the Spirit of the Lord came upon Othniel so that he judged Israel and went out to war against Cushan-rishathaim.

The imagery of the Spirit coming upon a person is analogous to the Old Testament phrase that the hand of the Lord came upon a person. The hand of the Lord "functions as a metaphor of the urgent, compulsive, often overwhelming force with which God operates in an individual's or a group's experience." Block states, "In the book of Judges when the *ruah yhwh*, 'Spirit of the Lord,' comes upon individuals, it signals the arresting presence and power of God, often of individuals who are unqualified for or indisposed to service for him. In the present instance the empowering presence of the Spirit of God transforms this minor Israelite officer from Debir into the ruler of Israel and the conqueror of a world-class enemy."[21] Block does not equate Othniel's ability to wage war directly with the Spirit; instead, he links the Spirit with the salvation of the nation. While he is correct that the Spirit is sent upon Othniel to save captive Israel, the other side of the coin is that the captors are vanquished, and this is done by the power of the self-same Spirit. The Lord gave Mesopotamia into Othniel's hand and the land had

19. Schneider, *Judges*, 38–39.

20. Ibid., 38–42; Matthews, *Judges and Ruth*, 56–57.

21. Block, *Judges, Ruth*, 154–55.

rest for forty years. The Spirit waged war through Othniel to free Israel and to judge the king of Mesopotamia. In the first instance in Judges of the Spirit coming upon a person, that person is empowered to attack the enemy and bring liberation to Israel.

Likewise, in Judg 6–8, the Gideon narrative recounts another instance where the Spirit came upon a person and empowered him to fight Israel's oppressors. In the beginning of the narrative Gideon was too afraid to tear down an altar to Baal in the daytime, instead opting for the cover of darkness to perform his deed. In 6:34, however, the Spirit came upon Gideon, after which he boldly sounded a trumpet to gather the Abiezrites to follow him. The Spirit transformed Gideon from a fearful man into a man of action, one that would free the Israelites from their captivity and oppression. It is not Gideon himself who is able to gather a fighting force together, for although God calls Gideon a mighty warrior in 6:12, the people are ready to kill Gideon in 6:30 for tearing down the pagan altar. It is only by the Holy Spirit that Gideon is able to gather an army to himself, for the Spirit that is upon Gideon causes the people to respond to him.[22] As God used Gideon to judge the nations that were oppressing Israel, the Holy Spirit provided the means whereby he was able to accomplish the task set before him.

The downward spiral continued as the story of Jephthah recounts how the Spirit came upon him before he went to fight the sons of Ammon. In preparation for the battle, he made a vow to God that he would sacrifice the first thing that emerged from his tent upon the battle's successful completion. As he returned victorious from the conflict, his daughter emerged from the tent and he eventually sacrificed her after giving her two months to mourn.[23] Nowhere in the text does God ever instruct Jephthah to make a vow to him in exchange for victory, nor is any indication given that God condoned Jephthah's action. Most likely, the story is given to show the deteriorating state of the nation, for even as the Spirit moves upon a judge to accomplish his purpose, the judge acts in a manner that is not in accordance with the Spirit.

Samson is similar to Jephthah, for God used him to accomplish his purposes, but he does not evidence a character that is in accord with God's nature.[24] God's purpose for moving in Samson's life, as indicated in Judges 14:4, was to provoke the Philistines to war in order for God to free the Is-

22. Ibid., 272.

23. Ibid., 375–79.

24. Williams, *Judges and Ruth*, 56–58.

raelites from oppression. The narrative of Samson and the Spirit's working in his life occurs in 13:25, 14:6, 19, 15:14, and ends in 16:29–31 when God brings final judgment upon the Philistines.

In 14:6, Samson killed a lion with his bare hands after the Spirit rushed upon him. Then, in 14:19, after his wife tricked him to reveal the answer to a riddle, Samson charged to Ashkelon and killed thirty men after the Spirit came upon him. On another occasion in 15:14, his own people bound him with ropes and handed him over to the Philistines out of fear of retaliation. When the Philistines came out from Lehi to get him, the Spirit rushed upon him and he broke the ropes that were around him, picked up a donkey's jawbone, and killed one thousand men. These are shocking acts of violence that are easy to pass by when reading, but to have been there would be a different story. It is the Spirit who enabled Samson to accomplish these violent acts of judgment against the Philistines. Apart from the Spirit, Samson would have been powerless to accomplish anything.

At the end of his life, Samson requested from God that he strengthen him one more time in order to avenge himself upon the Philistines. In the famous scene where the Philistines are sacrificing to Dagon, they call for Samson to be brought for their entertainment. He is placed at a location in the building close to support columns that he is able to topple, thus killing the gathered Philistine rulers. While the text does not explicitly state that the Spirit empowered Samson in this feat, it is a logical conclusion from his request in 16:28 for God to give him strength that he recognized his feats of strength earlier in life had been empowered by the Spirit. At this moment, therefore, Samson requests the Spirit to come upon him one last time to allow him to avenge himself upon the Philistines for his gouged-out eyes. Even in his last act, Samson thought only of himself, but God still empowered him with the Spirit to liberate Israel from its oppressor.

While the nation slowly spiraled downward from God, the Spirit still acted within the nation to liberate it from its oppressors. He came upon the judges to empower them to military victories that released the nation from oppression. The preceding four examples clearly reveal the Spirit's involvement in the judgment of those nations that stood in opposition to God and his plans. While no text directly states that the Spirit defeated the oppressing nations, the indication is clear that each judge only accomplished his victory because of the Spirit's empowerment.

The Spirit and Judgment in Isaiah

In numerous prophecies relating to Israel's coming redeemer Isaiah highlights a direct link between the Messiah's mission to establish justice upon the earth and his empowerment by the Spirit. As argued earlier, the establishment of justice entails the elimination of injustice and those individuals who seek to maintain injustice in God's creation. John 3:16 is clear that out of his love God sent his Son to redeem creation. Equally clear is John 3:17–21 in which those people who are evil flee from God's light because they love darkness, injustice, and unrighteousness, and they therefore refuse to come into the light to have their deeds exposed so as to be able to put aside injustice in favor of justice. If the Spirit's anointing of Jesus was the prerequisite for him to proclaim liberty to the captives, then it logically follows that he will also carry out the condemnation of those who refuse to come into the light by the same Spirit. His entrance into the world with the accompanying empowerment by the Spirit is a single act that creates two groups of people, those who come into the light and those who refuse. Jesus, in the Spirit's power, liberates those who come to him and condemns those who refuse his offer of salvation.

Jesus was empowered by the Spirit to proclaim the favorable year of the Lord and to break the chains of bondage under which the people were living. Many expected him to break the physical chains of Roman occupation and therefore they looked for a Messiah that would ride into Jerusalem on a warhorse, not a donkey.[25] Jesus, however, understood his Spirit anointing as a call to first break spiritual chains and then, having accomplished that, work to end the external chains of oppression that feed upon those internal ones.[26]

Isaiah 11 is one of the most beautiful and poignant passages in the Bible relating the coming Messiah and his empowerment by the Spirit to accomplish his mission. He will judge with righteousness and fairness for the poor and the afflicted. At his coming, the animal kingdom will experience peace as one-time predators and prey take to reposing with each other. The curse placed upon the earth at the Fall will be reversed as humanity and the rest of creation returns to a state of harmony. This return to harmony is Paul's theme in Rom 8 where creation groans as in childbirth waiting for the revealing of the sons of God. In addition, God's children groan waiting

25. Wright, *New Testament and the People of God*, 159–61.

26. Matt 23:25–26.

for their inheritance, and deep within each believer, the Spirit himself groans and intercedes for the saints according to the will of God. The shoot from the stump of Jesse will accomplish this return to harmony because the Spirit will rest upon him.[27] The Spirit will empower him to judge fairly, for he will see the hearts of people, not merely their outward actions.

In Jesus, the promise of Isa 11 finds its fulfillment. From his birth, he was filled with the Holy Spirit, but at his baptism, the Spirit descended upon him to commission him for his ministry. In Luke 4:18–19 Jesus proclaims he is the fulfillment of Isa 61:1–2 in which the Lord's Spirit will anoint the Messiah to preach good news to the poor and to bring liberation to the captives. This scene is often presented as the paradigm regarding the Spirit's work in relation to the Messiah, but what is often overlooked is Isa 11:4, in that the Messiah will, in addition to judging the poor in righteousness and deciding with equity for the meek, "strike the earth with the rod of his mouth, and with the breath of his lips he shall kill the wicked." The connection between God's breath and the Spirit will be given in chapter 4.

Likewise, Isa 61:2 states that the Messiah would proclaim both the year of the Lord's favor and his day of vengeance. If the Spirit is the power that enables the Messiah to judge righteously, then should not the same Spirit empower him to strike the earth with the rod of his mouth and slay the wicked with his breath? Motyer suggests that the rod and the breath in Isa 11:4 are shorthand for the king's power to make decisions. It is the king who can condemn a person. He does, however, understand the reference to the Spirit in the passage as a reference to the Holy Spirit and is therefore able to write, "breath/'spirit' or 'wind' is a powerful, invisible force. When the reference is to the Lord's Spirit, there is constantly the suggestion of power to effect change, to impose the divine will and order on things (Ps 33:6). So, the King's word is full of divine efficacy."[28]

In fact, the rod of the mouth and the breath of the lips are phrases connected with the Holy Spirit in other parts of the Bible. Neve argues convincingly that Isa 11:15 is a reference to the parting of the sea in Exod 15:8–10 and retold in 2 Sam 22:16. While the account in Exodus speaks of the wind as moving the sea back, 2 Sam refers the action to the blast of the breath of God's nostrils. Therefore, the meaning of *ruach* in Isa 11:15 is not wind,

27. Montague argues that Isa 11:2 applies to the baptism of Jesus. Montague, *Holy Spirit*, 41.

28. Motyer, *Prophecy of Isaiah*, 120–23. Similarly, Wildberger writes, "The Spirit of Yahweh gives the king the abilities to carry out the demands of his office." Wildberger, *Isaiah 1–12*, 471.

but Spirit, viewed symbolically as breath. Additionally, Isa 11:15 mentions that God will wave his hand over the river, thus lending more weight to the translation of *ruach* as breath and not wind.[29]

Isaiah 28:5–6 presents a similar idea when the prophet relates, "In that day the LORD of hosts will be a crown of glory, and a diadem of beauty, to the remnant of his people, and a spirit of justice to him who sits in judgment, and strength to those who turn back the battle at the gate." Calvin does not see this verse as referring to the Holy Spirit, but instead as a reference to the civil magistrate's ability to govern.[30] Motyer asserts that the verse does not refer to the Holy Spirit, but to God's power of judgment.[31] Young, however, argues, "The language does not mean that God fills the judges with a spirit of judgment, but rather that He Himself becomes that Spirit of judgment. There is clear reflection on 11:2. He who places upon the Messiah the sevenfold Spirit will place Himself upon judges as the Spirit who brings forth true judgment."[32] Likewise, Alexander posits that the *ruach* in the verse is not a mere influence, but a reference to God himself.[33] For Montague, this verse is connected with Isa 4:4 and Mic 3:8. The Spirit is the power that will enable judges to rule honestly.[34]

Likewise, Isa 32:15–16 declares that when the Spirit is poured out on the barren land the fields will become fruitful, with justice and righteousness dwelling in the land. The Spirit being poured out foreshadows the Pentecost event foretold in Joel 2:28–29. It is because he is poured out that justice will exist in the land, and while this verse speaks to the positive aspects of his work, the corollary to that work is that the barrenness of the field will disappear, as well as injustice and unrighteousness. Young writes, "When justice and righteousness are found, it is because the Spirit has been poured out from on high, for these are the gifts of God alone."[35]

The Spirit's being poured out picks up an allusion to water that had already been introduced in Isa 30:28 where God's *ruach*, translated as breath, is "like an overflowing stream that reaches up to the neck; that will sift the

---

29. Neve, *Spirit of God in the Old Testament*, 44–52.

30. Calvin, *Commentary on the Prophet Isaiah*, 2:275.

31. Motyer, *Prophecy of Isaiah*, 230

32. Young, *Book of Isaiah*, 270.

33. Alexander, *Commentary on Isaiah*, 475.

34. Montague, *Holy Spirit*, 39.

35. Young, *Book of Isaiah*, 399. Similarly, Kaiser acknowledges that the Holy Spirit will establish justice and righteousness in the land. Kaiser, *Isaiah 13–39*, 334.

nations with the sieve of destruction." The connection of *ruach* with water in this verse speaks to the condemnation of the Assyrians. In 32:15, a water metaphor is again applied to the *ruach* as he is poured out on the barren land in order to bring fruitfulness and healing. The Spirit's double work is presented when the two verses are connected, with him both sifting the nations and bringing healing to the land.[36]

Isaiah presents a picture of the coming Messiah being empowered by the Spirit to accomplish his task of liberation. This liberation will be accomplished as he pours out the Spirit upon the fallen creation, since the Spirit will abide upon him permanently. It is in the Spirit's power that he proclaims the favorable year of the Lord, but also the day of the Lord's vengeance. The Day of the Lord will be either a day of great blessing or of destruction depending upon each person's relationship to the Messiah. Having examined the Spirit's role in empowering the coming Messiah, it is now possible to move to Jesus' own words during the Farewell Discourse concerning the Spirit's role in convicting the world of sin, righteousness, and judgment.

The New Testament

Having investigating the passages that relate the Spirit and the Messiah with judgment in the Old Testament we now move to the New Testament. We will first highlight the Spirit's role in the judgment rendered upon Ananias, Sapphira, and Elymas. Following that the Farewell Discourse will reveal the Spirit's role in convicting the world of sin, righteousness, and judgment. It will be shown that the Spirit will continue the work that Jesus started during his ministry, in which the light of the world discloses those who are opposed to that light and who refuse to come to the light for forgiveness. While the Son was sent to save the world, his entrance into it also created the standard by which those who reject his offer of salvation will be judged. As the Spirit-anointed Messiah, he was empowered to be the world's liberating judge, and he related that the Spirit would continue his work once he had been glorified. Finally, Paul's statements in Gal 3:17 and Rom 8:13 that set in contrast the Spirit and the flesh will be considered. In these passages, he instructs believers to kill the old nature by the Spirit's power. The dual aspects of liberation and condemnation are evidenced as the Spirit works sanctification in a believer's life. The believer is to produce the fruit of the

36. Montague, *Holy Spirit*, 40.

Spirit that is in accord with his new nature, while at the same time, by the Spirit's power, he is to continually kill the old nature that stands in opposition to God.

The Spirit and Judgment in Acts

One of the more shocking stories in the Bible, the death of Ananias and Sapphira, displays the Holy Spirit's role in judgment, even though it is not explicitly stated.[37] The church was in its infancy and encountered a breach of trust within its membership when a couple conspired to test the Holy Spirit, resulting in a swift and decisive condemnation of their actions.

In contrast to Barnabas, who sold a field that he owned and gave the proceeds to the fledgling Christian community in Jerusalem, Ananias and Sapphira sold a piece of property, but conspired to withhold a portion of the profits while claiming that they were giving the entire amount to the church. One might have expected Peter to reprimand the couple, but quite unexpectedly, Ananias is struck dead and three hours later his wife suffers the same fate. Having put the Holy Spirit to the test by lying to him resulted in this couple coming under God's condemnation in order for them to serve as an example to the newly formed church.

In Acts 5:3 Peter asks Ananias why he had lied to the Holy Spirit. The conflict that Luke presents is not primarily between the couple and Peter, although that conflict is how it appears on the surface, but is instead between the Holy Spirit and Satan.[38] The couple was not together when they brought the money to Peter, for as he questioned Ananias Peter told him that he lied to the Holy Spirit, whereupon Ananias fell down and breathed his last. The text does not state that God was the direct cause of death, but the implication is so strong that it is hard to miss. In addition, Luke makes a subtle play on words between Ananias' death and the Holy Spirit, when he writes that Ananias breathed his last. As the Spirit is God's breath, and it is the Spirit that breathes into a person the breath of life, Ananias, who had challenged God's breath, breathes his last one. The Spirit removed from

37. For an overview of the various issues involved in this narrative see Kienzler, *Fiery Holy Spirit*, 101–20. Also see Marguerat, "La Mort d'Ananias et Saphira," 209–26. Marquerat's article seeks to draw a parallel between Acts 5:1–11 and Gen 3, and while that effort is beyond the scope of this investigation, the article gives a concise overview of the various interpretive techniques employed in explicating the passage.

38. O'Toole, "'You Did Not Lie to Us," 197–98; Dunn, *Acts of the Apostles*, 64.

Ananias the very gift he needed to continue living. Calvin states that the Spirit gave Peter the dart that shot and killed the couple.[39]

Sapphira came to Peter three hours after her husband died and he confronted her with the same question. Unlike Ananias, who was given no chance to repent of his lie, Peter asked Sapphira how much money they received from the sale of the property. She lied to Peter, and ultimately to the Holy Spirit, and he asked her why she wanted to put the Spirit to the test. Because of her deception she fell at Peter's feet and breathed her last.

Polhill is correct when he writes:

> The church is a holy body, the realm of the Spirit. By the power of this spiritual presence in its midst, the young community worked miracles, witnessed fearlessly, and was blessed with incredible growth. The Spirit was the power behind its unity, and its unity was the power behind its witness. However, just as with God there is both justice and mercy, so with his Spirit there is also an underside to his blessing. There is his judgment. This Ananias and Sapphira experienced. The Spirit is not to be taken lightly. As the Spirit of God he must always be viewed with fear in the best sense of that word (*phobos*), reverent awe, and respect.[40]

The Spirit's work in condemnation is not explicit in this short story, but the implications are clear. The Acts of the Apostles could just as easily, and probably more descriptive of the true nature of the power behind the work described, be called the Acts of the Holy Spirit, for he is the motivating agent behind the work that is accomplished. Jesus had ascended to the Father's right hand and from there he poured out his Spirit upon the earth. The church was moving forward in the Spirit's power, and Luke is careful to relate each progressive stage of the church to his activity. It is therefore quite appropriate that here, in the condemnation of the couple's deception, the Spirit played a central role. While the sentence may seem harsh, one must keep in mind that the actual conflict was not only between the couple and the church, but was between God and Satan, the divine community of believers as called together by the Spirit and the forces of darkness that stand in opposition to him.

Ananias and Sapphira, like Uzzah, lived at one of the crucial epochs in salvation history and therefore their actions were met with a greater punishment. A temporal perspective on this story might lead one to question

---

39. Calvin, *Commentary Upon the Acts of the Apostles*, 199.

40. Polhill, *Acts*, 160. Haenchen, *Acts of the Apostles*, 237.

God's goodness, but if one considers the issue from an eternal perspective then it is quite conceivable to suggest that in the couple's death God is using their evil for its maximal good. By dying as an example to the church their evil became a warning and God used them for his ultimate glory. Here in the church's infancy, a clear stand was taken between the encroaching darkness and God's holiness as evidenced in the Spirit.

Like the encounter of Ananias and Sapphira with the Holy Spirit, so also Elymas encountered the Holy Spirit in his attempt to stop Paul from preaching the gospel to Sergius Paulus. While Elymas was not killed for his interference, he was struck blind for a time as a punishment for his actions. As in the case of the couple, the Holy Spirit is vital to the narrative, though he is not directly credited with the execution of the sentence passed upon Elymas.

In Acts 13:4–12 the proconsul Sergius Paulus summoned Paul to relate the gospel to him. Elymas, a magician connected with the proconsul, sought to keep him from hearing Paul's message and was temporarily blinded because of his attempt to impede the gospel. As Elymas, also called Bar-Jesus (son of the savior), sought to obstruct Paul, who was filled with the Holy Spirit, Paul rebuked this son of the devil and informed him that the hand of the Lord was going to be upon him and that he would be blind for a season. As in the Ananias narrative, Elymas was not confronting Paul only, but was also confronting the Holy Spirit who empowered Paul's message and work.[41] Kienzler rightly concludes "the Spirit is not only the inspirer of the words of judgment but is also involved in effecting the blindness itself."[42]

The connection between the Spirit and condemnation in this passage is not explicit, for while Paul is filled with the Holy Spirit when he makes his proclamation, the text does not directly state that the Holy Spirit caused the blindness, attributing the blindness instead to the hand of the Lord. The phrase "hand of the Lord" occurs two other times in Luke's writing, the first in Luke 1:66 in relation to John the Baptist and the second in Acts 11:21 in relation to the successful expansion of the gospel.[43] Immediately after his birth, John's story spread throughout the hill country of Judea and the people pondered what this could mean because the Lord's hand was upon him. Luke had already related in 1:15 that the Spirit would be upon John from his mother's womb and therefore, the reference in 1:66 is most likely

---

41. Polhill, *Acts*, 293.

42. Kienzler, *Fiery Holy Spirit*, 186.

43. Luke's use of the Lord's hand recalls Moses' confrontation with Pharaoh. Dunn, *Acts of the Apostles*, 177.

an indication of the Spirit's presence in John's life. A stronger connection between the hand of the Lord and the Spirit will be presented in chapter 5. The second occurrence of the phrase is in Acts 11:21, where those dispersed over the persecution of Stephen had great success in spreading the gospel. Luke recounts that the hand of the Lord was with them and a great number believed. It is the Spirit that draws a person to Christ, who convicts him of his sin and places him in the community of faith. The disciples were able to have great success in their mission because the Spirit was with them. In a similar manner, the Spirit was with Paul, and through Paul's word, he struck Elymas blind, condemning him for his obstruction of his work.

Polhill interprets the hand explicitly as the "power and Spirit" of God, while others like Haenchen and Dunn only describe the hand as the power of God.[44] Luke Johnson is indicative of the unwillingness to state the obvious concerning who the "hand of the Lord" refers to when he writes that the hand "signifies the presence of divine power that validates their testimony."[45] The book of Acts makes it abundantly clear that the validating power of the gospel proclamation is the Holy Spirit. One reason Dunn and Johnson might be reluctant to directly call the hand of the Lord the Holy Spirit is that they both refer the phrase back to 1 Sam 5:6, 9, in which the Philistines took the Ark of the Covenant, whereupon the hand of the Lord was heavy upon them and God smote them with tumors. Could it be that having referred the hand of the Lord back to this passage—and the obvious implications of condemnation that those verses carry—has caused these two commentators to shy away from the obvious reference to the Holy Spirit in Luke's description of the success of the evangelistic endeavors of these early converts? The answer appears to be yes, but the text nevertheless points to the two outcomes of the work of the Spirit, both salvation and condemnation.

Both of these short narratives describe in graphic fashion the execution of judgment upon people by the Holy Spirit. Ananias and Sapphira are struck dead for their testing of the Spirit, while Elymas is blinded for his attempt to obstruct the Spirit's progress in spreading the message of salvation.

---

44. Polhill, *Acts*, 271; Haenchen, *Acts of the Apostles*, 366; Dunn, *Acts of the Apostles*, 155.

45. Johnson, *Acts of the Apostles*, 203.

The Spirit's Convicting Work in John's Gospel

Another passage that stands out in relation to the Spirit's role in judgment is John 16:8–11, where Jesus related to the disciples that when the *Paraclete* comes, he would convict the world concerning sin, righteousness, and judgment. The Spirit is not restricted to operating only within the church, as if the church had a monopoly on his activity or as if it served as a straitjacket that confined his actions, but he is active in the entire creation.[46] While these verses appear to give a straightforward presentation of what the Spirit does concerning judgment, the verse's interpretation has been notoriously difficult to understand.[47]

Jesus stated that the *Paraclete* would convict the world regarding sin, righteousness, and judgment. The world is convicted concerning sin because they have not believed in Jesus, concerning righteousness because he is going to the Father and they will not see him anymore, and concerning judgment because the ruler of this world has been judged. While on the earth, Jesus convicted people of these three things by his purity showing people their sin, by his righteousness showing them their false righteousness, and by his truth showing them that they were children of the father of lies, the devil and that the devil's judgment was their judgment.

The Spirit convicts the world concerning sin because it does not believe in Jesus.[48] This verse can be understood in three ways. The first is that the Spirit will convict the world of wrong ideas of sin. The second is that he will convict the world because they do not believe and their unbelief is a classic illustration of their sin. The final option is to see unbelief in Jesus as the only sin under consideration. More than likely, John was not making a sharp distinction between any of the options. Instead, unbelief is the root of all sin. Since the guilt is relational, only a change of allegiance can remove it.

A person in the world can never know Jesus by definition, since the world is the sphere estranged from and hostile to him. The verdict given in John's gospel is that light has come into the world, but the world has loved

---

46. Morris argues that this is the only passage in the Scripture that speaks of the Holy Spirit performing a work in the world, as opposed to in believers. While he is correct that this verse reveals that the Spirit operates outside the church, he has failed to consider the other references to the Spirit's work in judgment that I have highlighted. Morris, *Gospel According to John*, 618–19.

47. Brown, *Gospel According to John (XIII–XXI)*, 711. See also Carson, "Function of the Paraclete," 548.

48. Morris, *Gospel According to John*, 619.

darkness and refused to come into the light to receive forgiveness. While on the earth, Jesus was the light that enlightens every man, and although he left the earth physically at his ascension, the sending of the Holy Spirit continued his work of exposing the world's sin. The Holy Spirit brings people to conviction regarding their rejection of God, but this conviction does not necessarily lead to salvation; it instead leaves the sinner with no option but to recognize his error.[49] The sin of which the Spirit convicts is the rejection of Jesus, from which all other sins stem, and if one removes that sin, then all others are forgiven. The Spirit convicts the world of sin in two manners. One is that he procures a guilty verdict against the world and the second is that he drives that guilty verdict home to the unbeliever on a personal level.[50]

When a sinful world encounters the Spirit, a destabilization takes place. For the individual, this can result in repentance or in a hardening to God. If a person refuses to succumb to the Spirit's convicting power he is not left unaffected in his decision, but it begins to ripple through his life. His refusal to accept forgiveness, to drink from the water that is available in Christ, leaves him restless, thirsty, and unfulfilled. This lack of contentment will often play itself out in various destructive tendencies. Likewise, the Spirit's work of convicting the world regarding sin constantly destabilizes the systems the world seeks to create in order to establish its own security and salvation. The world's various systems, from governments to families, which are built upon shifting sand, will continually fail as long as they are not built upon the rock of Christ's redemption in the Spirit's power. Christ's Spirit serves to call into question all false saviors and ethical systems. The Spirit convicts the world of its sin, and that conviction is driven by the world's rejection of God's love as revealed in Jesus Christ.[51]

The Spirit convicts the world regarding righteousness in that its righteousness is inadequate. Instead of righteousness referring to the righteousness of Christ, which would force the *hoti* clause to be explicative, Carson suggests that John employs a touch of irony, something for which his gospel is known, by stating that the Spirit will convict the world of its false righteousness.[52] The world lives under the false assumption that its righteousness is enough to curry God's favor. Jesus rebuked this false understanding of righteousness repeatedly during his ministry by declaring that unless a

49. Aloisi, "Paraclete's Ministry of Conviction," 65–66.

50. Morris, *Gospel According to John*, 619–20.

51. Moltmann, *Spirit of Life*, 142–43.

52. Carson, "Function of the Paraclete," 558–61.

person's righteousness exceeded that of the Pharisees' then he could not get into heaven. Isaiah, one of Jesus' most quoted Old Testament prophets, stated that the world's righteousness is like filthy rags.[53]

Jesus' resurrection is the vindication of his statements during his life and an indictment upon his opponent's false accusations. The resurrection proved Jesus to be right and his opponents wrong in their understanding of him.[54] With the ascension, he has gone to be with the Father, sending the Holy Spirit to continue the work of revealing to the world that its righteousness is as filthy rags. The Jewish leaders condemned Jesus to death as a blasphemer, while Pilate saw him as a potential leader of a rebellion, a nuisance to be dispensed with to avoid a riot. The world's judgment on Jesus was that he was a sinner who deserved to die, and that in the crucifixion he was indeed cursed by God. The resurrection, however, exposed to the world the falsity of its judgment. It was the religious and political leaders of the day, as well as the masses, whose judgment was proven wrong, whose supposed righteousness was broken upon the reality of his resurrection.

Finally, the Spirit convicts the world about its own judgment because the devil has been judged. Jesus had already shown the disciples that the devil was the father of all lies, of all wrong judgment. The world's judgment of itself is that it is safe and secure. The world falsely believes that it is full of life, when, in fact, he revealed it was dead. The world loves darkness and mistakes the darkness for light. Jesus' life, death, and resurrection judge the father of wrong judgment, and hence, the world's judgment is wrong since it gains its judgment from the devil.[55] Not only does the Spirit reveal that the world has judged wrongly regarding Jesus, but in Satan's judgment on the cross the Spirit judges those who are aligned with him. This judgment, which carries an eschatological flavor, is proleptically fulfilled in the present. Whoever does not believe in Jesus Christ is condemned already.[56] While this condemnation is effective in the present, it gains its orientation from the future final judgment.[57]

On the cross, the devil was defeated in the victory of the Son of God. What to the world's eyes appeared to be the death of an upstart revolutionary

53. Isa 64:6.

54. Brown, *Gospel According to John (XIII–XXI)*, 712–13; Morris, *Gospel According to John*, 620.

55. Carson, *Gospel According to John*, 534–37.

56. John 3:18.

57. Pannenberg, *Systematic Theology*, 3:610–20.

with aspirations of divinity was in fact the defeat of death itself, the over-coming of the barrier between God and his crowning creation. The Spirit convicts the world of this judgment inasmuch as the world has aligned it-self with the devil. The Father's judgment against all rebellion and idolatry that was given to the Son is applied to the world, and the individuals within it, in the Spirit's power.

Hebrews 9:14 intimately connects the Spirit with the Son in the cruci-fixion itself when it reveals that Jesus offered himself to the Father through the eternal Spirit. There is debate as to whether or not the Holy Spirit is the correct reference in this verse. The phrase "eternal spirit" is not a typical name for the Holy Spirit, but it is not inappropriate as a designation for him. Many commentators see this as a reference to the Holy Spirit by mak-ing a connection with Isa 61:1–2.[58] The Spirit was upon Jesus to inaugurate his ministry and the reasoning is that the same Spirit is empowering Je-sus during the crucifixion. All of the major English translations capitalize Spirit, thus throwing their support behind the interpretation that this is a reference to the Holy Spirit. In the context in Hebrews, the offering is for the forgiveness of sins, but the verse nonetheless shows that Jesus offered himself to the Father in the Holy Spirit. Just as the Spirit anointed him to carry out his ministry, he went to the cross under the Spirit's power, thus connecting the Spirit with the judgment rendered upon Satan and subse-quently upon humanity.

Under this interpretation of Jesus' words in the Farewell Discourse, the Holy Spirit will continue the very work that Jesus did while on the earth. Borchert writes, "The Paraclete's task here then is portrayed in the presence of the disciples and in the Johannine court of God like a counselor and judge in bringing to just judgment the world and its rebellious prince. This section then is not unrelated to the way Jesus has earlier been pictured as having been given the authority to render all judgment by the Father (cf. 5:22)."[59] Of course, this work was not something that the Spirit was previously uninvolved in, for Jesus carried out his entire ministry under the Spirit's anointing and power. In a sense, Jesus and the Spirit switched places after the resurrection and ascension. While on the earth, Jesus was the pri-

---

58. For those who contend that the Holy Spirit is the referent in this verse see Lane, *Hebrews 9–13*, 240; Kistemaker, *Exposition of the Epistle*, 251–52; Bruce, *Epistle to the He-brews*, 205–6; Ellingworth, *Epistle to the Hebrews*, 457. Attridge argues that the phrase is not in reference to the Holy Spirit, but to the spiritual nature of Jesus' sacrifice. Attridge, *Epistle to the Hebrews*, 250–51.

59. Borchert, *John 12–21*, 167.

mary agent in convicting the world of sin, righteousness, and judgment. After the ascension, the Father and the Son sent the Spirit as the primary agent in convicting the world.

The Holy Spirit does not do this work on his own, but accomplishes it through the church. It is the church, in the Spirit's power, that convicts the world of sin, righteousness, and judgment, through its actions and words. This work, like Jesus' work, is not one of condemnation, but of life. The church is not sent to tell the world it is going to hell, but instead to reveal to it the Father's great love. If, however, the world rejects God's offer all that is left is condemnation and death. While the Holy Spirit will provide comfort and guidance to those who belong to Jesus, he will also execute the Father's condemnatorial judgment given to the Son upon those who reject him.

The Spirit and the Flesh in Paul

Two final verses that deserve consideration regarding the Spirit's role in judgment are Gal 5:17 and Rom 8:13. Galatians 5:17 declares that the Spirit's desires are set in opposition to the flesh's desires, as the flesh is set in opposition to the Spirit. The believer finds himself in the midst of a struggle that calls for his allegiance to one side or the other. In verse 18, Paul gives the believer hope when he states that if the Spirit leads someone, he is no longer under law. Betz declares, "In the battle between the forces of flesh and Spirit there is no stalemate, but the Spirit takes the lead, overwhelms, and thus defeats evil."[60] The Spirit ensures the defeat and condemnation of the flesh for those who are in Christ.

In Rom 8:13, Paul increases the opposition between the two by stating that it is the Christian's duty to put to death the deeds of the body and that this mortifying of the body's misdeeds is accomplished by the Spirit. The Spirit's role in putting to death the body's misdeeds relates him to the condemnation of that which stands in opposition to God. The desires of the flesh represent those things that are opposed to God, whether openly immoral or secretly so. The murderer and the prideful moralist are both equally fulfilling the flesh's desires as they seek to establish their fulfillment and security upon their own terms.[61] Paul does not leave the option open

---

60. Betz, *Galatians*, 281.

61. Barth writes, "The vast display of noble and ignoble human vitality, all the actual realization of human positive and negative capacities, in fact, all which we name 'Life' (Bios), is—*after the flesh.*" Barth, *Epistle to the Romans*, 293.

for people to establish their own salvation, but instead insists that people put aside the works of darkness in favor of the fruit of the Spirit. The life that the Spirit imparts to the believer will result in works that are in accord with that life. Conversely, the death in which the unbeliever finds himself will result in deeds that are in accord with that death. The believer who has the Spirit of Christ dwelling in him is obligated to put to death those deeds of the old nature that linger on.[62] Through the process of sanctification, the Spirit empowers the believer to destroy continually those tendencies and actions that are incongruous with God's kingdom.[63]

As the believer continually kills the flesh, the Spirit gives life to his mortal body because of Christ's resurrection. The Spirit imparts to the believer the life of the age to come, and puts to death the deeds that belong to the current age.[64] The warning given in Rom 8:13 is clear: either destroy the deeds of the body by the Spirit's power and live, or live according to the flesh and die. While the text does not explicitly state that the Spirit will impose the death sentence upon the unbeliever, it is clear that he puts to death the old nature. This death sentence on the old nature is accomplished by the believer's participation in Christ's crucifixion, which is itself accomplished by the Spirit.

Conclusion

God the Father works through God the Son in the power of the Spirit. This understanding of God's working in the world is the Trinitarian ground for the Spirit's work in judgment. But not only can it be shown that the Spirit works in judgment as a logical outworking of Trinitarian theology, it is also evident from direct scriptural passages. Having established that the Spirit has a part to play in God's judgment, we can now move in the next four chapters to explicating four motifs or symbols that the Bible employs to describe both the Spirit and judgment.

---

62. "It is the energy of the divine Spirit, not the energy of the flesh, that enables the believer to put the body's deeds to death." Morris, *Epistle to the Romans*, 312.

63. The Greek verb suggests continual action. Mounce, *Romans*, 180.

64. Swete states that the "Spirit, which kills the flesh, brings you life." Swete, *Holy Spirit in the New Testament*, 218. Moo correctly relates that a fine balance is established by Paul in which the believer works in cooperation with God's Spirit to mortify the deeds of the flesh. Moo, *Epistle to the Romans*, 495–96.

3

The Spirit and Divine Fire

FIRE IS A FASCINATING thing. It can provide warmth on a cold night to chase away the chill, yet it can also burn down the house it is heating. Fire can provide light to dispel the darkness, yet that same light can find us if we are seeking to hide. Fire can refine silver, purging off the dross, but silver and dross may have a different opinion about the fire itself. The silver is refined and used by the smelter, while the dross is discarded. Fire is a basic need of humanity, but with all the wonderful benefits fire provides it has a dangerous side, an uncontrollable aspect. Warmth can turn to burning, a soft glow into a raging inferno, and when this happens fire ceases to be beneficial to humanity and becomes destructive. It is therefore appropriate that fire is used as a symbol of God's beneficial presence and that it also describes his judgment. Likewise, the Spirit provides wonderful blessings to humanity, but he can also be a consuming fire who actualizes God's judgment in the world.

To prove the thesis that the Spirit actualizes God's judgment under the symbol of fire, the following chapter will begin by investigating how fire is used in scripture in relation to judgment. Once I have shown that fire serves as a symbol of divine judgment I will show that the Spirit is also described by the symbol of fire. The bulk of the chapter will be committed to showing that not only is the Spirit described symbolically as fire, but that he is also connected with fire as a symbol of God's judgment.

Fire in the Bible

God is a consuming fire![1] The fire of God's presence burns all with which it comes into contact, purifying some and destroying others. Numbers 11:1 relates that the fire of God destroyed those who grumbled against Moses, while in Isa 6:6, a burning coal cleansed Isaiah's unclean lips. It is clear that "fire is viewed theocentrically in the Old Testament as a representation of the mysterious, unapproachable, terrifying and yet gracious glory of Yahweh in revelation, and also as means and established image of His judicial action."[2]

As Moses approached the burning bush, fire as a representation of the presence of God must have deeply embedded itself into his consciousness. This representation was expanded to Israel while they stood at the foot of Mount Sinai as it was engulfed by smoke and fire. As they moved about in the desert for forty years, they were guided by the pillar of cloud by day and of fire by night. The tying of God's presence with fire graphically illustrated his nature, in that he is both protective and destroying. The same element that is most desperately needed by man can become most destructive when misused or neglected. Likewise, the symbolical presence of God as fire connotes his loving kindness, a love that seeks to save his people, and his absolute holiness that can allow no transgression of his nature to pass by as inconsequential.

Israel's *cultus* used fire for several purposes, not the least of which was to assist in the offering of sacrifices to Yahweh. A fire was to be burning continually on the sacrificial altar.[3] It purified articles such as gold and silver, so that before these articles could be considered ceremonially clean, they must be passed through fire.[4] Additionally, it destroyed those things that were sanctified to keep them from becoming profane. A classic example of this procedure is the instruction in Exod 12:10 to burn any of the leftover Passover lamb. It is by fire that pagan altars are to be destroyed, along with the enemies of the Lord.[5] The use of fire in the *cultus* would assuredly remind the people of the fire of God's presence.

In the majority of passages in the Old Testament when fire is related to God, it speaks of his judicial wrath. Genesis 3:24 relates that a cherubim and a flaming sword that turned in every direction barred Adam and Eve from

1. Heb 12:29
2. Lang, "πῦρ," 6:937.
3. Lev 6:2, 6.
4. Lev 13:53; Num 31:23.
5. Deut 13:16–17; Josh 6:24; 1 Sam 15.

returning to the garden. For the first couple, it was impossible to return to Eden by the way they left, for fire blocked the entrance. Furthermore, Gen 19:24 recounts Lot's flight from Sodom and Gomorrah as fire from the Lord rained down upon the cities. Punishment by fire becomes a recurring theme within the Bible, both in a figurative and a literal sense.[6] While it might have been possible to view this fiery punishment as capricious and uncontrolled, the Jewish people understood that the God who presented himself in and by fire was in control of its effects. Fire was not a blind force, but was in God's hand.[7]

In the prophetic writings, the fire of judgment was transferred from a strictly temporal framework to an eschatological one. The coming Day of the Lord, a day that the Israelites had looked forward to as a day of vindication, was reinterpreted by Amos as a day of judgment for the nation.[8] At the end, God would come to judge both the Gentile nations and his own chosen people, and it was his own who were to be considered first in the judgment. Joel writes that in the Day of the Lord, blood, fire, and columns of smoke will be signs of judgment.[9] Whereas God judged the world by water in the time of Noah, his final judgment will be by fire. This fiery judgment is most notably developed in the apocalyptic writers and carried forward into the New Testament in 2 Pet 3:7. The judgment oracles of the prophets repeatedly attest to God's judgment of both the nations and Israel by fire, temporally and eschatologically.

In the New Testament, fire is not an element in theophanies, for in the revelation of Christ fire gives way to flesh as the fullness of God among his people. This is not to argue that fire is not employed in a minor sense in the New Testament to represent God, for in Rev 1:14–15 the eyes of the risen Christ are like flames of fire, and his feet are like bronze that has been heated. Nevertheless, the imagery of a fiery cloud and a burning bush does not continue into the New Testament.

In the Gospels, Jesus speaks frequently of the fires of hell, but never of fire as temporal judgment. He is concerned, in line with the Baptist, to warn people that the axe is already at the root of the tree, and there is coming a time in which those who are in rebellion against God will be chopped down and thrown into the fire. In Luke 9:51–56, as Jesus was traveling to

---

6. Dan 7:10 and 2 Pet 2:6.

7. Lang, "πῦρ," 6:936.

8. Heschel, *The Prophets*, 33–34.

9. Joel 2.30.

Jerusalem to celebrate his last Passover, he sent disciples ahead of him into a Samaritan village to make arrangements, but the Samaritans would not accommodate the group because they were heading to Jerusalem. James and John took this insult quite personally and asked Jesus if they should call down fire from heaven to consume the village. Jesus does not discount that God has done this type of action in the past, but rebukes the two disciples by informing them that he did not come to destroy lives, but to save them.

This is the only instance in the Gospels in which the Old Testament understanding of temporal punishment by fire is evident, and here it is rejected as a proper method of dealing with those who are opposed to God's chosen.[10] Kienzler makes an astute observation when he shows that in Acts the Spirit falls upon the Samaritans when Peter and John come to them after their baptism. Instead of God sending fiery punishment upon the Samaritans, as John initially requested, God baptizes the Samaritans in the Spirit to show their inclusion in the church.[11]

The only other possible New Testament correlation of temporal judgment and fire occurs when John the Baptist warns the crowds gathering around him to flee from the wrath to come. He then informs them that he indeed baptizes with water, but one is coming who will baptize them with the Holy Spirit and fire. The surrounding context speaks of the eschatological judgment of the people, and it is therefore likely that the reference to baptism in the Holy Spirit and fire refers to an eschatological baptism, with the caveat that within the New Testament the age to come has broken in upon the current age and therefore this baptism, which is eschatological in nature and origin, is taking place temporally in the decisions people make regarding Christ.[12]

As previously mentioned, Jesus does use fire in an eschatological manner to refer to the fate of those who come under condemnatory judgment, those who are consigned to Gehenna.[13] At the end of the age, Jesus will send forth his angels to gather up those who commit lawlessness in order

10. Green, *Gospel of Luke*, 405–6.

11. Kienzler, *Fiery Holy Spirit*, 157–58.

12. Matt 3:1–12. The present execution of eschatological judgment is displayed most clearly in the Gospel of John, especially John 5:19–29.

13. Mark 9:43. Gehenna is a reference to the Valley of Hinnom outside of Jerusalem in which child sacrifice had taken place in Israel's past. The valley was believed to be the place where God would purify the nation through fire. The name became a proper noun over time for the place of eschatological punishment. Böcher, "γέεννα," 239–40; Jeremias, "γέεννα," 657–58; Baird, *Justice of God in the Teaching of Jesus*, 221–23.

to throw them into the fires of hell.[14] In Luke 12:49–59, Jesus relates how he came to bring fire upon the earth. While the mission of Jesus was for salvation, the process of salvation involved the sifting of the peoples, with the end result being salvation for some and condemnation for others. Jesus' presence upon the earth created a division within humanity between those who are for him and those who are against him. The fire motif is used to portray both the creation and revelation of that division.[15]

Paul, like Jesus, employs fire in a strictly eschatological manner. For Paul, however, fire is not understood as only punitive, but also as purgative. 1 Corinthians 3:10–15 reveals that in the consummation believers will pass through a fire that will test their works. The salvation of the individual is not in question, but how he has served God. Fire will test the nature of his work, and it will burn away all those works that cannot withstand it, so that some may be left with nothing but themselves.[16] 2 Thessalonians 1:7 states that when Christ returns with his mighty angels in flaming fire he will bring comfort to those who have been afflicted and affliction to those who have been afflicting the church.[17]

The closest Paul comes to connecting temporal punishment and fire is in Romans 12:20 where he admonishes believers to treat their enemies with kindness, and in effect heap burning coals upon their heads. While one can interpret the coal in this verse as temporal punishment from God, it most likely refers to an eschatological judgment that awaits those who fail to repent. A valid alternative, however, points to an ancient custom in which a person who is seeking reconciliation and forgiveness will approach the one they have offended with a pot of burning coals on his head. The pot was to symbolize contrition and repentance.[18] If one adopts this interpretation, then the meaning changes from fire being punitive to signifying restoration of broken fellowship.

Fire does appear in the book of Revelation as a temporal judgment, but this judgment is so intimately tied up with the end time judgment that the two are virtually synonymous. The second beast of Rev 13 is able to make fire come down from heaven in the same manner that God does in the Old Testament. Fire also comes out of the mouths of the two prophets

14. Matt 13:41–42.

15. Green, *Gospel of Luke*, 507–12.

16. Orr and Walther, *1 Corinthians*, 173.

17. Morris, *First and Second Epistles to the Thessalonians*, 198–202.

18. Moo, *Epistle to the Romans*, 787–90.

in Rev 11:5, destroying all those who oppose them. At the end, the lake of fire becomes the final abode of the Devil, the false prophet, the beast, and all those whose names are not written in the Book of Life.[19]

In references to the eschatological age, the symbol of fire in the Bible is gradually replaced by that of light. While no clear reason is given for this switch, it might be that in the coming age, the dual activity of God as both redemptive and destructive is removed for those who are saved. Zechariah 2:5 relates that in the age to come Jerusalem will not have a wall around it, but God himself will be a fire around the city and the glory within it. For those outside the city, God is only perceived as fire, a fire that bars them from the glory within. For those inside the city, he is perceived as a protector from intruders and as the city's very glory.[20] In Rev 21:23, Jesus is represented as light for the people who are in the New Jerusalem.

While fire was predominately used for destructive punishment, without recourse to reform, often, as in 1 Cor 3, it is presented as purifying the people. When God brings punishment upon his people, his intention is for their reform and purification. As fire smelts the dross from silver, so God's punishment is described as smelting the dross of the nations and of individuals.[21] Isaiah 4:4 declares that by a Spirit of judgment and of fire, God will purge the filth of Zion and establish his presence over the entire nation. Ezekiel presents a similar understanding when he declares that God will gather his people into Jerusalem and there blow on them his fierce wrath and anger. God's rationale for this action is that the people had become dross. Whereas they were intended to be silver and gold, they had instead corrupted their ways and broken their covenant. It was therefore necessary to bring judgment upon them in order to purge away the dross, to refine the silver so that it was pure once again.[22]

Not as prevalent as punishment, both destructive and purifying, fire is related to the gracious visitation of God.[23] Within the *cultus*, it was fire that signified God's acceptance of sacrifice. In the confrontation in 1 Kgs 18 between the prophets of Baal and Elijah, it was fire from God that vindicated Elijah. For Elijah this fire was salvation, but for the prophets of Baal, the same fire was their defeat and failure. At the end of his career, Elijah is

---

19. Rev 20:10.

20. Calvin, *Zechariah and Malachi*, 62–63.

21. 1 Pet 1:7.

22. Ezek 22:17–22.

23. Lang, "πῦρ," 937.

caught up to heaven by a fiery chariot. As already mentioned, the pillar of fire led the Israelites on their wanderings. While this pillar aroused a deep sense of fear within the people, it also served as a constant reminder that their God was with them and was leading them in their journey.[24]

It has been shown that fire is used throughout the Bible to represent both God's protective and purificatory presence and a means of the execution of his condemnatory judgment. Fire has a more literal temporal aspect of judgment in the Old Testament, while the New Testament presents fire in an eschatological manner. In both cases, fire retains the personal nature of judgment in that it is God's presence that brings forth both salvation and condemnation. Closely related to the motif of fire is the motif of God's breath, which is often referred to as fiery.

The Spirit and Fire

The Spirit is a consuming fire! From the pillar of fire by night to the seven lamps that burn before God's throne, the Bible employs fire as a symbol for the Spirit. The Spirit, like fire, consumes, judges, purifies, softens, illuminates, and inflames. Within all these analogies between fire and the Spirit, it is the one between fire and judgment that goes uncorrelated. To present a complete picture of the Spirit's work, however, this crucial aspect must not be eliminated, but must instead be broken open and exposed so that the full force of fire's symbolic use in relation to the Holy Spirit might come to be appreciated. The following section will ground the thesis that the Spirit executes the Son's judgment by investigating several biblical passages that relate the Holy Spirit and judgmental fire. Initially, however, a brief defense will be made for the often assumed connection between the two.

Fire as a Symbol of the Spirit

Beginning in the Old Testament, one encounters the pillar of fire that guided the Israelites during their desert wandering, not only providing guidance and protection, but also being intimately related to God's revelation to Israel.[25] In Exod 19, when Moses ascended Mount Sinai, the pillar descended

24. "Much like the activity of the *ruach*, the pillar serves to guide, protect, reveal, and even judge people to fulfill the work of Yahweh." Hildebrandt, *Old Testament Theology*, 72–76.

25. Hildebrandt, *Old Testament Theology*, 72–76.

to enshroud it. Likewise, it would descend upon the Tent of Meeting when Moses entered to hear from God. The pillar also provided protection for the Israelites as they fled from the Egyptians, moving from in front of the nation to rest behind it in order to serve as a barrier that the enemy could not cross.[26] When the Tabernacle was complete, the pillar came to rest upon it and the Lord's glorious presence dwelt with Israel. The Temple eventually replaced the Tabernacle as the location of God's presence on earth, and subsequently, the church replaced the earthly Temple in Jerusalem as the location of God's presence. It is now in the church that the Holy Spirit has come to dwell.[27]

As one moves from the beginning of the biblical text and the history of redemption to its conclusion, the symbolic connection between fire and the Holy Spirit continues. In Rev 4:5, John had a vision of seven lamps burning before God's throne. These seven lamps are the seven Spirits of God, having already been introduced in Rev 1:4 as part of the greeting to the seven churches. Additionally, the seven spirits appear a final time in 5:6 in relation to the seven horns and eyes of the slain lamb. They are the seven spirits of God sent out into the entire world, and while the phrase "seven spirits" is somewhat ambiguous in that in no other place in Scripture is the Holy Spirit described as the seven spirits of God, many commentators agree that the reference to the seven spirits or the sevenfold spirit is a reference to the Holy Spirit.[28] Here, in this vision, where symbolism reigns supreme, the symbolic use of fire captures the Spirit's nature.

The main line of argument in favor of these verses referring to the Holy Spirit revolves around the following points. First, the verse contains a backward look to Zech 4:2, 10. In Zech 4:2, seven lamps on a lampstand are described as the word of the Lord to Zerubbabel that it is by the Spirit's power that the Temple will be rebuilt. Zechariah 4:10 furthermore equates the seven lamps with the seven eyes of the Lord that range back and forth throughout the earth. John has adopted Zechariah's imagery in his description of the Spirit.

Additionally, John is referring to the list in Isa 11:2 in which the coming Messiah would be endowed with seven qualities from the Spirit. The

26. Exod 14:19–20.

27. Fee, *First Epistle to the Corinthians*, 146–50.

28. For those supporting the seven spirits as a reference to the Holy Spirit, see Osborne, *Revelation*; Kistemaker, *Revelation*, 82; Ladd, *Commentary on the Revelation of John*, 24; Beale, *Book of Revelation*, 189–90. For those holding a different view see Mounce, *Book of Revelation*, 44–48; Aune, *Revelation*, 34–37.

Masoretic Text does not list seven, but the Septuagint does. While there are those who reject the passages in Revelation as referring to the Spirit, their arguments that the spirits refer to the angels of the churches or to the seven principal angels of God does not carry the day. Nowhere in Revelation are angels referred to as spirits, and there is no firm evidence for the incorporation of Judaic angelology in the book of Revelation.[29]

In Acts 2:3 fiery tongues appeared above the heads of the disciples as the Holy Spirit filled them, causing them to speak in languages they had not previously learned so that the gathered people heard them in their own language. Fire symbolized the Spirit at this most important of moments in salvation history in which the prophecy of Joel 2:28 was fulfilled. As the new age in which the Spirit is poured out on all flesh arrived, the imagery of fire was employed to symbolize his work.

It is clear from the foregoing brief discussion, that the Bible depicts the Holy Spirit in conjunction with fire. There is no argument that fire is one of the main symbols of the Holy Spirit, but resistance might be encountered when relating the imagery of fire as judgment to the Holy Spirit. While fire describes the nature of God's judgment, the connection between this symbolic use of fire and the Holy Spirit has not been adequately established.

It must be made clear that the use of any symbol is not univocal, so that every possible symbolic use of fire can be automatically ascribed to the Spirit. To make such a facile connection would undermine the symbol's power and rob it of its use. For example, the symbol of a lion is used both to describe Jesus and Satan. One would not want to argue that since Jesus is symbolically described as a lion then those passages which speak of the work of Satan as a lion must also apply to Jesus. In the same manner, it would not be legitimate to argue that since the Holy Spirit is symbolically described as fire, then every symbolic use of fire must apply equally to the Holy Spirit. What must be done is to show that the Bible employs the symbol of judgmental fire in conjunction with the Holy Spirit's work. Having established this connection, only then can one make the further connection between the symbol of judgmental fire and the Holy Spirit, even in those passages that do not directly mention him.

In order to accomplish the connection between fire in relation to condemnation and the Holy Spirit an investigation will be made into several passages. First, Isa 4:4, and corresponding verses in Isaiah, will be highlighted to show a direct connection between the Holy Spirit and judgmental

---

29. Yarnell, *God the Trinity*, 211–17.

fire. In the New Testament, the statement of John the Baptist that Jesus would baptize in the Holy Spirit and fire will serve as the primary text from which to understand the relationship between the two. Next, Jesus' statement regarding the baptism he must undergo and the fire he casts upon the earth will come under discussion. Finally, Paul's use of fire in relation to the judgment of believers will be extrapolated to unbelievers as a logical conclusion of the Last Judgment.

The Spirit and Judgmental Fire in the Old Testament

In Isa 4, the prophet is describing the great Day of the Lord in which the Branch will be glorious, creation will be set right, and all those in Jerusalem will be called holy. Before this happens, however, Isa 4:4 says there must be a sifting of the righteous and the unrighteous, for the filth and bloodshed of Zion must be purged, as so much dross from silver, with the purgation taking place by a *ruach* of judgment and burning. Verse 4 clearly portrays judgment as discrimination, for the righteous will remain to enjoy God's presence and fellowship, while the unrighteous are removed. The question naturally arising at this juncture in an attempt to delineate the Holy Spirit's work in judgment is to determine if Isa 4:4 is describing his work, or if the phrase is a periphrastic construction in which *ruach* is a means of stating that there will be a process of judgment and burning.[30]

The Hebrew word *baar* can mean both sifting and separating completely; however, the Septuagint translated the word as *kausis*, and hence the NASB, RSV, and ESV translate as spirit of burning, while the NIV translates the phrase as spirit (Spirit) of fire. The idea behind fire or burning obscures somewhat the emphasis upon the sifting that takes place in the judgment, but does capture the completeness of the task. It is therefore quite acceptable to translate the Hebrew along the Septuagintal line as burning or fire since within the context of the verse it is obvious that a separation is taking place.

In determining how to understand *ruach* in this verse, one has to make a decision about the nature of the *ruach* in the Old Testament in general. Based upon the further revelation of the New Testament it is appropriate to go back into the Old Testament to seek to discover references to the Holy Spirit that might not have been explicit before the New Testament revelation. Isaiah 4:4 is a perfect candidate for this type of investigation. While the NASB, ESV, and NIV (though the NIV does give the capitalized form in

---

30. Oswalt, *Book of Isaiah: Chapters 1–39*, 146.

a footnote) do not capitalize "spirit" thus indicating that the translators do not perceive this to be a reference to the Holy Spirit, it will be argued that their conclusion is wrong.[31]

While *ruach* can be translated as wind or breath, there is nothing within the context of Isa 4 that would argue for one of these translations. The most obvious translation is that of Spirit.[32] God will bring about purification through his Spirit, and in light of Isa 28:6, which speaks of the spirit of judgment, *ruach* should be translated as Spirit, not as storm or great wind.

John Calvin rearranged the word order of Isa 4:4 to emphasize that it is the judgment and fire of the Spirit that is purifying. He does not treat how this purifying affects the unrighteous, but only states that the judgment and fire of the Spirit purifies the redeemed. Calvin writes, "In this expression there are two things to be observed; first, that the purification of the Church is accomplished by the Spirit; and secondly, that from the effects which he produces the Spirit receives the name, sometimes of *judgment*, and sometimes of *burning*; as if he had said, The *judgment* of the *Spirit*, The *burning* of the *Spirit*."[33] Furthermore, a correlation exists between this verse and the baptism of the Holy Spirit and fire that John the Baptist attributed to Jesus.[34]

Isaiah 4:5–6 lends further evidence to the argument that it is the Holy Spirit who is being described in 4:4, in that after Jerusalem's purification is completed a canopy will be established over Zion that will be a cloud by day and a fire by night. This canopy is reminiscent of the pillar that guided the Israelites and rested upon both the Tabernacle and the Temple. As already argued, there is an intimate relationship between the pillar and the Holy

---

31. Keil and Delitzsch, *Isaiah*, 154–55.

32. Kaiser, *Isaiah 1–12*, 87–88. Woods, *"Finger of God" and Pneumatology*, 21.

33. Calvin, *Commentary on the Prophet Isaiah*, 156–57.

34. Jerome, *Isaiah 1–39*, 37. See also Davies and Allison, *A Critical and Exegetical Commentary*, 317; Beasley-Murray, *Baptism in the New Testament*, 37–38; Dunn, *Baptism in the Holy Spirit*, 12; McDonnell and Montague, *Christian Initiation and Baptism*, 4–5. Wildberger does not understand Isa 4:4 as a historical event, but as an eschatological event, and he furthermore makes the connection with Jesus' baptizing in the Holy Spirit and fire stating the "Spirit of Yahweh is God's power which judges and brings salvation." Wildberger, *Isaiah 1–12*, 170–71. Eisler also makes the connection between the two, but sees both as referring to wind. Eisler, *Messiah Jesus and John the Baptist*, 276. His argument for the statement of John referring to wind will be addressed and refuted in a subsequent section. What is to be noted is that he does see a connection between Isa 4:4 and John's statement, even though he misinterprets both.

Spirit, and Isaiah is declaring that after the Spirit purges Jerusalem, he will then establish himself as the protector of the redeemed people.[35]

Isaiah 30:27–33 provides another example of the close connection between judgmental fire and the Spirit. While the connection uses another symbol of the Spirit, the breath of God, thus placing this verse in a less prominent position than Isa 4:4, it will be shown that God's breath is a standard Spirit symbol and therefore that this verse refers to his work. Additionally, in 30:30 yet another Spirit symbol, the Lord's arm, is incorporated into the description of the impending condemnation. Yahweh's anger is burning and his tongue is like a consuming fire. His *ruach* is a consuming fire that sifts the nations. Like a torrent of brimstone, the *ruach* will set afire the unrighteous and their deeds. Alexander argues that the *ruach* could refer to God's Spirit, while Wildberger translates it as wind and Kaiser does not call the *ruach* the Spirit, but does describe it as a hypostasis.[36] Calvin makes the right observation as he relates the *ruach* to the Spirit when he writes, "They will be plunged into the deep by the 'Spirit' of God, or rather, that the 'Spirit' himself is like a deep torrent which shall swallow them up."[37]

Isaiah 33:11 picks up the same theme when God warns the people that his breath will consume them like fire. Isaiah then asks who can live with this fire, this continual burning. In answer, he does not say that no one can, but instead he describes a person who walks righteously, speaks sincerely, rejects unjust gain and bribes, does not listen to tales of bloodshed, and closes his eyes from looking upon evil. This type of person will find refuge in the impregnable rock. Only a person who has fled for refuge to the rock that is Jesus Christ can live with the Holy Spirit's continual burning. The very holiness of God's presence burns and consumes that with which it comes into contact, but in Christ, humanity experiences the Holy Spirit's fire as comfort and protection. The Spirit purifies those who are in Christ, but for those outside of Christ who have given birth to chaff in their life, the Spirit is a consuming fire that condemns their rebellion.

---

35. Young, *Book of Isaiah*, 186.

36. Alexander, *Commentary on Isaiah*, 485; Wildberger, *Isaiah 1–12*, 197–99; Kaiser, *Isaiah 1–12*, 307. It is difficult to understand how Wildberger and Kaiser, who both affirm that Isa 4:4 refers to the Holy Spirit, do not see the Holy Spirit at work in this passage.

37. Calvin, *Commentary on the Prophet Isaiah*, 380. Calvin offers a split here. Is perdition a place that the Spirit puts people, or is the Spirit the place where people are put who are condemned?

The Spirit and Judgmental Fire in the New Testament

Having established the connection between the Holy Spirit and judgmental fire in the Old Testament writings, it is now necessary to move into the New Testament to demonstrate God's continued revelation in regard to the Spirit's role in judgment as it relates to fire. This will be accomplished by first investigating John the Baptist's statement about Jesus' baptism, then Jesus' own statement as it relates to the baptism he must undergo, and finally Paul's reference to an eschatological fire that all believers must pass through in order to have the quality of their works tested.

Baptized in the Holy Spirit and Fire

The scorching wind blows through the valley where a shaggy man dressed in camel's hair warns the gathered masses to repent, for the kingdom of heaven is at hand. The wind, heated even more than normal by the mountains that loom on either side of the Jordan serves as an apt reminder of the Day of the Lord that burns like a furnace.[38] The man proclaims he is merely a forerunner, a pointer to one who is greater than he, to one who will not baptize in water only, but who will baptize in the Holy Spirit and fire.[39] In the crowd were those who had already undergone his baptism, those waiting for it, and those whom he described as a brood of vipers.[40] To some, the baptism in the Holy Spirit and fire would result in life, to others, death. Webb makes the salient point that within the passage context trumps a strictly grammatical understanding vis-à-vis who John was addressing with the baptism of Jesus. Webb correctly argues that the "you" of John would refer to all those present at the time of his declaration, not just those already baptized. John's declaration of Jesus' baptism would then entail both purification for some and destruction for others.[41]

There has been much debate as to whether or not John spoke of one or two baptisms by Jesus, as to whether he would baptize in the Holy Spirit

---

38. Mal 4:1.

39. Matt 3:11 and Luke 3:16 have "Holy Spirit and fire," while Mark 1:8 and John 1:33 only have Jesus baptizing in the Holy Spirit. In addition, Acts 1:5 only mentions baptism in the Holy Spirit.

40. Matt 3:1–12.

41. Webb, *John the Baptizer and Prophet*, 291–92. B. M. F. Van Iersel further contends that it is appropriate to view the Spirit as both gracious and condemning. Van Iersel, "He Will Baptize You," 132–41.

and fire, in a fiery wind of judgment, in just the Holy Spirit, or only fire.[42] One needs to investigate each option put forward in order to form a conclusion regarding the meaning of John the Baptist's declaration. The latter, that he would only baptize in fire, is based upon an incomplete understanding of his message in which John is viewed as being exclusively a harbinger of condemnation. Those who hold this position must first perform a rather tortured exercise in textual surgery to eliminate the reference to the Spirit. Mason rejects the inclusion of Spirit in John the Baptist's message based on the preconceived notion that the Holy Spirit can have nothing to do with condemnation. Since John's message was one of condemnation, there is by default no place for the Spirit within his message.[43] Dunn correctly points out that this option is not viable as there is absolutely no manuscript support for fire having existed independently in the passage.[44]

Furthermore, proponents of the view must eliminate all aspects of redemption from John's message, for he only proclaimed condemnation in their opinion. Briggs argues that the original Aramaic only contained fire. He offers no proof for this contention, but alludes to the hypothesis that the Evangelists would have added Holy Spirit after Pentecost.[45] T. W. Manson makes a similar argument for the addition of the Holy Spirit onto John's original statement of a baptism only in fire.[46] Bultmann is less dogmatic, but still holds that Matthew and Luke added to the original saying of John found in Q.[47]

A slightly different version of this argument contends, "The *pneuma hagion* is a stormy wind of judgment, holy, as sweeping away all that is light and worthless in the nation."[48] Within this modified version, *pneuma* is maintained as part of John's declaration, but it is understood as wind, not Spirit, so that it is usually argued that John only spoke of a baptism in wind (*pneuma*) and fire, and the church later added holy in the light of the Pentecostal outpouring of the Spirit and the tongues of fire in Acts 2:3.[49]

---

42. For an exhaustive overview of the options and those holding to each position see Dunn, "Spirit-and-Fire Baptism," 81–92; Meier, *Marginal Jew Volume Two*, 29–38.

43. Mason, "Fire, Water and Spirit," 163–80.

44. Dunn, "Spirit-and-Fire Baptism," 84.

45. Briggs, *Messiah of the Gospels*.

46. Manson, *Sayings of Jesus*, 40–41.

47. Bultmann, *History of the Synoptic Tradition*, 246.

48. Bruce, *Matthew*, 84.

49. This view is also espoused by Flowers, "ἐν πνεύματι ἁγίῳ καὶ πυρί," 155–56;

There is no manuscript support for the reduction of Holy Spirit to simply spirit, and while it is possible to translate *pneuma* as mighty wind, in the New Testament *pneuma hagion* refers specifically to the Holy Spirit and it is therefore difficult, if not impossible, to accept this translation of the phrase.

The previous option understood John the Baptist as presenting a message of condemnation and warning to the nation of Israel. He was a prophet of doom and destruction, with no hope of redemption. While it is true that his message entailed condemnation, it is equally true that he understood that the Messiah would offer salvation, gathering his wheat into the barn and burning up the chaff with fire.[50] What is more important in the process of gathering wheat: the chaff or the wheat? Obviously, the farmer is concerned with the wheat, with its purity and its storage, and therefore to place the emphasis in this statement upon the chaff is to fail to recognize the purpose of winnowing.

Vincent Taylor argues that the original wording only contained a reference to fire because of the close proximity of the winnowing reference. He makes the flawed assumption that the winnowing reference is only about condemnation. He writes, "In this context a reference to the fire as judgment is natural. Probably, then, the reference to the Holy Spirit has been introduced under the influence of the Christian practice of baptism."[51] Taylor's argument makes little sense in that he suggests that Matthew and Luke added a reference to the Holy Spirit that would refer to redemption to a statement from John the Baptist that only mentioned condemnation. If they were willing to change his message to this extent, it would seem more likely that they would have dropped the "fire" reference completely.

Dunn is correct when he gives priority to the Matthean and Lukan source and then argues that Mark abbreviated their fuller statement to his more condensed one.[52] Additionally, Webb has convincingly argued that the winnowing fork is in actuality a tool used to move wheat that has al-

---

Schweizer, "With the Holy Ghost and Fire," 29; Best, "Spirit-Baptism," 236–43; Eisler, *Messiah Jesus and John the Baptist*, 275–76; McDonnell and Montague, *Christian Initiation and Baptism*, 4–5; Barrett, *Holy Spirit and the Gospel Tradition*, 125–26. Bock notes that in the Acts 2 account of Pentecost, the tongues of fire do not baptize the people, but spread out among the people. The people are not baptized in the fire, and therefore, to see this verse as a fulfillment of the statement from John the Baptist is misplaced. Bock, *Luke 1:1—9:50*, 322–24.

50. Matt 3:12.

51. Taylor, *Gospel According to St. Mark*, 157.

52. Dunn, *Baptism in the Holy Spirit*, 85.

ready been winnowed into storage and that the imagery John is portraying is of a person who has already completed the winnowing process and is moving the chaff and the wheat to its final location. Webb posits that John saw his baptism as the actual winnowing and Jesus' baptism as the removal of the already winnowed wheat and chaff.[53]

The Messiah was coming to gather a people to God's kingdom, and in the process there will be those that are not fit for that kingdom, who are only fit for burning, but they are not the reason for the winnowing.[54] Luke 3:18 ends the section on John the Baptist's teaching with the statement "with many other exhortations he preached the gospel to the people." That is not quite the description one would expect of a person who was only preaching destruction.

Another group of commentators retain the "and fire" in Matthew and Luke, but they fail to understand the fire as condemnatory, but instead, in spite of the condemnatory thrust of the passage, conceive of it as exclusively purificatory.[55] Cyril of Alexandria wrote, "The blessed Baptist added to the word *spirit* the active and meaningful phrase 'and with fire.' This was not only to imply that through Christ we shall all be baptized with fire but to indicate through the designation *fire* that the life-giving energy of the Spirit is given."[56] Morris represents a modern exegete who propounds this interpretation based upon his preconceived notion that the Holy Spirit is not involved in condemnation. While he acknowledges that there is only one baptism spoken of by John, in Holy Spirit and fire, the inclusion of Holy Spirit dictates how one should understand the reference to fire. This interpretation goes completely against the surrounding context in which both redemption and condemnation are in view.[57]

Their presuppositions regarding the Spirit's work will not allow him to function in a condemnatorial capacity, and for this reason they must perform not textual, but exegetical surgery to redefine the "fire" in John's statement from one of condemnation to one of only purification. The path that excludes the Holy Spirit from John's statement and understands his message as all condemnation and the path that understands fire as exclusively purificatory are both based upon a misconstrued conception

53. Webb, "Activity of John the Baptist's," 104–10.

54. Beasley-Murray, *Baptism in the New Testament*, 31.

55. Chrysostom, *Homilies of S. John Chrysostom*, 153–54.

56. Cyril, *Matthew 1–13*, 47.

57. Morris, *Gospel According to Matthew*, 61–62.

of the Spirit in relationship to condemnation. The first approach seeks to eliminate the Spirit from John's statement because they understand that the Spirit is purely gracious, while the latter group seeks to limit the symbolic range of the word fire to include only purification because they understand the Spirit likewise.

The reading that retains both "Spirit" and "fire" as an original proclamation of John and that furthermore understands the fire to refer primarily to condemnation is preferable. Within this option, however, there is debate as to whether or not the Holy Spirit and fire is the same thing and as to whether there are one or two baptisms administered. Those who separate the Spirit from the fire, wishing to understand them as two separate and distinct entities or agencies, argue for two separate baptisms, while those who equate the two tend to argue for one baptism, but often stop short of stating that the baptism in the Holy Spirit can be either condemnatory or purificatory, depending on the recipient's relationship to Jesus.

Gundry writes, "Those producing good fruit will receive the gift of the Holy Spirit. Those producing bad fruit will suffer unending punishment."[58] Additionally, Blomberg argues that those who accept Christ receive the Holy Spirit, while those who reject him receive a convicting power for punishment.[59] He is quite explicit about the role of the Spirit in redemption, but does not ascribe the work of condemnation to the Spirit. Bock argues that those who accept Christ receive the Spirit, but those who reject him are thrown to the wind.[60] This is quite an evasion of the obvious in that Bock does not translate *pneuma* as wind, but as Spirit, but then suggests that the unredeemed are thrown to the wind by adopting the wheat and chaff symbol. He would have been more consistent to write that the unredeemed are thrown to the Spirit.

Origen understood the reference to refer to two lustrations, arguing that those who repent are baptized in the Holy Spirit, and after death, Christ in the river of fire near the flaming sword will baptize them again.[61] He disconnected the fire from the Spirit, thus allowing him to retain the pure graciousness of the Spirit. Webb makes an argument similar to Origen's,

58. Gundry, *Matthew*, 49.

59. Blomberg, *Matthew*, 80.

60. Bock, *Luke: 1:1—9:50*, 324.

61. Origen, *Homilies on Luke*, 103–4. Dunn, in his article "Spirit-and-Fire Baptism," argues Origen held to the view that the baptism in fire refers to the eternal punishment of the wicked. He does not offer a reference for this view of Origen's, but Origen's homily on Luke 3:16 contradicts Dunn's statement. Dunn, "Spirit-and-Fire Baptism," 6.

but the Messiah will baptize those who repent with the Holy Spirit, and the unrepentant he will baptize with fire that will destroy and remove them from the righteous. Even though he keeps the "fire" in the baptism of the Messiah, he likewise dissociates it from the Spirit.[62] Splitting the baptism in Holy Spirit and fire into two distinct and separate baptisms is difficult to maintain on exegetical grounds, but is instead driven by a reduction of the Holy Spirit's ministry to only acts of redemption.

Chrysostom equated Spirit and fire, and thus held to one baptism, but he interpreted the phrase so that the fire of the Spirit is a gracious outpouring with a purifying element.[63] Many modern scholars do not support this interpretation, however, not concerning the correlation of the Spirit and fire, but upon Chrysostom's emphasis upon the Spirit's graciousness in John's proclamation.[64] John's message was primarily of a destructive judgment and the bestowal of the Spirit at Pentecost, which was not a destructive event, resulted in the reduction of John's message to the Markan version in which the Messiah only baptizes in the Spirit. Dunn, in contradistinction, recognizes the dual nature of the judgment of the Messianic baptism when he writes:

> Taken together these facts suggest that what John held out before his hearers was a baptism which was neither solely destructive nor solely gracious, but which contained both elements in itself. Its effect would then presumably depend on the condition of its recipients: the repentant would experience a purgative, refining, but ultimately merciful judgment; the impenitent, the stiff-necked and hard of heart, would be broken and destroyed.[65]

In Dunn's analysis, John the Baptist only proclaimed one baptism that would be in Holy Spirit and fire. He argues, "The future baptism is a single baptism in Holy Spirit and fire, the ἐν embracing both elements. There are not two baptisms envisaged, one with Spirit and one with fire, only one baptism in Spirit-and-fire."[66] Nolland puts forward an opposite position in

---

62. Webb, *John the Baptizer and Prophet*, 289–95. Patzia likewise argues for the retention of "fire" as being original in the proclamation of John, but does not correlate the Spirit with fire. The baptism in the Spirit is only for the redeemed, while that in fire is for destruction. Patzia, "Did John the Baptist Preach," 21–27. Others who follow this line of argumentation are Nolland, *Matthew*, 146–47; Scobie, *John the Baptist*, 69–72; Taylor, *Immerser*, 139–41; Meier, *Marginal Jew Volume Two*, 37.

63. Chrysostom, *Homilies of S. John Chrysostom*, 153–54.

64. Dunn, "Spirit-and-Fire Baptism," 87.

65. Ibid., 86.

66. Dunn, *Baptism in the Holy Spirit*, 11–12. For those holding a similar view see

which he argues that the idea of one baptism is based upon reading *baptizo* as a noun, when it is used as a verb in the text. As a noun, it would refer to only one baptism, but as a verb, it could refer to two separate baptisms. There is no grammatical necessity for it to refer to only one.[67] While this argument is valid, it does not overcome the contention of Dunn and the others that John's reference to "you" is inclusive and that both terms, Holy Spirit and fire, are governed by a single preposition as a compound object.

When John told the crowd about the baptism in Holy Spirit and fire, he was addressing the entire crowd that was composed of those who had accepted his baptism and those who had refused. The Messiah's baptism was to be upon all people, not just those who had undergone John's baptism.[68] With the inclusion of all present in the coming Messiah's baptism, there would be a need for both redemption and condemnation in it. There was the wheat to store and the chaff to burn. If you hold to a single baptism, as Dunn and others have correctly argued, and you take John's message in its own context, then you are driven to conclude that the single baptism in "Holy Spirit and fire" is a baptism in a single agent that contains within itself both redemption for those who have accepted the Messiah and condemnation for those who have rejected him. Both redemption and condemnation are included in the Father's judgment given to the Son and executed by the Spirit, symbolically described as fire.

While the equation of the Holy Spirit as condemnatorial fire goes against the commonly held view of the Spirit as the Comforter of John's Gospel and the deposit and seal of salvation for those who are in Christ, one should not allow this presupposition of the Spirit's activity to limit his full work. The lack of direct discussion of the relation of the unredeemed to the baptism in the Holy Spirit should not be surprising since the thrust of the Bible's message is on the redeemed wheat and not the condemned chaff. Therefore, the question that must be asked is how can one move forward with John's statement and construct an interpretation that is faithful to the text and what it reveals about the Holy Spirit?

Blomberg, *Matthew*, 80; Davies and Allison, *Critical and Exegetical Commentary*, 317; Gundry, *Matthew*, 49; Beasley-Murray, *Baptism in the New Testament*, 38–9; Taylor, *Immerser*, 141; Bock, *Luke 1:1—9:50*, 323.

67. Nolland, *Matthew*, 147.

68. Taylor notes that in Mark 1:8 John was referring only to those that he has already baptized as evidenced by the aorist, which denotes an action that has already taken place, while Matthew and Luke have the present tense and thus John is referring to all those present. Taylor, *Immerser*, 141.

Kraeling's redefined understanding of the Holy Spirit within an Old Testament framework and of the baptism of the unredeemed in the Holy Spirit will serve as a foundation from which to proceed in order to elucidate the understanding that John's message presented the coming Messiah's baptism as one in which all people will be baptized in the single baptism of the Holy Spirit and fire, but with radically different results depending on each baptizand's relationship to the baptizer.[69]

In traditional Christian teaching, the Holy Spirit is the power of God that inspires and transforms creation. While this is a correct understanding of his work, it fails to elucidate his role in routing the forces of evil; a routing that is necessary and complementary to his role in bringing God's kingdom to actuality. This routing of evil is clearly displayed in the exorcisms performed by Jesus in the Spirit's power. It is in the Spirit that Jesus is able to bind the strong man and plunder his house.

John's statement declares that if a person does not repent in his baptism then the Messiah would baptize him in his fiery breath or Spirit. Second Thessalonians 2:8 offers a similar phrasing where Jesus' breath will consume the lawless one. While this paraphrase captures the judgmental nature of the baptism and the correlation between the Spirit and fire, it does not fully capture the Spirit's redeeming nature. Kraeling's assessment is correct, even though his emphasis is skewed toward condemnation.

From the Messiah's fiery breath Kraeling returns to the Old Testament's use of fire as both purifying and destructive. First-century Judaism turned the symbolic use of fire in the Old Testament into a reality and at the same time, the description in Dan 7:10 of a river of fire flowing from the Ancient of Days was employed to describe God's judgment upon the wicked.[70] If one allows that John would have been familiar with these symbols, then his baptism in the river Jordan takes on added symbolism. John was inviting people to baptism as an act of pre-judgment in which they accept God's judgment on their actions and attitudes so that at the actual judgment in the river of fire, which is the Holy Spirit, they would be redeemed, not

---

69. Kraeling, *John the Baptist*, 115–22.

70. Marshall shows how the symbolic baptism in fire could be used in the same phrase as the literal baptism in water. Fire was often pictured as a flowing stream or a lake. Additionally, the Spirit is often described in liquid terms, such as being poured out or gushing forth. It is, therefore, quite natural for John to employ the idea of baptism in the Holy Spirit and fire in reference to the work of the Messiah. Both ideas would fit with the normal use of the word baptize. Marshall, "Meaning of the Verb 'to Baptize,'" 130–40.

destroyed.[71] By participating in John's baptism, the individual comes into agreement with God on his sinful condition and his need for redemption.

The same symbolism is present in Christian baptism. The person's submersion in water symbolizes his participation in the death and burial of Christ; as he rises from the water the new life of which he is a part in Christ is symbolized as he overcomes condemnation with redemption. He receives purification, not destruction, in passing through God's judgment. Under this construction, John the Baptist would have understood baptism in the Spirit and fire as God's coming judgment through which all people will pass. The result of that passage will depend upon one's relationship to the Judge. Additionally, given the nature of the Spirit presented in the Old Testament in passages such as Isa 4:4, as well as the understanding of the Qumran Community that the Spirit would execute judgment, it is quite likely that John would have conceived of the Spirit as executing the Messiah's judgment in some capacity.[72]

The above construction remains true to the context in which John the Baptist's statements were made and incorporates the Old Testament theme that the Spirit is actively involved in the punishment of the unredeemed. Here at the beginning of Jesus' ministry, before the Holy Spirit comes upon him to empower him for his mission, John proclaims that Jesus would baptize everyone in this same Spirit and that Jesus' baptism would effectuate the separation of the wheat from the chaff at the end of the age. Jesus' baptism in the Holy Spirit and fire was not something that he stood outside of, but was itself a baptism that he would undergo. He would take upon himself the Father's judgment in order to defeat death by entering into it and rising from the dead. The baptism that Jesus administers is the baptism that he himself went through. This will be highlighted further in the final chapter in which the Spirit's role in the crucifixion is addressed.

---

71. Kraeling, *John the Baptist*, 114–18.

72. Geldenhuys writes, "The Messiah will through the Holy Ghost consume sin and the sinners insofar as they cling to sin. In this way, those who persist in sin will be destroyed, but those who sincerely confess their sins and flee to Him for refuge will be purified from sin to their own salvation, and delivered from its penalty and power." Geldenhuys, *Commentary on the Gospel of Luke*, 140.

The Spirit, Fire on the Earth, and Jesus' Baptism

Jesus proclaimed in Luke 12:49–50, "I came to cast fire upon the earth; and would that it were already kindled! I have a baptism to be baptized with, and how great is my distress until it is accomplished!" In this passage, he is referring to the division that his impending death will create, with an obvious reference back to the baptism in the Holy Spirit and fire.[73] In the present verse, Jesus' desire to cast fire upon the earth, and his subsequent reference to a baptism, points to his desire to pour out the Spirit, with the resulting division that the Spirit's inundation would cause.[74] Jesus came to establish peace on earth, but that peace must come through righteous judgment, for the Spirit "will judge people's hearts to determine who will enter the kingdom and who will face the fire."[75] It is the Spirit who will "mediate the 'judging' message of the kingdom."[76]

Additionally, Jesus stated that he has a baptism to undergo before he will be able to cast this fire upon the earth because he "does not stand over against the world as fiery judge, but that he also must make his way through the end-time distress for which it is his task to set ablaze the refiner's fire."[77] In his death, he would face the inundation of God's judgment carried out in the Spirit's power.[78] Having passed through the fire of the Spirit, he would then be able to cast the Spirit upon the earth, therefore allowing the Spirit to perform his role of convicting the world of sin, righteousness, and judgment. Jesus himself must be baptized in the Holy Spirit and fire as he takes upon himself the punishment due fallen humanity.[79]

---

73. Fitzmeyer, *Gospel According to Luke*, 996.

74. The following commentators understand fire as a reference to the Spirit. Bock, *Luke 9:51—24:5*, 1192; Marshall, *Gospel of Luke*, 546; Ellis, *Gospel of Luke*, 182–83; Geldenhuys, *Commentary on the Gospel of Luke*, 336. As an example of a commentator who separates the baptism in the Holy Spirit and fire into two baptisms and interprets the reference in v. 49 to only fire and judgment see Stein, *Luke*, 364.

75. Bock, *Luke 9:51—24:5*, 1192.

76. Ellis, *Gospel of Luke*, 183.

77. Nolland, *Luke 9:21—18:34*, 708.

78. Ellis understands that the baptism refers to Jesus immersion "through the eternal Spirit" in the waters of death. He gives a reference to both Heb 9:12–28 and Mark 10:38, 45. Ellis, *Gospel of Luke*, 183.

79. Bock rejects two options for the baptism in favor of it referring to divine judgment. The first option is martyrdom, which is too broad an idea for the present passage. The second is an allusion to either John's or Christian baptism. Jesus had already undergone John's so that is eliminated. Christian baptism is not something thrust upon

The result of the fire being cast upon the earth is division; father against son, mother against daughter, family member against family member. The act of decision creates division, with Jesus' baptism serving as a necessary precursor to the baptism of the world in the Holy Spirit and fire. Jesus must be glorified before he can send the Spirit, and according to John, his glorification is achieved at the cross. Once Jesus returned to his Father, he sent the Holy Spirit, and "the presence of the Holy Spirit in the life and proclamation of the church produces division before it produces unity."[80]

The Spirit, Judgmental Fire, and Believers' Works

In 1 Cor 3:10–17, Paul offers a glimpse into the final judgment of those who are part of God's Temple.[81] In an argument dealing with the division created in Corinth over people aligning themselves with various personalities, Paul relates that no one can lay another foundation than the one he laid: Jesus Christ. He warns that how a person builds upon this foundation will be shown at the Final Judgment when each person's work will be tried by fire. If they built with flammable materials like wood, hay, and stubble, their works will burn up, but they will be saved. If, however, they built with flame retardant materials like precious stones, then they will have a reward along with their salvation. The works of those within the church will pass through fire, and the fire will reveal the works' inner nature. Here one encounters the positive side of God's judgment, but it retains the reality of purifying and purging. There is no hint of eternal separation from God for those who make it through the fire with little to spare, with nothing but their self. This judgment focuses only on the redeemed.[82]

The fire is not a literal fire, for it will not test literal wood and jewels, but is a symbolic fire that will test the individual's various works. At the end of the age, Christians will pass through a fire, a fire that Calvin explicitly relates to the Holy Spirit.[83] Godet does not make the connection as explicitly,

---

someone, nor is it construed as humiliation, so it is also eliminated. Bock, *Luke 9:51– 24:5*, 1193–194.

80. Talbert, *Reading Luke*, 144.

81. Orr and Walther, *1 Corinthians*, 173.

82. Fee, *First Epistle to the Corinthians*, 144.

83. Calvin, *Commentary on the Epistles*, 138–40. He writes, "Paul having spoken of doctrine metaphorically, now Paul also applies metaphorically the name of *fire* to the very touchstone of doctrine that the corresponding parts of the comparison may

but states God's "Spirit will thoroughly explore the fruit due to the ministry of every preacher."[84] The Holy Spirit will purge the Christian of those works not fit for the Age to Come. The Son is the judge of the work, but the Spirit is the one who carries out the process of actualizing the Son's judgment within the church. While this verse is a description of the judgment the church will pass through at the end of the age it is not outside the bounds of reason, and in fact it is a logical conclusion that unbelievers will also encounter the same judgment. Their judgment will also concern their work, with the difference being that since they are not redeemed, they will not make it through the fire with their own self.[85] When the unbeliever encounters the judgmental fire that is the Holy Spirit, he will suffer destruction.

Conclusion

Having established a connection between the Holy Spirit and condemnatorial fire, it is now possible to move to the next symbol of the Spirit, God's breath. Like fire, the breath of God reveals both blessings and curses for creation. God's breath gives life to humanity, renews the face of the barren ground, and revives the dead bones in Ezekiel's vision, but it also scorches the earth and destroys God's enemies.

---

harmonize with each other. The *fire*, then, here meant is the Spirit of the Lord, who tries by his touchstone what doctrine resembles *gold* and what resembles *stubble*. The nearer the doctrine of God is brought to this fire, so much brighter will be its luster. On the other hand, what has had its origin in man's head will quickly vanish, as stubble is consumed in the fire."

84. Godet, *Commentary on 1 Corinthians*, 186.

85. Rom 2:5–11.

4

The Spirit and God's Breath

As ADAM LAY LIFELESS in the dust from which he was created, God breathed into him the breath of life transforming him from a lifeless statue to a living man. Thus the Bible introduced one of its most powerful symbols for the Holy Spirit: God's breath. The same breath appears in Ezek 37 in the valley of dry bones, as it gives new life to dead Israel, accomplishing its resurrection. It is also God's breath that Jesus breathes upon the disciples after his resurrection in John's Gospel, telling them to receive the Holy Spirit. As God's breath brought life to inanimate Adam and breathed life into the dry bones of dead Israel, so too, Jesus breathed the new life of the age to come, the Holy Spirit, into the disciples. As already shown, both the Hebrew *ruach* and the Greek *pneuma* have breath as a primary translation. Therefore, it is quite natural for breath to serve as a symbol of the Spirit. Additionally, the Hebrew *neshamah,* whose primary translation is breath, is often used in a parallel fashion with *ruach.*[1]

God's breath as an image of the Holy Spirit has been a common symbol throughout Christian history, being linked to the benefits and grace that the Spirit bestows upon believers. The famous hymn "Breathe on Me, Breath of God" is a testament to the believer's desire to have God's Spirit sanctify him as God's breath fills him with new life, empowering him to act faithfully in his relationships. While this is undoubtedly the major thrust of the imagery of God's breath, it fails to capture those passages that utilize the symbol for condemnation. While God's breath is refreshing to those who

---

1. Mitchell, "Old Testament Usage of Nešama," 177–87.

are in Christ, that same breath carries the smell of death for those who have rejected the salvation available to them.[2]

The Bible presents the Holy Spirit under the symbol of God's breath as executing God's judgment. The defense of this thesis will begin by proving that the Holy Spirit is symbolized as God's breath in both the Old and New Testament. The valley of dry bones in Ezek 37 offers a wonderful example of the ambiguities of *ruach* as it is variously translated breath/spirit/wind, with a conclusion that the symbol of breath is linked to the Holy Spirit. Additionally, Job has several instances where God's breath and Spirit appear in a parallel fashion. In the New Testament three passages will be addressed. First, Jesus' breathing upon the disciples in John 20:22 will show that the Spirit is connected with the breath of Jesus. Second, Paul's claim in 2 Tim 3:16, that all Scripture is God-breathed, will be related to the claim in 2 Pet 1:21, that the Holy Spirit carried along those men in the past who spoke for God. After laying a firm foundation for the Spirit's symbolic description as God's breath, an explication of those verses that directly relate his breath to condemnation will be undertaken. Finally, a connection will be established between God's breath, the sword of the Spirit, and the sword/rod that comes from Jesus' mouth with which he slays God's enemies.

The Spirit and God's Breath in the Old Testament

The valley of dry bones in Ezek 37:1–14 mixes all three of the primary meanings of the word *ruach*: spirit, wind, and breath.[3] While the ambiguity of the word is present in the text, if one wishes to grasp the full significance of Ezekiel's vision, one must place it in its literary context between chapters 36 and 39 in order to sort out the various uses of *ruach*.[4] In 36:27, God informs the people that he will put his Spirit in them so that they will be able to follow his statutes. The nation was under punishment for forsaking God, but he was going to act to restore the nation for his name's sake; and his action was to give a new heart, one of flesh and not of stone, a heart

2. 2 Cor 2:14–16.

3. Block is correct in stating, "In spite of its simplicity, the use of the term *rûah* creates ambiguity. The shift in meaning from v. 1 is obvious, but it is difficult to decide whether *rûah* should be interpreted as 'spirit' or 'breath.' In any case, *rûah* represents the divine animating force without which no life is possible." Block, *Book of Ezekiel*, 376.

4. Allen argues that chapter 37 is placed in its present location in order to amplify 36:27. The repeated use of *ruach* in chapter 37:1–14 will forcefully recall its use in 36:27. Allen, *Ezekiel 20–48*, 187.

given by the indwelling of his Spirit. Likewise, in 39:29, after recounting the punishment that was to come upon the nation for its disobedience, God declared that he would not hide his face anymore, but would instead pour out his Spirit upon Israel. The outpouring of the Spirit would constitute the nation's return to a relationship of obedience and blessing. In the middle of these two references to the Spirit's work in renewing the nation is the valley of dry bones that depicts the nation as dead and in need of resurrection.

The word *ruach* appears in 37:1, 5, 6, 8, 9, 10, and 14, with v. 1 being a clear reference to the Holy Spirit. The Spirit (*ruach*) of God brings Ezekiel out to the valley. In v. 5 God declares that *ruach* shall enter the dead bones and they shall live. The major English translations employ breath as the appropriate reference here with the ESV, NET, and NIV offering Spirit as a possible alternative. There is clearly a reference to the Gen 2:7 account of God breathing into Adam the breath of life, and it therefore is correct to understand *ruach* as breath in this verse.[5]

Likewise, breath is the most appropriate translation in vv. 6, 8, and 10, with v. 8 being more amenable to Spirit replacing breath, but still not being the most obvious translation. In v. 9, Ezekiel is commanded to prophecy to the *ruach* to come from the four *ruach*, so that the *ruach* may breathe upon the bones.[6] Here, while breath is still an appropriate translation, a shift has been made to a more personalized tone in which the *ruach* can be addressed and commanded.[7] Zimmerli does not see this address as personal, but to a force that pervades the entire universe. In contrast to Eccl 12:7, which states at death a person's body returns to dust and the Spirit returns to God who gave it, Zimmerli does not equate the *ruach* as coming from God. While one does not want to overemphasize the personal nature of the *ruach* because it is addressed, Zimmerli fails to connect this verse adequately with v. 14 in which the *ruach* is given a more personal tone when it is described as "My Spirit." Within this verse, the prophet begins the transition that he will complete in v. 14 which reveals that the *ruach*

---

5. Block, *Book of Ezekiel*, 379.

6. The breath will come from the four winds or directions. The winds could be a literal reference to something like the scorching sirocco that blows in off the desert or to the divine breath that blows in every corner of the earth. Ibid., 377. Cooper states, "It was clearly God's Spirit who was to give breath to these corpses, and Ezekiel was given the extraordinary task of summoning him." Cooper, *Ezekiel*, 324.

7. Zimmerli, *Ezekiel*, 2:261.

(breath) that he has been discussing the entire time is none other than a symbol for God's Spirit.[8]

Starting in v. 11, God reveals to Ezekiel the meaning behind the symbolism of the dry bones and their reconstitution. The bones are the house of Israel that is suffering under exile. The question posed to Ezekiel is, can the nation rise from its death? Can these bones live again? The answer given is that God will open their graves, raise them to life, and put them back in their land. In v. 14, God declares that he will put his *ruach* within them and then they will know that he is God. At the point when the *ruach* is given to the nation, they will be able to fulfill the requirements of their relationship.

It is clear that Ezekiel was using God's breath as a symbol for God's Spirit in the same manner that the dry bones were a symbol for Israel.[9] Cooper states, "Paul makes a similar argument in a more didactic manner in Rom 7:13–25 and 8:1–17. Without the enabling, life-generating presence of the Holy Spirit, Paul was unable to live the life of a believer. There was nothing in him that would give him life, but in the Spirit, Paul was given the power of rebirth, the power to live in covenant faithfulness with God."[10] Here is a joining of God's breath and Spirit in such a tight connection that it is nearly impossible to miss. Likewise, the allusion back to Gen 2:7 further confirms the Spirit's role in the initial creation of humanity.[11]

The book of Job is a treatise on suffering and the goodness of God. Job is commended by God to Satan as a righteous man, yet Satan challenges God's assertion. Job only loves God because God has provided for him so well; remove the blessings from God and he will curse God, so says Satan. God allows exactly this to happen to Job, and as the book unfolds the reader comes to see that while Job questions why he is suffering, he never curses God. Job's troubles are compounded by his friends who insist that he is suffering because he is a sinner, but they cannot overcome Job's responses to their claims.

---

8. Keil and Delitzsch argue that the "divine Spirit of life" is in view in this verse. Keil and Delitzsch, *Biblical Commentary on the Prophecies of Ezekiel*, 120. Allen sees a connection between v. 9 and John 20:22. Jesus breathes new life into the disciples, and in a similar manner new life is breathed into the dry bones. Allen, *Ezekiel 20–48*, 188.

9. Block, *The Book of Ezekiel*, 382.

10. Cooper, *Ezekiel*, 325.

11. In addition to the Gen. 2:7 connection, Allen further connects the account to Gen. 1:2 in which "the *ruach* of God hovered over the raw elements of the world, waiting to transform them into a living cosmos." Allen, *Ezekiel 20–48*, 185.

As Job's three friends finish their speeches, the young Elihu enters the discussion and in Job 33:4, he states that the Spirit (*ruach*) of God made him and the breath (*neshamah*) of the Almighty gave him life. In v. 6 he makes an allusion to Gen 2:7 when he states that he also was made from clay. Here is a synonymous use of the two main Hebrew terms for breath: *ruach* and *neshamah*. It is clear from the context that *ruach* should be interpreted as Spirit; otherwise, *neshamah* becomes a pointless redundancy. Elihu is clearly equating God's breath and Spirit, for it is indeed God's breath who gives life to humanity according to Gen 2:7, but Elihu clarifies that this breath is God's Spirit and not merely a wind issuing from him. He is not claiming to have supernatural powers because God's Spirit made him but on the contrary, he is employing the idea to show that he is just like every other person.[12]

Job 34:14, making a connection like 33:4, proclaims that if God should so choose to gather to himself his breath (*neshamah*) and his Spirit (*ruach*), all flesh would perish and man would return to dust. God's Spirit is the power of life that sustains creation, so if God were to withdraw his Spirit the very creation would cease. In Job 32:8, Elihu refutes the idea that wisdom is given by age, and instead argues that wisdom and understanding come from God's Spirit and breath.[13] Finally, Job states in 27:2–3 that "as God lives, who has taken away my right, and the Almighty, who has made my soul bitter, as long as my breath is in me, and the Spirit of God is in my nostrils, my lips will not speak falsehood, and my tongue will not utter deceit." While the translators of the ESV fail to see this as a reference to the Holy Spirit, there are those who see God's breath (*ruach*) as a reference to the Spirit and the first as a reference to the breath of life within a person. This breath is the natural phenomenon of respiration, but it is supported and maintained by God's breath.[14]

---

12. Reyburn, *Handbook on the Book of Job*, 606.

13. Tur-Sinai, *Book of Job*, 459; Hartley, *Book of Job*, 434; Reyburn, *Handbook on the Book of Job*, 595; Alden, *Job*, 318–19. Alden remarks in a footnote that the NIV offers Spirit as a minority translation. All the above commentators argue that the Spirit in this verse has some reference to the Spirit within a person, but they also argue that wisdom and intelligence come from God.

14. Dhorme equates the breath of God with Gen 2:7 and defines it as the principle of life. Dhorme, *Commentary on the Book of Job*, 380. Tur-Sinai also relates the idea to Gen 2:7, but translates *neshamah* as God's Spirit. Tur-Sinai, *Book of Job*, 386–87. Habel likewise recognizes *neshamah* as a reference to God's Spirit, but does not emphasize a connection with the Holy Spirit. Habel, *Book of Job*, 380.

The Spirit and God's Breath in the New Testament

In John 20:22, Jesus appeared to the disciples after his resurrection and informed them that as the Father sent him, so he in turn is sending them. John's entire Gospel attests to the fact that the Father sent the Son in the Spirit's power. Likewise, Jesus told his disciples that they too would not be sent in their own strength, but would be given the same Spirit that rested upon him. By his death and resurrection, Jesus had become the bestower of the Spirit on the entire world. He then breathed upon the disciples, instructing them to receive the Holy Spirit.

John's use of breath is an allusion to Gen 2:7 where God breathes into inanimate Adam, bringing him to life. In a similar manner in Ezek 37:9–10, the prophet is commanded to call for the breath from the four winds to enter the inanimate bodies in order to restore them to life.[15] In this graphic illustration, Jesus showed that the Holy Spirit he gave to his disciples, to bring them into the new life that he himself is, comes from him personally. His breath in this scene is a symbol for the intimate connection between himself and the Spirit he bestows.[16] His act of breathing on the disciples was to teach them that the Spirit not only proceeded from the Father, but that he also proceeded through the Son. The symbolic impact of God's breath reaches its zenith in this act, with the fullness of the Trinity on display as the Son, who has been sent by the Father in the power of the Spirit, breathes the same Spirit into the disciples that are being sent by the Son. While this verse in and of itself is enough to establish the connection between the imagery of God's breath and the Holy Spirit, it will be beneficial to strengthen the claim by examining the other New Testament passages that treat God's breath and Spirit as synonymous.

A further line of evidence that supports the connection between God's breath and the Holy Spirit is the doctrine of the inspiration of Scripture. Second Peter 1:20–21 states, "Knowing this first of all, that no prophecy of Scripture comes from someone's own interpretation. For no prophecy was ever produced by the will of man, but men spoke from God as they were carried along by the Holy Spirit." The relationship between the Holy Spirit and God's breath is established in the correlation of 2 Pet 1:21 with 2 Tim

---

15. For those who posit a connection with Gen 2:7 and Ezek 37:9–10 see Beasley-Murray, *John*, 380; Morris, *Gospel According to John*, 747; Brown, *Gospel According to John*, 1037; Boulnois, "Le Souffle et l'Esprit," 3–37.

16. Carson, *Gospel According to John*, 652.

3:16 in which Paul declares, "All Scripture is breathed out by God."[17] The Greek word *theopneustos* is the underlying word from which the translation "breathed out by God" is derived. God breathes out the Scriptures, or to put it another way, God is the source of the Scriptures. There have been some who have taken *theopneustos* in an active sense and argued that the Scriptures breathe out God, but this view has been rejected by the majority of scholars.[18] Paul, in showing the benefit and usefulness of Scripture to Timothy, declares that all Scripture owes its origin to "the divine breath, the Spirit of God."[19]

The Spirit and God's Breath in Judgment

It is time to connect God's breath as a symbol of the Spirit and his breath as a symbol of judgment together. In doing this, we can see that the Spirit, under the symbol of God's breath, carries out God's judgment upon the world. We will begin by looking at evidence from the Old Testament, then move to Paul's description of how the lawless one will be destroyed by the breath of Jesus, and finally arrive at John's description of Jesus in the book of Revelation.

Within the symbol of God's breath, there is not only the prospect of life, but also of condemnation. There are numerous verses directly relating to God's breath as a destructive force that carries out his wrath and vengeance. Job 4:8–9 states, "As I have seen, those who plow iniquity and sow trouble reap the same. By the breath of God they perish, and by the blast of his anger they are consumed." Eliphaz, in responding to Job, argues that Job is experiencing suffering because he has plowed iniquity in some manner. Eliphaz then relates this suffering personally to God. He is not content

17. The NIV and ESV's "breathed out by God" catch the force of the Greek more closely than the NASB's "inspired by God." Mounce attests this connection as the closest parallel between the two verses. Mounce, *Pastoral Epistles*, 566.

18. Warfield offered the standard rejection. Warfield, *Inspiration and Authority of the Bible*, 245–96. See also Goodrick, "Let's Put 2 Timothy 3:16 back in the Bible," 484–85; House, "Biblical Inspiration in 2 Timothy 3:16," 57–61.

19. Hendriksen, *Exposition of the Pastoral Epistles*, 302. In addition to 2 Tim 3:16, which is the only occurrence of *theopneustos*, other Scripture appeals to the same idea. Exod 20:1; 2 Sam 23:2; Isa 8:20; Mal 4:4; Matt 1:22; Luke 24:44; John 1:23, 5:39, 10:34–5, 14:26, 16:13, 19:36–37, 20:9; Acts 1:16, 7:38, 13:34; Rom 1:2, 3:2, 4:23, 9:17, 15:4; 1 Cor 2:4–10, 6:1, 9:10, 14:37; Gal 1:11–12, 3:8,16,22, 4:3; 1 Thess 1:5, 2:23; Heb 1:1–2, 3:7, 9:8, 10:15; 2 Pet 1:21, 3:16; 1 John 4:6; and Rev 22:19.

to argue that suffering was a natural result of iniquity. Eliphaz leaves no room for a distant, uninvolved God whose wrath is nothing other than the inevitable result of sin in a cause-and-effect universe. Quite the opposite is the case, for God directly causes the suffering of those who plow iniquity by blowing his breath on them. Clines writes, "God is not only the architect of the moral processes of the universe, but consciously their executor. The 'breath of God' betokens his personal involvement in retribution."[20] Furthermore, his breath is linked with his anger in that his breath is destructive because it embodies his anger. Eliphaz captures in this verse the condemnatorial nature of God's breath, and by linking God's breath to the Spirit, one is able to conclude that the Spirit is active in executing God's judgment upon iniquity.

Isaiah 30:27–28 declares that God's lips are full of fury and his tongue is like a devouring fire, while his breath is like a torrent that reaches to the neck. His breath will sift the nations in a sieve of destruction and put on their jaws a bridle that will lead them astray. Here, God's breath is the means whereby he will destroy the Assyrians who have captured his people. Not only is the breath symbol used, but it is also combined with the imagery of a river of fire.[21]

In Isaiah 40:7–8 the *ruach* withers the grass of the field, with the grass serving as a symbol for the people. Oswalt understands this verse as referring to the Holy Spirit's action.[22] Robert Jenson does likewise when he comments, "The Lord's Spirit is his life as he transcends himself to enliven other reality than himself; for central example, it was the Lord's *ruach* that blew about the waters and the Egyptians to accomplish the Exodus. Since the Lord is the God he is, the movement agitated by his life is absolute, is either creation or destruction." In defense of his statement that the Spirit is destruction, Jenson points the reader to Isa 40:6–7.[23]

The NASB and NIV do not, however, understand *ruach* as a reference to the Holy Spirit by their translation of *ruach* as "breath," while further evidence is given in Ps 104:30 for the tendency to translate *ruach* as breath

---

20. Clines, *Job 1–20*, 127. See Habel, *Book of Job*, 126.; Hartley, *Book of Job*, 108; Tur-Sinai, *Book of Job*, 78–80. Dhorme sees a connection between this verse and Hos 13:15, Ezek 17:10, 19:12 and 2 Thess 2:8. The passage in 2 Thess 2:8 will be treated in a subsequent section. Dhorme, *Commentary on the Book of Job*, 46.

21. The Holy Spirit is reflected in the symbol of water throughout the Bible, and like the other symbols under investigation, water is both purifying and destructive.

22. Oswalt, *Book of Isaiah: Chapters 40–66*, 53.

23. Jenson, *Triune God*, 86.

in those passages that deal with judgment, but as "Spirit" in those that deal with renewal. Psalm 104:29 states that when God takes away a man's breath, the man dies, but when God sends his Spirit (*ruach*) the face of the earth is renewed. It makes perfect sense to translate *ruach* as "breath" here, but "Spirit" is chosen instead. A more consistent translation, one that considers the context, would be beneficial.

Furthermore, in Isa 40:13, a mere five verses from the use of *ruach* translated as breath, the NASB translates it as Spirit, and the NIV translates it as "mind" with a footnote that offers Spirit as an alternative. Reluctance to ascribe judgment to the Spirit apparently drives the choice of translation. The texts, however, show that the Spirit both renews the face of the earth and withers the grass of the field. Here one encounters the dual nature of God's judgment as the Spirit withers the old in the process of creating the new.[24]

In 2 Thess 2:8 Paul writes, "Then the lawless one will be revealed, whom the Lord Jesus will kill with the breath of his mouth and bring to nothing by the appearance of his coming." This verse reveals how the symbol of a rod or a sword is employed to describe the Holy Spirit executing judgment as symbolized by Jesus' breath. This verse is a clear reflection of Isa 11:4, which declares that the Spirit-empowered Messiah would "strike the earth with the rod of his mouth, and with the breath of his lips he shall kill the wicked." The Lord's breath is powerfully effective, bringing to an end the embodiment of evil and opposition to God.

Ernest Best argues that the breath is not a reference to the Spirit because the Spirit is not a destructive force in Paul's message.[25] While it is true that the Spirit's role in condemnation is not the focal point of Paul's proclamation, or of any other writer for that matter, that does not preclude a verse from referencing his work in condemnation. The salvific work of both Christ and the Spirit is what is in the foreground of the New Testament narrative, with the inevitable condemnation for those who stand in opposition to that salvation in the background. The argument that a verse about condemnation does not refer to the Spirit because the Spirit does not condemn runs a circular course that will only continue to dig a deeper rut, when what is needed is to allow the symbol of the Lord's breath, which is

---

24. Calvin, *Commentary on the Prophet Isaiah*, 210.

25. Best, *Commentary on the First and Second Epistles*, 303. Best contends the breath of his mouth is not something weak or minor as evidenced in Ps 33:6. Best's reference to Ps. 33:6 is interesting in that this verse argues in favor of the breath in 2 Thess 2:8 being the Holy Spirit. The breath is not a word coming out of Christ's mouth, but is an image of war (Rev 19:15) where the breath is a fierce weapon, as in Isa 30:27 and Rev 2:16.

overwhelmingly understood as a symbol for the Spirit, to carry its weight in this verse referring to the destruction of the lawless one.

Additionally, Best gives a nod to Rom 8:13 in which Paul tells his readers that if they by the Spirit put to death the deeds of the flesh they will live, but concludes that this is not a strong enough parallel to warrant the verse under investigation to be understood as a reference to the Spirit.[26] In the Romans passage, it is clear that when a person lives in the Spirit's power then that person will kill those actions that stand in opposition to God. As has been demonstrated, exegetical issues regarding the understanding of the Spirit have often been decided based upon a presupposition that the Spirit is not involved in condemnation. If one removes this fallacy, then 2 Thess 2:8 makes perfect sense as a reference to the Spirit as the effective power within Jesus' words.

Paul has taken the idea from Isa 11:4 and has related Jesus' victory over the Lawless One to his possession of the Spirit, as does the text in Isaiah. The breath of his mouth recalls the sword of the Spirit, which is the word of God in Eph 6:17 and Heb 4:12, or the two-edged sword from his mouth in Rev 1:16.

> The jump from the sword's connoting the word of the Lord to Paul's substitution of the phrase speaking of the spirit of the Lord, entailing Paul's omission of the word 'sword' itself, is not too difficult to account for. By saying breath of his mouth, Paul is trying to show that it is done effortlessly; a mere breath defeats the enemy. In the verse, pneuma does not refer to power to give life, but to destruction. Only in Rom 8:13 does Paul have this idea of the spirit. In Rom 8:13 and 2 Thess 2:8 pneuma appears in the dative without a preposition like through or by, as that by which something disordered is killed. The result of the destruction is the New Creation. The very 'negative' use of pneuma in v. 8b (as an instrument of death) hints at the process of transformation which is contingent on the purging out (to death) of what is disordered or evil.[27]

The coming of the Lord, his appearing, and the Spirit cannot be separated, although they are not the same thing. When the Lord comes the Spirit is present; the two cannot be disconnected.

The connection between 2 Thess 2:8 and Isa 11:4 is clear, and it is most likely that Paul was drawing his imagery of the Lord's breath as a weapon

---

26. Ibid. He does not give a reason for why it is not strong enough.

27. Giblin, *Threat to Faith*, 89–94.

from the Isaiah passage.[28] While Paul used the symbol as a weapon, Isa 11:4 speaks of both the rod of the Messiah's mouth and the breath of his lips that are used to strike the earth and slay the wicked. The passage describes the actions of the shoot that will spring from the stump of Jesse, upon whom the Spirit of the Lord will rest. It further reveals that he will judge fairly for the poor and afflicted and slay the wicked with the breath (*ruach*) of his mouth. The mere word of the Messiah will be enough to judge the earth, for his word is dynamic, powerful, and effective because God's Spirit rests upon him.[29]

At the end of Paul's letter to Ephesus, he instructs his readers to equip themselves with various items of God's armor (Eph 6:10–17). There is the belt of truth and the breastplate of righteousness. In addition, they are to put on the helmet of salvation and carry the shield of faith. Lastly, they are instructed to wield the sword of the Spirit, which is the word of God. The one offensive weapon that Paul exhorts his readers to utilize is God's word. This word is described as a sword that gains its effectiveness from the Spirit.[30] The Spirit is not described as the sword, but as the power that makes the sword mighty. He is the agent that gives the sword its bite, which makes the edge of the blade sharp so as to accomplish its task effectively.[31] The word of God is the instrument the Spirit uses in the believer's life to defeat the schemes of the devil. Ephesians 6:17 makes a strong connection between God's word, a sword, and the Spirit. The word of God is the good news of the gospel, but as already shown, this good news is also the means of defeat for those who stand in opposition to it.[32] The Spirit who empowers the word actualizes this defeat.

Like Paul, in the book of Revelation John also acquires the theme of a weapon coming forth from the Lord's mouth that will judge the world. In Rev 1:16, as John encounters Jesus in his vision, he beholds him with a sharp sword coming out his mouth. It would appear that John has established a connection with Isa 11:4, but has changed the metaphor from a rod to a sword, possibly in connection with Isa 49:2 in which the Servant

---

28. Martin, *1, 2 Thessalonians*, 243.

29. Wildberger, *Isaiah 1–12*, 471–79.

30. Lincoln, *Ephesians*, 451. Barth states, "Whether a traditional or a freshly inspired 'word of God' is in mind, this 'word' can be called the cutting edge of the Spirit—but it must be maintained that the word itself, not the Spirit, is the sword." Barth, *Ephesians*, 776–7. See also O'Brien, *Letter to the Ephesians*, 481–83; Fee, *God's Empowering Presence*, 729.

31. Schnackenburg, *Ephesians*, 279.

32. Lincoln, *Ephesians*, 451.

recounts that God has made his mouth like a sharp sword.[33] Here, in Revelation, John combines the two images so that a sword proceeds from Jesus' mouth. The sword is a common symbol for the tongue and therefore the reference is most likely to Jesus' words. Additionally, the sword is a metaphor for judgment and hence the sword from his mouth is the word of condemnation that he speaks against the world.[34] Likewise, it is the word that continuously comes forth from his mouth that brings judgment. It is not a one-time spoken word that ceases to exist, neither does it come forth intermittently, but it continuously comes forth.[35] As the sword, Jesus' word continually proceeds from his mouth, so too does the Spirit continually proceed through the Son.

The final two verses in Revelation that relate the sword of the mouth to condemnation are 19:15, 21. These verses appear in one of the more graphic scenes in the book as Jesus rides forth from heaven on a white horse to make war against those who stand opposed to him. John recounts that from his mouth proceeds a sharp sword with which to strike the nations and that he will rule them with an iron rod. The close connection between the sword and the rod in this verse further establishes the connection with Isa 11:4 in which the breath of the Messiah's lips is the effective agent of condemnation. In v. 21, after the beast and false prophet have been thrown into the lake of fire, those who remain are said to be slain by the sword coming from Jesus' mouth. The imagery draws together Isa 11:4, 49:2 and Ps 2:9 into a unified whole.[36]

John 12:46 states that Jesus' words will be what will judge a person on the last day. Jesus is confident in the effectiveness of his word because he has only spoken that which the Father told him to speak. The words that he spoke are those words that have proceeded from the Father. It would seem that he left little room for the Spirit in this statement, that all that is taking place in judgment is between the Father and the Son, but later, in John 16:12–15, Jesus revealed the Holy Spirit's work in relation to his words. He told his disciples that he had much more to tell them, but they could not bear it at that time. However, once he had been glorified and the Spirit of truth, the Holy Spirit, had come, then the Holy Spirit would guide them into all truth because he would not speak on his own, but would take Jesus'

---

33. Osborne, *Revelation*, 92.

34. Aune, *Revelation*, 98.

35. Kistemaker, *Revelation*, 97.

36. Beale, *Book of Revelation*, 961–63.

words and declare them to the disciples. As Jesus spoke what the Father told him, so likewise the Spirit would speak only those things that the Son instructed him.

John 16:12–15 presents a beautiful image of the Trinitarian relationships, in that the Father gives his word to the Son, who is the Word, then the Son reveals that word to creation, and in doing so reveals himself, but only in the power of the Spirit. The Father is the source of the word; the Son, who is the Word, is the one who takes what the Father has told him and delivers it to the world, and the Spirit is the means whereby the word becomes actualized in a person's life. The Spirit's role in the Farewell Discourse in relation to the transmission of Jesus' words to the believing disciples can be extrapolated to all of humanity, both those who believe them and are judged not guilty and those who reject them and are judged guilty. In both cases, the Spirit actualizes and empowers the judgmental word of the Son.

Conclusion

Having established both fire and breath as symbols that pertain to the Holy Spirit and that relate the Spirit to judgment, an investigation into the symbols of God's finger, hand, and arm will be undertaken. This investigation will establish, as in the previous two symbols, the Spirit's role in condemnation.

5

The Spirit and God's Hand

ANOTHER MOTIF OF BOTH the Spirit and judgment needing elucidation is God's arm and hand. While the two words, hand and arm, are not strictly synonymous, their frequent overlap in use makes it feasible to treat them as one motif.[1] Most texts that employ the motif of the arm or hand of God do so within the context of God as a warrior who is either protecting his people or carrying out a campaign against those who are opposed to them. This representation of God as a warrior is most clearly demonstrated in the Exodus event in which his arm delivers the people from the oppression of Egypt while simultaneously punishing the Egyptians for their oppression. As is readily apparent, God's arm functions as a motif of the execution of judgment, with the same dual result.

In Ezek 20:33–38, God declares that with his outstretched arm he will bring Israel out from the nations in which they had been scattered and enter into judgment with them in order to establish his kingship. His arm will place the people in a position in which they can be judged. This judgment will purify the nation by removing the rebels from among them.

In several verses, God's arm almost attains a hypostatic existence, similar to wisdom in Prov 8. Isaiah 63:11–14 asks:

> Where is he who brought them up out of the sea with the shepherds of his flock? Where is he who put in the midst of them his Holy Spirit, who caused his glorious arm to go at the right hand of Moses, who divided the waters before them to make for himself an

1. The origination of the idiom is uncertain, but it might have derived from the other cultures surrounding the Israelites, who often portrayed their gods in poses in which the arm and hand were represented as carrying out the will of the deity. Hoffmeier, "Arm of God," 378–87.

everlasting name, who led them through the depths? Like a horse
in the desert, they did not stumble. Like livestock that go down
into the valley, the Spirit of the LORD gave them rest.

The arm of the Lord is portrayed as an entity that has been placed
alongside Moses.[2] Additionally, God's arm and his Spirit are intimately connected in this passage. This connection will be investigated further in Jesus'
reference in Luke 11:20 that he casts out demons by the finger of God, and
Matthew's parallel passage in 12:28 in which he records that Jesus said he
would cast out demons by the Spirit of God. These passages will be used
to argue that God's finger is synonymous with the hand and the arm of
the Lord, and further that the finger is the Holy Spirit, who carries out the
judgment of the Father given to the Son.[3]

In addition to God's arm/hand serving as a means of describing his
warrior nature, it also served as a symbol for his protection. Ezra 8:22 states,
"The hand of our God is favorably disposed to all those who seek Him, but
His power and His anger are against all those who forsake Him." While
God's hand proved terrifying to the surrounding nations and even to the
nation of Israel at times, it was understood that his hand was also protective
and that it is from his hand that blessings were dispensed.

In order to explicate the connection between God's hand and the Spirit, this chapter will begin with God's finger and its connection to the Spirit
in the gospels of Matthew and Luke. From there, we will connect God's
finger with his hand and arm, showing that all three are used as a symbol
of God's judgment. We will then connect God's finger/hand/arm with his
Spirit, with the intention to show that the Spirit actualizes the judgment of
God's mighty arm.

God's Finger as a Symbol of the Spirit

In Luke 11:20, Jesus declared that he cast out demons by the finger of God,
while in Matthew's parallel account in 12:28 he related that he did his exorcisms by God's Spirit. The link between God's finger and Spirit in these

---

2. There is some disagreement among scholars as to whether the arm refers to the
people of Israel or to God. For a defense of the former interpretation see Young, *Book of
Isaiah*, 3:484–85. For those who hold that the arm is that of God's see Blenkinsopp, *Isaiah
56–66*, 255; Westermann, *Isaiah 40–66*, 385–89.

3. Wall, "Finger of God," 144–50; Klingbeil, "Finger of God in the Old Testament,"
409–15.

two passages will serve as an entry point to investigate the symbol of God's hand and arm in relation to the Holy Spirit. Initially, those passages in the Old Testament that employ the finger of God will be addressed, leading to a deeper look into Luke and Matthew's exorcism accounts. Having established a connection between God's finger and his Spirit, it will be possible to extend the connection to God's hand and arm. Once a connection is made between God's finger, hand, and arm, a further connection will be established between God's finger/hand/arm and the Holy Spirit vis-à-vis judgment.

The phrase "finger of God" in the singular only appears three times in the Old Testament. The first is in the response of Pharaoh's magicians to the third plague in Exod 8:19 in which Moses changed dust to gnats. The magicians declared that it is by the "finger of God" that Moses performed this feat, thus admitting that it was beyond their powers to duplicate his sign, and therefore, it was only by the power of a god that he produced gnats from dust. Interestingly, this first use of the phrase "finger of God" comes in the context of a judgment upon Egypt.[4] In Exod 7:4, God tells Moses that He will put his hand upon Egypt and will bring out the Israelites by great acts of judgment. The synonymous use of the "hand of God" and the "finger of God" is evident in the two passages.[5] God will liberate his people while simultaneously condemning the Egyptians, accomplishing both by his hand, which is synonymous with his finger.

The next occurrence of the phrase is in relation to the giving of the Law on Sinai. Exodus 31:18, paralleled in Deut 9:10, records that God wrote out the Ten Commandments on a stone tablet with his own finger. Augustine makes the conjecture that if one member of the Trinity should be singled out in the event of the writing of the Law, then it might be the Spirit. He states, "But if it is allowable, without rash assertion, to venture upon a modest and hesitating conjecture from this passage, if it is possible to understand it of one person of the Trinity, why do we not rather understand the Holy Spirit to be spoken of, since the Law itself also, which was given there, is said to have been written upon tables of stone with the finger of God, by which we know the Holy Spirit to be signified in the Gospel."[6]

4. Klingbeil, "Finger of God in the Old Testament," 409–15. Couroyer makes an interesting interpretation of Exod 8:19 by arguing that the finger of God is in reference to the rod of Aaron. Couroyer, "Le 'Doigt de Dieu,'" 481–95. Durham rejects Couroyer's interpretation as based upon too thin an argument, and further argues that "finger of God" is a typical Hebrew anthropomorphism. Durham, *Exodus*, 108–9.

5. Hamerton-Kelly, "Note on Matthew 12:28 par Luke 11:20," 167–69.

6. Augustine, *Trinity*, 2.26.

Having recently been delivered from Egypt by the "finger of God," now the Israelites are given the law, the ethical and relational benchmark for their relationship with Yahweh, by the same "finger of God."[7]

Paul, in 2 Cor 3, makes a pointed distinction between the Siniatic law written on tablets of stone and the new Covenant in Christ written on the heart. The law written on stone tablets by God's finger, or, as is being argued, the Holy Spirit, was an external law that brought death because it did not provide the power with which to accomplish its fulfillment. The New Covenant, written not on stone but on a heart of flesh by the Spirit, provides the means wherewith the person is able to fulfill its demands.[8] Both the Old and New Covenants were written by the Holy Spirit, the first that leads to condemnation and the second that leads to justification.

While not in the singular, like the previous instances of the phrase, Ps 8:3 equates the work of creation with God's fingers, while three verses later in v. 6 the work of creation is ascribed to God's hands. Additionally, Ps 33:6 ascribes creation to both God's word and breath.[9] Furthermore, one finds in Gen 1:2 a description of the Spirit's involvement in the creation of the world. These verses serve as part of the foundation for the Trinitarian description of creation in that God the Father speaks creation into being, while the Son (Word) who is the effective agent of creation works in the power of the Spirit (finger/hand/breath) to actualize that which the Father is creating through the Son. In other words, the Father creates through the Son in the power of the Spirit.[10] While the Old Testament writers were most likely not conscious of God's Trinitarian nature, the Old Testament

7. Weinfeld argues based upon the distinction between Exod 8:15 and Ps 8:4, 7, that the use of finger instead of hand denotes an extraordinary activity of God. Weinfeld, *Deuteronomy 1–11*, 408.

8. Hughes is correct in his argument that Paul is not deprecating the Siniatic Law in itself, but only that the Law was not able to save people due to the weakness of the people, not the Law. The Law came with glory, but the new Law in Christ comes with greater glory. Both Laws are written by the Holy Spirit, the distinction is between how the recipient is empowered by the Spirit. Hughes, *Paul's Second Epistle to the Corinthians*, 90.

9. The breath of God was a favorite description of Basil of Caesarea for the Holy Spirit and he argued convincingly in his writings that the Spirit was operative in creation in conjunction with the Son. Basil, *On the Holy Spirit*, 62–63.

10. Grenz, *Theology for the Community of God*, 133–39. While Erickson rightly ascribes creation to the Trinity, he casually notes that many of the Old Testament passages that support his claim are difficult to determine whether they refer to the Holy Spirit or to God's breath. While the interpretation of *ruach* as Spirit or breath in these verses may be in question, God's breath is his Spirit and therefore the verses offer no impediment to an understanding of the Trinitarian nature of creation. Erickson, *Christian Theology*, 398–99.

has a Trinitarian thrust to it.[11] The distinction between God and his finger is therefore to be understood as more than poetic description, but leaning toward an ontological distinction within the Godhead.

The Old Testament's use of God's finger sets the stage for the move into the New Testament and Jesus' ministry in which he claimed that he cast out demons by God's Spirit/finger. This equation of the Spirit and the finger between Matthew and Luke offers an avenue to investigate the relationship between God's finger, hand, and arm with the intention of connecting all three phrases with the Holy Spirit.

According to Luke 11:20, Jesus cast out demons by the finger of God, while Matt 12:28 records that it was by the Spirit of God he performed exorcisms. The quest for the original saying, while helpful, often becomes a distraction, and it is therefore necessary to correlate the two sayings, viewing them as complementary, not contradictory, by connecting the themes of God's Spirit and finger.[12] In line with Dunn's premise of oral tradition, it is most likely that Jesus made these statements on numerous occasions and that therefore he used both sayings.[13] He cast out demons by the Spirit of God, described symbolically as the finger of God.

Luke states that in the event of the exorcism the kingdom of God had come upon the people. The exorcism is in itself an act of judgment upon the inhabiting demon. God's finger brings deliverance to the possessed and exile to the possessor. While the kingdom's advent is often viewed from the perspective of the freed captive, it is necessary to understand that the freedom gained came through the vanquishing of the oppressor. When faced with God's finger, the demon had no choice but to succumb to the judgment passed upon it.[14] In Matthew, Jesus stated that he cast out demons by the Spirit of God, and this verse, even more so than the one in

---

11. Knight, *Biblical Approach to the Doctrine of the Trinity*.

12. There has been much ink spilled within Synoptic studies over which logion should have priority, who borrowed from whom, and the ramifications of the difference. Yates, "Luke's Pneumatology and Lk. 11, 20," 295–99; Wall, "Finger of God," 144–50; Van Cangh, "Par L'esprit de Dieu," 337–42; Nolland, *Luke 9:21—18:34*, 639–41; Hamerton-Kelly, "Note on Matthew 12:28 par Luke 11:20," 167–69; George, *Etudes sur L'Oeuvre*; Couroyer, "Le Doigt de Dieu," 481–95; Dunn, *Jesus and the Spirit*, 44–53; Rodd, "Spirit or Finger," 157–58; Woods, *"Finger of God" and Pneumatologys*; van der Horst, "Finger of God," 89–103.

13. Dunn, *Jesus Remembered*, 192–254.

14. Klingbeil makes a similar observation regarding Pharaoh and God's judgment upon him. Klingbeil, "The Finger of God in the Old Testament," 413–14.

Luke, presents clear evidence that the Spirit is involved in judgment, both redemptive and condemnatory.

The parable of the binding of the strong man serves as an interpretation on the purpose of the exorcism. Jesus, in casting out the demon, had first to bind the strong man, Satan, in order to carry out his mission. It is clear that Jesus binds Satan in the power of the Spirit. Morris describes the exorcism as the defeat of the demon.[15] The Holy Spirit, as Jesus' efficacious power, released the captive and condemned the captor. The Spirit accomplished the freedom the Son proclaimed in his inaugural speech in Nazareth recorded in Luke 4:18 in which he declared the release of captives and the favorable year of the Lord.[16]

While it is obvious that both passages in Matthew and Luke are related, the equation of the Holy Spirit and the finger of God must be justified. Hamerton-Kelly argues that Q had spirit and Luke changed it to finger. He rests his argument upon three Old Testament passages, Ezek 8:3, 37:1, and 1 Chr 28:11–19, which treat God's Spirit and hand as synonymous. From this correlation of the two themes, he further argues that finger is a variation of hand, and hence Luke has adopted the Old Testament connection between God's Spirit and his hand.[17] While Dunn argued in his treatment that Spirit is original, he similarly concluded that God's Spirit and hand are equivalent concepts in numerous passages such as Ezek 3:14, 8:1–3, and 37:1, Ps 8:3 in connection with Ps 33:6, 1 Kgs 18:12 in connection with 2 Kgs 2:16, 1 Chr 28:12 in connection with 28:19, and Isaiah 8:11. He further writes that "the equation, finger of God=power of God=Spirit of God, is one which arises directly out of the Hebrew understanding of God's action, and one which was obvious to either Matthew or Luke when he altered the Q original."[18] I.

15. Morris, *The Gospel According to Matthew*, 317. Blomberg states that "God in Christ is decisively defeating the devil." Blomberg, *Matthew*, 203.

16. Smeaton offers a thorough overview of the anointing of the Son in the Spirit from conception to glorification. Smeaton, *The Doctrine of the Holy Spirit*, 116–36.

17. Hamerton-Kelly, "A Note on Matthew 12:28 par Luke 11:20," 167–69. Woods presents a strong case against the connection that Hamerton-Kelly makes by asserting that the Spirit is never connected with miracles, but only inspiration in these texts and that therefore it is an unfounded move to see the Spirit as working in the miracles of the Exodus tradition. While his point is worth noting, it is ultimately unconvincing in arguing for why God's finger or hand should not be understood as referring to the Spirit in those passages that do not involve prophetic inspiration and proclamation. In fact, one could argue that the miracle of the third plague was nothing other than a proclamation of God's power over Pharaoh. Woods, *The "Finger of God" and Pneumatology in Luke-Acts*, 161–62.

18. Dunn, *Jesus and the Spirit*, 46.

Howard Marshall likewise concludes that the Old Testament equated God's hand and Spirit, and therefore Matthew and Luke make the same point.[19]

With the equation of God's finger and Spirit in Matthew and Luke established, it is not a great step to make the connection between his hand and Spirit as already shown. This is a connection that is not novel for Luke, for there are numerous passages in the Old Testament that relate God's hand to the Spirit as already cited. In order to elaborate more fully this connection, the following section will investigate those passages that connect God's finger and hand. Once a connection is made between his finger and hand, a further connection will be shown between his hand and arm. Once all the preceding connections have been established, the connection between his finger/hand/arm and the Holy Spirit will be demonstrated.

The Finger's Connection to God's Hand and Arm

The first link in the skeleton is to establish the synonymous nature of God's finger(s) and hand(s). While this link is natural and can almost be assumed, as the finger is the natural extension of the hand, there is scriptural support for the equation. As already mentioned in Exod 3:20, God told Moses that he would stretch out his hand against Egypt and because of his judgments, Pharaoh would grant the Israelites their freedom. At the conclusion of the miracle of Exod 8:19, the magicians equated the gnats with God's finger, establishing a link between God's hand and finger.[20] The early church made the connection between God's finger and hand, as well as the Spirit's writing on the stone tablets, as evidenced in the *Epistle of Barnabas* (c. 80–130 CE), which relates that the two tablets of the covenant "were written in the Spirit by the finger of the hand of the Lord."[21]

The handwriting on the wall in the fifth chapter of Daniel provides a further connection between God's hand and his finger. Belshazzar openly challenged Yahweh by ordering that the utensils seized from the Temple in

19. Marshall, *Gospel of Luke*, 475.

20. Horst argues that both God's Spirit and finger mean the power of God, as does the phrase "hand of God." van der Horst, "Finger of God," 90–91. Childs states that the finger in Exod 8:12 is a synecdoche for hand or power of God. Childs, *Exodus*, 129. For others who make a similar connection between the use of God's finger and hand see Dunn, *Jesus and the Spirit*, 46; Nolland, *Luke*, 640; Hamerton-Kelly, "Note on Matthew 12:28 par Luke 11:20," 168.

21. *Epistle of Barnabas* 14.2. Credit for this reference goes to Woods, *"Finger of God" and Pneumatology in Luke–Acts*, 99.

Jerusalem be brought into his festivities. After he drank from the vessels, he praised the gods of gold, silver, bronze, iron, wood, and stone. Immediately, the fingers of a hand appeared and wrote a message on the wall that caused great terror to fall on Belshazzar. The message proclaimed the end of his reign as king. Daniel 5:5 does not reveal who sent the fingers, but 5:24 confirms that God sent the hand from his presence. The same finger that wrote on the wall of Belshazzar's palace turned the dust to gnats in Egypt and wrote on the stone tablets at Sinai.[22]

Collins argues that the hand is a divine emissary, but that it is not to be correlated with either the plague narrative or the Sinai account in which the finger is not visible.[23] While Collins is correct about the invisibility of the finger in the plague narrative, he gives no basis for the invisibility of the finger in the Sinai account. If his argument is from silence, then the argument can cut both ways because the account does not say the hand was invisible. Therefore, given the unique nature of the manifestation, it is most likely that the finger of God in the plague narrative and at Sinai is also the same finger that writes out the response to Belshazzar's false worship. The finger/hand of God pronounces God's judgment upon Belshazzar.

Before moving on to establish the connection between God's hand and Spirit, it is necessary to move up one body part and solidify the connection between God's hand and his arm. *Yad*, the most common term employed for the hand in Hebrew, most often denotes the hand only, but it is not clearly differentiated from the wrist or the arm. In the Exodus narrative, all three body parts are used to describe God's power to liberate captive Israel. Deuteronomy 26:8 states, "And the LORD brought us out of Egypt with a mighty hand and an outstretched arm and with great terror and with signs and wonders." Jeremiah 27:5 reiterates this same theme where God related to Jeremiah that he made the earth with his outstretched arm. Jeremiah elaborates on the theme of God's outstretched arm in 32:21, after restating in 32:17 that God made the earth with his outstretched arm, by directly connecting God's strong hand and outstretched arm to the Exodus.

While the finger is definitely the least emphasized of the three parts, God's hand and arm appear in numerous places in parallel structure, with the clear implication that they are referring to the same thing and

---

22. Calvin argues, "This was really God's hand, being sent from his sight as a certain testimony of his wrath." Calvin, *Commentaries on the Book of the Prophet Daniel*, 342. Goldingay and Lacoque equate the hand in Dan 5:5 with the finger at Sinai. Goldingay, *Daniel*, 114; Lacoque, *Book of Daniel*, 95–96.

23. Collins, *Daniel*, 241–47.

are interchangeable.[24] Having established the relationship between God's finger and hand in Scripture, it is now possible to relate God's hand and arm, which are more ubiquitous phrases in the Bible, to the Holy Spirit, and to thus complete the circle back to the Gospels' correlation between God's Spirit and finger in which Luke's use of finger is connected with a general Old Testament theme of the finger/hand/arm of God being the means of God's deliverance and condemnation.

The Spirit's Connection to God's Hand and Arm

In 1 Chr 28:12, 19 God's Spirit and hand are related as David is giving to Solomon the plans for the building of the Temple. According to v. 12, David received the plans for the Temple from the Spirit of the Lord who placed them in David's mind. The RSV, ESV, and NASB translate this verse so that *ruach* refers exclusively to David's mind, while the NIV translates it so that the Spirit imparts the plans to David's mind.[25] Johnstone argues for a parallel between David/Solomon and Moses/Bezalel, for just as Bezalel carries out the plan for the Tabernacle that was divinely given to Moses, so also Solomon carries out the plan for the Temple that was divinely given to David. Myers argues that *ruach* is not used in reference to a human being in Chronicles, but he was corrected by Braun who showed that it was used in both 2 Chr 21:16 and 36:22. While Braun is correct that the Chronicler can use *ruach* to refer to a human's spirit or mind, that does not prove conclusively that in this instance the reference is to David's mind alone, especially in light of 28:19 where it is explicitly stated that the hand of the Lord was upon David. As has already been shown in other passages, the hand of the Lord and the Spirit can be used synonymously. The NIV has best captured the sense of the verse with its translation. In v. 19, David declared that he received all the plans for the Temple "in writing by His hand upon me." The imagery switches from the Holy Spirit delivering the knowledge of the Temple to David to God's hand writing upon David the plans for the Temple.

---

24. The other verses in the Bible that connect the hand and the arm of God are Deut 4:34, 5:15, 7:19, 11:2, 26:8; 1 Kgs 8:42; 2 Chr 6:32; Pss 44:3, 89:13,21, 98:1, 136:12; Isa 62:8; Jer 21:5, 32:21; Ezek 20:33–38.

25. In agreement with the NIV translation is Myers, *1 Chronicles*, 190; Thompson, *1, 2 Chronicles*, 191–92; Johnstone, *1 and 2 Chronicles*, 280.

Likewise, Ezekiel closely correlates God's hand and Spirit. Beginning in 3:12–14 he described how the Spirit carried him away and how the hand of the Lord was strong upon him. This description of the Spirit taking someone away can also be found in 1 Kgs 18:12 and 2 Kgs 2:16. While is it debated whether in this verse *ruach* should be translated as wind or Spirit, Block has offered a convincing argument for Spirit as the proper understanding. His two main arguments for understanding *ruach* as Spirit is that the Temple visions of chapters 8–11 are bookended with references to the *ruach* transporting the prophet; within the visions, each time the prophet is taken to a new location he writes that "he then brought me to . . . " thus affirming that the *ruach* is not to be understood as a mere wind. Furthermore, most convincing is 37:1, which reads, "The hand of the Lord was upon me, and He brought me out by the Spirit of the Lord and set me down in the middle of the valley; and it was full of bones." This verse clearly reveals the *ruach* as God's Spirit.[26]

In 8:1–3 the connection is even stronger as Ezekiel described a vision in which the hand of the Lord fell upon him, a phrase similar to how the Spirit is described as falling on the Judges and other prophets. Subsequently, Ezekiel saw a man that appeared as fire from the waist down and from his waist upward, there was brightness. This man stretched out a hand and grabbed Ezekiel by the hair and the Spirit lifted him up between heaven and earth, bringing him in a vision to Jerusalem. The description of the man resembles John's vision of Jesus on the isle of Patmos in Rev 1:13–14 and again in chapter 4, and therefore it is not unreasonable to assume that Ezekiel had a vision of the Son and that the hand was a vision of the Spirit, the one who executes the Son's work in the world.[27]

One final verse in which Ezekiel connects the hand and the Spirit is 37:1, the beginning of the famous valley of dry bones vision. The hand of the Lord was upon Ezekiel and the Spirit of God brought him out and placed him in the valley of dry bones. As in the previous verses, the hand and the Spirit are tightly connected so that the only conclusion one can

---

26. Block, "Prophet of the Spirit," 34.

27. While the primary imagery behind the Rev 1 image is from the book of Daniel, the reference in Ezekiel can further be seen as relating to this vision. Cooper makes the connection between the fire in the theophanies in Ezek 1:26–27 and Rev 4. Cooper, *Ezekiel*, 71. Brownlee also makes a connection between Ezekiel's vision and John's in Rev 4. Brownlee, *Ezekiel 1–19*, 16.

make is that the hand of the Lord served as a colloquial expression, at least for Ezekiel, for the Spirit of the Lord.[28]

Isaiah related in 8:11 that a strong hand was upon him or that God spoke to him with strength of hand, instructing him not to walk in the ways of the people of Judah. While this verse does not explicitly describe the hand as God's, the reason for this is that the use of the Lord's hand as code for prophetic inspiration had become quite widespread so there was no need to identify whose hand it was.[29] Alexander argues that God's hand is connected with inspiration in this verse and that it is equivalent to expressions such as "in the Spirit" in Rev 1:10, "in a trance" in Acts 11:5, and "in power and in the Holy Spirit" in 1 Thess 1:5.[30]

The prophet warned Israel in Isa 31:3 not to make an alliance with Egypt, for "the Egyptians are man, and not God, and their horses are flesh, and not spirit." The contrast established is not between corporeality and immateriality, but between two types or sources of power. The Egyptians will rely on their earthly power, but in truth that is not power at all, for all power derives ultimately from God. Isaiah then related that "when the LORD stretches out his hand, the helper will stumble, and he who is helped will fall, and they will perish together." The implication is clear. The power to withstand the coming assault against the nation will not be found in Egypt, but in God, specifically his *ruach*. If the people do not rely on God's power, and instead opt to seek protection from Egypt, then God will stretch out his hand, that is, he will extend his power, his Spirit, and both Egypt and the nation will perish.[31]

A final passage connecting God's arm with the Holy Spirit is Isa 63:10–12.[32] The prophet is recounting how the Israelites rebelled against

28. Block, "Prophet of the Spirit," 33–34; Zimmerli, *Ezekiel*, 2:259.

29. Wildberger, *Isaiah 1–12*, 356–57. Zimmerli sees a similar connection between God's hand coming upon a prophet and the way in which the Spirit is described as falling upon the Othniel and Jephthah in Judg 3:10 and 11:29. Zimmerli, *Ezekiel*, 1:118.

30. Alexander, *Commentary on Isaiah*, 189.

31. Wildberger gives an overview of the various exegetical conclusions that have been reached concerning this verse, specifically the relation of *ruach* to God's nature. There are three main options: 1) One is able to ascertain from this passage that God is Spirit; 2) the verse attempts to draw an antithesis between spirit and matter, thus establishing a metaphysical dualism; 3) Spirit is understood as a reference to God's power that shaped history. It is not the military power of Egypt, symbolized by its horses, that will shape history, but the power of God, understood as *ruach*. Wildberger, *Isaiah 28–39*, 211–15.

32. This is one of the clearest Old Testament passages that present the Spirit as a personal agent. Westermann, *Isaiah 40–66*, 388; Oswalt, *Book of Isaiah*, 607–8; Alexander,

God during the desert wanderings, grieving God's Holy Spirit, so that he turned against them and became their enemy. The question is then asked, where is the God who walked with the people in the days of old, who brought them out of Egypt? Isaiah 63:11b–12 asks, "Where is he who put in the midst of them his Holy Spirit, who caused his glorious arm to go at the right hand of Moses, who divided the waters before them to make for himself an everlasting name?"[33] Isaiah clearly declared that God placed his Holy Spirit in the midst of the people. This is most likely a reference to the Shekinah glory exemplified in the pillar of fire and cloud. He then equated God's Spirit with his glorious arm that went at the right hand of Moses.[34] Moses was empowered by the Spirit to accomplish the liberation of the Israelites. Additionally, a reference is made to the parting of the Red Sea, a miracle that has already been connected with God's breath and hence with the Holy Spirit. Here, Isaiah has made a direct connection between the arm of God's salvation, the power with which God works in the world to accomplish his purposes, and the Holy Spirit.

One Body, Many Parts

In using "finger of God" to describe God's power in Jesus' exorcisms, Luke was employing a connection that already existed in his time. In the foregoing discussion, one could get the impression that the Spirit acts independently of the Son. This impression must be banished, for the Spirit does not act as an independent agent of the Godhead, but as the effecting power of the Father and the Son. The Son initiates the work of the Father, and the Spirit fulfills that work. Furthermore, the equation of the arm of the Lord with the Suffering Servant of Isa 53 gives further strength to the argument that one cannot separate out the workings of the Trinity.

In Isa 53, the question is asked to whom the arm of the Lord has been revealed, and then the prophet moves immediately to describe the arm that

---

Commentary on Isaiah, 421.

33. While Young suggests the conjunction "and" should be added to the verse so that the reference is to Moses' arm and not God's, this is arbitrary and unnecessary. Young, *Book of Isaiah*, 3:484.

34. Alexander recognizes the potential ambiguity in the verse regarding whether the arm refers to God or Moses, but concludes in favor of God. Alexander, *Commentary on Isaiah*, 423. Blenkinsopp, Oswalt, and Westermann all agree that the reference is to God's arm. Blenkinsopp, *Isaiah 56–66*, 252; Oswalt, *Book of Isaiah: Chapters 40–66*, 608–9; Westermann, *Isaiah 40–66*, 388–89.

until this time had been understood as the power of God working through the natural events of history and in miracles. It was the arm of the Lord that not only delivered the people from their oppressors, but that also brought punishment upon the people when they disobeyed. Here the arm appears, but not in a manner that the people expected. They were looking for a great warrior, but instead they were given a young plant that had no majesty. The arm of the Lord, God's power to deliver his people, became flesh and dwelt among them.[35] Jesus is the visible, tangible arm of God. Being the arm, one can make the connection that he is also the visible, tangible hand of God in the world.

Having established the connection between God's arm, hand, and finger, and furthermore having argued that in Jesus all these anthropomorphisms used to describe the power of God became incarnated, it is possible to see the intimate connection between the Son and the Spirit. Isaiah 63:7–14 reinforces this intimate connection, in which it describes the Holy Spirit as being in the midst of the people during the exodus. Furthermore, 63:12 states that God put his glorious arm at the right hand of Moses. It was the Holy Spirit, the Lord's glorious arm, who empowered Moses to deliver the people from Egypt and to establish God's everlasting name.[36]

It was in the power of the Spirit that the Son carried out his ministry. It is the Spirit who executes the commands of the Son. The Son pours the Spirit out upon his people in order to deliver them from sin and death. The Trinitarian doctrine of proper operations is affirmed in this line of reasoning. The Father sends the Son into the world to deliver it from evil and, as a necessary corollary, to judge it. The Spirit comes upon the Son to empower him for his task and to be the executor of the Son's decisions.

While the Son is the visible arm of the Lord in the incarnation, in line with Irenaeus, the Spirit is also the Lord's arm. Irenaeus argues the Son and the Spirit are the two hands of God that work in creation. He writes, "For God did not stand in need of these, in order to the accomplishing of what He had Himself determined with Himself beforehand should be done, as if He did not possess His own hands. For with Him were always present the Word and Wisdom, the Son and the Spirit, by whom and in whom,

---

35. Oswalt, *Book of Isaiah: Chapters 40–66*, 381–82.

36. Westermann relates that this passage is the first step in the Old Testament in which the Spirit is beginning to be understood as the agent of all God's activities, not merely charismatic endowment. The use of Spirit in this context comes close to the New Testament usage. Westermann, *Isaiah 40–66*, 389.

freely and spontaneously, He made all things."[37] While his imagery might lead one to assume the Son is one hand, while the Spirit is the other, this assumption would not do justice to his attempt. He was arguing that it is the Son and the Spirit in conjunction that accomplish the Father's will.[38]

Conclusion

The finger bone is connected to the hand bone. The hand bone is connected to the arm bone. The arm bone is connected . . . well, you get the idea. When God's arm moves in the world it brings both redemption and condemnation. When God's arm moves in the world, this action originates from the Father and is carried out by the Son in the power of the Spirit. The Spirit is the connection point between God's arm/hand/finger and the world. The Spirit does not act apart from the Father and the Son, but brings to fulfillment their work.

Not only is the Spirit symbolized as the fire, breath, and arm of God, but he is also related to God's love and wrath. The next chapter will address the connection between God's love, his wrath, and the Spirit.

---

37. Irenaeus, *Apostolic Fathers*, 487–88.

38. Osborn reaches the same conclusion when he writes, "While the action of each of his hands is distinct, Irenaeus affirms nothing of one person which he does not affirm of another." Osborn, *Irenaeus of Lyons*, 92.

6

The Spirit: God's Wrath and Love

PAUL TELLS US IN Rom 5:5 that the love of God is poured into the hearts of believers by the Holy Spirit. John tells us in 1 John 4:8 that God is love. From these two verses it is not surprising that we would think of the Holy Spirit in terms of God's love for his creation and people. It is by the Spirit that God enlivens the world. It is God's breath that brings life to creation, energizing inanimate matter, bringing it to life. The Spirit is life and love, but there is also another aspect of that love that must be addressed. The Bible is clear that God is opposed to all that brings death and destruction into his creation. God's love calls forth his wrath when evil springs up in creation. God will not sit idly by in the face of evil, but moves into creation to bring redemption. Those who will not accept redemption, but instead seek to bring darkness, will experience God's wrath. And both God's love and wrath are actualized to creation in the Spirit.

In what follows we will present a biblical understanding of God's wrath such that his wrath cannot be separated from his love. Having established the nature of God's wrath I will then present two theological paradigms that when connected point to the Spirit's role in judgment. The first paradigm is that the Spirit is the mutual-love of the Father and the Son. This will be followed by exploring the understanding that God's wrath is the converse of his love, with both love and wrath begin connected to the Spirit. When the two paradigms are combined the Spirit's role in judgment is revealed.

God's Wrath

Since the eviction from the garden, God's wrath has been a topic of controversy. Within the covenant relationship between God and Israel, the Hebrews lived with a keen sense of both his love and wrath. The bifurcation proposed by Marcion of the God of the Old Testament and the God revealed in Jesus Christ was an early reaction within Christianity to the distaste that many people experience when confronted with a wrathful deity.[1] This separation is completely unfounded, and in fact, is highly destructive to both Jesus' message and the rest of the Bible. To whom was Jesus praying, if not to the God of the Jews, the God of the Old Testament? It will not do to erase the Old Testament's picture of God because it offends humanity's sensibilities, sensibilities that reduce love to sentimentality and justice to indulgence. As Erlandsson writes, "The wrath of YHWH is a personal quality, without which YHWH would cease to be fully righteous and His love would degenerate into sentimentality."[2] R. P. C. Hanson furthermore argues that a God without wrath is like the United Nations; "only able to use moral suasion over people, and hence as ineffectual as the United Nations in dealing with evil."[3]

It is not only Marcion who has attempted to make this disconnect between God's love and wrath, but scholars such as C. H. Dodd, Friedrich Schleiermacher, and Jerry Robbins have also found the doctrine of divine wrath to be unacceptable. For Dodd, the wrath of God is nothing more than the impersonal cause-and-effect relationship between sin and its results.[4] Though God established a moral universe, he is not directly involved in its maintenance. Schleiermacher presents a similar understanding in his rejection of God's wrath as a proper doctrine of Christianity.[5] Robbins argues that an impersonal moral system established by God in which evil

1. MacGregor, "Concept of the Wrath of God," 102. For an overview of ways in which people have attempted in modern times to avoid the concept of God's wrath see Nysse, "Dark Side of God," 437–46.

2. Erlandsson, "The wrath of YHWH," 115.

3. Hanson, *God: Creator, Saviour, Spirit,* 39.

4. Dodd, *Epistle of Paul to the Romans,* 45–51. See also Koch, "Is There a Doctrine of Retribution in the Old Testament?," 57–87;

5. Schleiermacher, *Servant of the Word,* 152–65. Paulson adopts a diametrically opposite understanding of God's wrath in which he argues that the church's proclamation in the power of the Spirit is the place where God's wrath is overcome. To overlook God's wrath or to deny it effectively eliminates the church's ministry of reconciliation. Paulson, "Wrath of God," 245–51.

is punished, but in which God does not get his hands dirty, is a much more credible concept than that of an angry deity that he argues the Bible espouses. What Robbins fails to consider is that if God established the moral order, then God is involved in the results, even if not directly, and therefore he is still indicted according to Robbins' view.[6]

The rejection of God's wrath as inappropriate to his nature cannot be found in Scripture, but is imported from without based upon prior philosophical considerations.[7] The attempt to emphasize God's love is commendable and proper, but the elimination of his wrath renders his love meaningless, or at least suspect, when joined with his righteousness and justice. This reduction of love to sentimentality throws God's role as judge into question: if he is unaffected by sin, how can he be moved to do anything about it? How can he both love the world and be just while simultaneously being unopposed to those elements within the world that seek to bring harm and destruction to it? While the modern tendency to downplay God's wrath may find some justification from its abuse by previous generations that sought to use it to frighten people into loving God, that reason does not warrant its wholesale rejection, for it is his wrath that impels him to seek justice in the world, and hence to bring judgment upon it. A God without wrath, without displeasure at the corruption and bondage of his creation, is one without love for that same creation.[8]

Before proceeding further, a brief mention must be made regarding the relationship between human and divine wrath.[9] While all talk of God

6. Robbins, "God's Wrath," 252–58. For a rebuttal of the impersonal understanding of wrath see Travis, *Christ and the Judgment of God*; Morris, "Wrath of God," 142–45.

7. Micka presents the different understanding of anger between Arnobius and his pupil Lactantius. Arnobius rejected God's anger based upon his prior philosophical commitments, while Lactantius accepts his anger from the biblical text and then argues for its logical necessity. Micka, *Problem of Divine Anger*. See also Erlandsson, "Wrath of yhwh," 111–16. For a rejection of the position that God does not have affective capacity see Oakes, "Wrath of God," 129–40.

8. "My claim is that the idea of divine love needs the truth in divine wrath as much as the latter needs the tenderness and care of God's compassion." Burrow, "Love, Justice, and Wrath of God," 397. See also Lane, "Wrath of God as an Aspect of the Love of God," 138–67.

9. Campbell presents a nuanced understanding of the relationship between anger, aggression, hostility, and hatred in which he argues that anger is not a necessary component of aggression, hostility, or hatred, and therefore, anger does not of necessity lead to destructive behavior. Just the opposite can be the case in that anger can actually lead to increased communication as people respond to the signs of anger that are being exhibited and adjust their behavior accordingly. Campbell, "Anger of a loving God." See also Baloian, *Anger in the Old Testament*.

takes place within the vehicle of language, and hence is subject to the limitations and distortions that language creates, it is doubly the case in relation to discussions of God's wrath. When applied to humanity, wrath is often understood as a negative attribute. It implies a loss of self-control, coupled with a desire for revenge or punishment that is oftentimes acted out. The Scriptures mention that humanity's wrath is an inappropriate reaction to unfavorable circumstances.[10] How then can this attribute be ascribed to God and not be understood as implying some type of imperfection?

One answer would be to ascribe the language of wrath to an unenlightened age that had to employ the concept to bring people to God, but that it is no longer valid or needed for modern Christians. Schleiermacher states, "We must notice first that we find in the vocation that Paul presents to us— the ministry of reconciliation—no cause for speaking of God's wrath."[11] While his route effectively eliminates the difficulty, it does so at the expense of the consistency of the biblical text. Paul had no problem talking about God's wrath, as can be seen in Rom 1:18–32. Likewise, the Old Testament prophets had no problem decrying the illegitimacy of humanity's wrath, while at the same time endorsing the legitimacy of God's wrath. In defense of this idea Heschel writes, "It is unlikely that the prophets, who never cease to proclaim the righteousness of God, should in the same breath ascribe to Him a morally reprehensible disposition, 'a defect in His justice.' As long as the anger of God is viewed in the light of the psychology of passions rather than in the light of the theology of pathos, no adequate understanding will be possible."[12] It is not the case that the attribution of wrath to God comes from a more barbarous age in which people were unaware of the problems of using this type of language about him.

Furthermore, humanity's wrath is diametrically opposed, for the most part, to love. It is an emotional response of irrationality erupting from unexpected circumstances, while God's wrath is held in restraint, publicly announced, explained in detail, justified by law, reversed by repentance, and stated with ample warning concerning its consequences. Where there is human wrath, there is no love. While this view is open to criticism, for often the greatest wrath involves those to whom one is closest, it is nevertheless defendable in that in the moment of wrath love is eclipsed and does not factor into the considerations made.

---

10. Prov 30:33; Eccl 7:9; Col 3:8; Jas 1:20.

11. Schleiermacher, *Servant of the Word,* 153.

12. Heschel, *Prophets,* 282.

In the case of God, his wrath and his love are never separated.[13] God's love tempers and restrains his wrath, and ultimately uses it as a tool to call people back to a right relationship.[14] God's love, in combination with his holiness, is the *raison d'etre* of his wrath.[15] If God did not love his creation, then he would have no reason to be wrathful. It is because of his deep love and the offense that sin gives to his love and holiness that his wrath exists and is applied to humanity.[16] There is no moment in which his wrath can be disassociated from his love, as if it could somehow overrule and eclipse his love or could exist apart from it.[17]

One must chart a different course in order to reconcile God's wrath with an understanding of human wrath. This course, like many others in theology, involves tightly defining God's wrath and highlighting where it differs from humanity's, while at the same time recognizing the connection between the two that allows the same word to be used of both.[18] As already mentioned, humanity's wrath is often irrational and out of the control of the person affected by it, while God's, on the other hand, is neither presented as an irrational response to a circumstance nor as a capricious act of a sadistic being.[19] His wrath is related to humanity's violation of his holiness in some form or another. God never loses control of himself or inflicts punishment on people capriciously.[20]

While God's wrath is related to specific violations of his will, there are passages in which it may appear capricious. The two major incidences that have been presented for the irrational and arbitrary nature of God's wrath are the execution of Uzzah at the Ark in 2 Sam 6:7–8 and the punishment inflicted after David's census in 2 Sam 24:1. A. T. Hanson offers these two examples as an early understanding of God's wrath in which it is not rationally or morally motivated. "So in the earliest part of the Old Testament, where the divine wrath is met with, it is thought of as not necessarily accountable or rational, or morally motivated."[21] He fails to consider that Uzzah's touch-

---

13. Carson, "God's Love and God's Wrath," 389.

14. Hanson, *God*, 45–46.

15. Burrow, "Love, Justice, and Wrath of God," 397.

16. Eichrodt, *Old Testament Theology,* 1:252–53.

17. Brunner, *Man in Revolt,* 187.

18. Williams, "Judging Judgment," 541–53.

19. Stahlin, "ὀργή," 5:397.

20. Erlandsson, "Wrath of YHWH," 112.

21. Hanson, *Wrath of the Lamb,* 1–3.

ing of the Ark was a direct violation of a previous command of God as to who can handle it, not to mention that an oxcart was not the proper means of transportation. Before one can argue that the execution was irrational or immoral one must consider the previous command from God, and when this is done, God's execution of Uzzah is neither irrational nor immoral.[22] While no direct explanation is given for God's anger in relation to his commanding David to take a census, the use of the word "again" allows one to travel back in the narrative, probably to 2 Sam 21:1–14, to find a previous instance of God's anger. In that account, there is a reason for his anger: Saul's sin against the Gibeonites. It is therefore reasonable to assume that God had a reason for his anger, even though the text does not disclose it.[23]

Within the Old Testament, there are numerous depictions of God's wrath, but by far the most prominent occurrence of it relates to punishment for disobedience.[24] In this connection, his wrath is either directly correlated with the punishment, so that the wrath and the punishment are virtually synonymous, or it leads to the execution of punishment.[25] This punishment is often presented in a vague fashion, so it is unclear by what means he executes his wrath upon the people, but several times his wrath is directly related to a current event or to a nation that he intends to use as an instrument.[26] People's actions can also turn away his wrath, so that it is not presented as a force that is irrational or out of control, but is instead something that humanity has at least some means of understanding.[27]

In juxtaposition to wrath as punishment, a few verses speak of wrath as a means of purification.[28] While a word study only reveals two passages in the book of Ezekiel in which wrath is related explicitly to purification in the Old Testament, the entire Bible repeatedly speaks of the purifying nature of chastisement. It is therefore not unreasonable to link the ubiquitous nature of remedial suffering, in which wrath is not explicitly mentioned, with those passages that clearly make the connection. Thus, the primary

---

22. Peterson, "Why Did Uzzah Die?," 3–8. See also Bergen, *1, 2 Samuel*, 329–32.

23. Bergen, *1, 2 Samuel*, 474–80.

24. Eichrodt, *Old Testament Theology*, 1:258–69; Stahlin, "ὀργη," 403.

25. Isa 34:2 and Jer 4:4. For a list of tools used for the disbursing of God's wrath in the book of Isaiah see Locke, "Wrath of God in the Book of Isaiah," 229–31.

26. Num 16:46 and Ezek 25:14–17.

27. Deut 9:7–29. Heschel, *Prophets*, 282; Kapelrud, "God as Destroyer," 33–38.

28. Ezek 20:33–38, 22:17–22.

purpose of God's wrath is to redeem those that have fallen away, to cleanse those polluted by the filth of the fallen world.[29]

God's wrath is intimately tied to the covenant established between Israel and himself.[30] It was the violation of this covenant that summoned forth his wrath. God entered into a relationship with his covenant people, a relationship in which he obligated himself to bless his people if they obeyed his commands and to punish his people if they failed to obey. It is within this reciprocal relationship confirmed at Sinai, and originally established with Abraham, that God in love seeks to redeem his wayward people. As already mentioned, his wrath arises out of his love. While love is a foundational aspect of his nature, wrath is not. Wrath only exists in the presence of rebellion and rejection of love.[31]

While the covenant community is the primary location of discussion of God's wrath in the Old Testament, his wrath also involves all people and their relationship to God. Adam and Eve were removed from the garden and barred from reentering after violating God's commands; the deluge destroyed the people in the time of Noah; fire and brimstone destroyed the citizens of Sodom and Gomorrah: the list could continue of the times God's wrath has been manifested against people other than Israel. The prophets are clear that those nations that have trespassed God's laws will experience his wrath. Although Israel is specifically targeted as an object of his wrath, it is also targeted as an object of his mercy.

There is a change in emphasis in relation to God's wrath in the move from the Old to the New Testament. In the Old Testament, temporal events primarily manifested God's wrath, while in the New Testament the focus is more often upon eschatological judgment. In other words, in the Old Testament, wrath ends in death, while in the New Testament, it ends in destruction.[32] Furthermore, the New Testament reduces the emphasis upon God's wrath and takes on a more impersonal nature.[33] This is neither to argue that the New Testament does not present God as being wrathful at sin, nor is it to suggest that God's wrath is a semi-independent force or entity alongside God such that the working of wrath can be distanced from God

---

29. Heschel, *Prophets*, 287–95.

30. Stahlin, "ὀργή," 403; Eichrodt, *Old Testament Theology*, 1:258–69.

31. Grenz, *Theology for the Community of God*, 642.

32. Stahlin, "ὀργή," 444. See also Aloysia, "God of Wrath?," 411.

33. Hanson, *Attractiveness of God*, 148; MacGregor, "Concept of the Wrath of God," 101–9.

himself.[34] The theme of God's wrath is not reduced in the New Testament, but is transformed.

When God's wrath is aroused, it is a lamentation.[35] The reason for his wrath is that he is not indifferent to suffering or injustice. He is not distant or unaffected by the injustice in the world, but is so intimately involved with creation that humanity's sins personally affect him. A god who impassibly observes the suffering in the world, unaffected by its actions, is a god that would do nothing about that suffering. God's action to redeem his creation is empowered by his love, and it is from this love that he kindles his wrath against those people that offend his love.

Far from being a negative aspect of God's nature, wrath signifies that he is not indifferent to the suffering in the world. What kind of god would not be outraged by the oppression in the world? What kind of love would it be that is not offended by those things that seek to destroy that love? James Cone poignantly states, "A God without wrath does not plan to do too much liberating, for the two concepts belong together. A God minus wrath seems to be a God who is basically not against anybody. All we have to do is behave nicely, and everything will work out all right."[36] One does not often find much difficulty with God's wrath among oppressed groups such as the poor and disenfranchised. The oppressed see his wrath as necessary for deliverance. They long for a God who is not indifferent to their plight. Those who are oppressors often seek to remove his wrath to either consciously or unconsciously remove the judgment looming over them. Those who are comfortable in the current world system see no need for its judgment, and hence, they seek the elimination of the wrath that necessitates the judgment.[37]

---

34. "'Law' and 'Wrath' are thus related, in St. Paul's thought, not to reconciliation but to redemption. As we have seen, they are not for him attributes of God's character; they are almost personified powers, which, owing to God their origin, act in partial independence of God, and are hostile to men as He is not." Cave, *Doctrine of the Work of Christ*, 43. MacGregor adopts a similar approach when he writes, "Wrath pictures anthropomorphically the divine retribution, inherent in such a universe, but working (may we say?) relatively independently of God's immediate volition." MacGregor, "Concept of the Wrath of God," 105.

35. Heschel, *Prophets*, 284.

36. Cone, *Black Theology of Liberation*, 131.

37. Burrow, "Love, Justice, and Wrath of God," 382.

The Spirit in Relation to God's Love and Wrath

While many theologians have employed the paradigm that the Spirit is the love of the Father and the Son, one who has used this paradigm in an intriguing manner is Stanley Grenz. He connects all the needed dots to show that the Spirit is both God's love and wrath, but he does not follow through and make this statement explicit. Grenz's work will therefore be used to give us an entry into the relationship between God's love, his wrath, and the Spirit. In an article dealing with the Spirit as the love of God Grenz writes:

> The Spirit's fundamental role within the divine life (i.e., the immanent Trinity) determines the role of the Spirit within the divine activity in the world (i.e., the economic Trinity). By being the bond between the Father and the Son, the Spirit completes the eternal immanent Trinity. In the same manner, the Spirit acts as the completer of the divine program in the world and hence the completer of the economic Trinity.[38]

He has adopted the postulate that the Spirit is the bond of mutual-love between the Father and the Son, and that this love, primarily encountered in the Spirit, is that which guides creation back to its Creator. While the article discusses the Spirit in relation to redemption, in his systematic work he makes the further connection between love and wrath when he states, "Those who undermine the love God pours forth for the world experience his love in the form of wrath."[39] His position both on the Spirit as the mutual-love of the Father and the Son and on God's wrath being how those who reject God experience his love clearly allows for the Spirit to have an active role in condemnation, but he never makes the connection within his writings. In order to undergird Grenz's conclusions regarding the mutual-love paradigm and the love-wrath paradigm, an investigation will be made into each, with the intention to synthesize the two ideas at the end, as Grenz has done in his systematic work, but with the inclusion of the Spirit's role in the synthesized scheme.

The Augustinian paradigm of the Spirit as the mutual-love of the Father and the Son is fairly well accepted in Western Christianity, being embraced by Benedict the sixteenth, Stanley Grenz, Robert Jenson, Wolfhart Pannenberg, Clark Pinnock, and David Coffey, to name only a few.[40]

38. Grenz, "Holy Spirit," 1.

39. Grenz, *Theology for the Community of God*, 95.

40. Ratzinger, "Holy Spirit as Communio," 324–37; Grenz, "Holy Spirit," 1–13;

Since the Spirit can be distinctively called the love of the Trinity, it becomes necessary to relate the conclusion that God's love and wrath are intimately connected, so much so that God's wrath is often described as God's spurned or rejected love. Wrath does not exist within the immanent Trinity, but comes into existence in relation to fallen humanity's rejection of his love. If this love is the Spirit, then God's wrath is intimately related to the Spirit.

In order to investigate the claim that God's wrath is poured out on people by the Spirit, it will first be necessary to establish Augustine's mutual-love paradigm. Once the paradigm is in place, then it will be necessary to move to Martin Luther's understanding of the *opus proprium* and the *opus alienum* of God, or God's proper and alien work. Here Luther contends that redemption is God's proper work and condemnation is an alien work that he must perform because of humanity's rejection of his love.

After establishing Luther's thesis and then connecting it with Augustine's proposal, as Grenz has done, albeit not explicitly, in his systematic work, it will be possible to conclude that the Spirit actualizes God's alien work to humanity. Or, to put it another way, the Spirit executes the judgment of the Son given to him by the Father upon those who refuse his offer of salvation. As already mentioned, while Grenz makes the connection between Augustine and Luther, he fails to follow through in his eschatology on the Trinitarian implications that he establishes, neglecting to assign to the Holy Spirit the role of carrying out the Son's judgment.

The Spirit as the Love of the Father and the Son

Augustine's influence upon the shaping of western Trinitarian thought cannot be overstated, setting the parameters of discussion for generations to follow in his work *The Trinity*.[41] Within the work, he attempted to trace out and defend the orthodox doctrine of the Trinity, while at the same time discovering new ways to relate the truths revealed within it. He is most famous for his psychological analogies for the Trinity.[42] One often overlooked area in his theology is the establishment of the Holy Spirit as the mutual-love of

---

Jenson, *Triune God*, 146–61; Pannenberg, *Systematic Theology*, 1:259–337; Pinnock, *Flame of Love*, 37–40; Coffey, "Holy Spirit as the Mutual Love," 193–229.

41. Fortman, *Triune God*, 139–50; Pannenberg, *Systematic Theology*, 1:315–19; Congar, "River of the Water of Life," 3:80–91.

42. Cunningham, *These Three Are One*, 90–107.

the Father and the Son.[43] While Augustine's establishment of the Holy Spirit as the bond of love between the Father and the Son has often been criticized for reducing the Spirit to an impersonal force, this criticism does not stand up under the full weight of his proposal.

While Augustine was the first to state clearly that the Spirit is the mutual-love of the Father and the Son, he developed this view from a minority position that existed among the early Fathers. While most of the Greek Fathers understood the Father as the source of unity within the Trinity, St. Epiphanius taught that the Spirit is the bond of the Trinity and the middle person between the Father and the Son. Gregory of Nyssa postulated that the Trinity was knit together by the unity of the Spirit, who was the bond of peace. There was therefore a lively tradition available from which Augustine could begin his investigation into the Spirit's role as the mutual-love of the Father and the Son.[44]

Augustine began his investigation by establishing the relationships between the persons of the Godhead. Within the Godhead, the only difference between each person is located in opposed relationships. The Father and the Son share the same essence with the only distinction being that the Father is not the Son, and the Son is not the Father. The very names of Father and Son contain within them the opposed relationship. One can say that the Son is the Son of the Father, or oppositely that the Father is the Father of the Son. However, when one speaks of the Holy Spirit he cannot make the same maneuver as regards opposed relations. The Spirit of the Father cannot be reversed to say the Father of the Spirit. The Father is only the Father of the Son, not the Spirit. Additionally, one can say the Spirit of the Son, but cannot reverse the order to say the Son of the Spirit. Scripture is clear that the Son is only the Son of the Father, not the Son of the Spirit.[45]

Since the name "Holy Spirit" in itself does not contain an opposed relation, but in fact, is a combination of two attributes that are common to the Godhead, holiness and spirituality, Augustine argued that another term was needed to establish the opposition of the relationship that exists between the Father, the Spirit, and the Son. While the name Holy Spirit is proper to the person of the Holy Spirit since he is the Spirit of both the Father and the Son, the name itself can also be applied to all the members of the Godhead since God is Spirit according to John 4:24. Just as all the

43. Coffey, "Holy Spirit as the Mutual Love," 1.

44. de Margerie, *Christian Trinity in History*, 110–16.

45. Augustine, *Trinity*, 5.13.13–16.

members of the Godhead are omnipotent, wise, and good, all the members are both spirit and holy, but the third person of the Trinity has been distinctively given the name Holy Spirit. Augustine writes that the "Holy Spirit is a kind of inexpressible communion or fellowship of Father and Son, and perhaps he is given this name just because the same name can be applied to the Father and the Son."[46]

The first title for the Holy Spirit for which he argued was gift, seeing as both Acts 8:20 and John 4:10 describe the Spirit as a gift.[47] Coffey correctly notes that nowhere in the Bible is the Spirit directly called gift. While John 4:7–15 and Eph 4:7–8 are used by Augustine to support his claim for the Spirit as gift, neither passage unequivocally makes this assertion, and even if one accepts Augustine's interpretation, neither passage has the "gift" being given by both the Father and the Son, but the Father only. The idea of the Spirit as the gift of the Father and the Son is built upon the *filioque* doctrine. While this is acceptable, it needs to be made clear that the Spirit as the gift of the Father and the Son is founded upon the *filioque* primarily, and then upon certain Scriptures interpreted in its light.

The Spirit is the gift of the Father and the Son, inasmuch as the Spirit proceeds from both of them. On an economic level, the Father and Son send the Spirit into the world to bring to completion the work the Son started. From this economic perspective, the immanent giving of the Spirit between the Father and the Son is established. The Father gives the Spirit to the Son who returns the Spirit to the Father.[48] If the Holy Spirit is understood as the gift of the Father and the Son, the first step to an opposed relationship is completed. Nevertheless, the terms Father and Son cannot be used in relation to the Spirit, so instead, Augustine spoke of the gift of the giver and the giver of the gift, inasmuch as both the Father and the Son give the Spirit to each other.[49] While the Spirit as the gift of the Father and the Son was Augustine's first move to establish the relationship of the Spirit

---

46. Ibid., 5.3.12

47. Ibid., 5.3.12–16; Coffey, "Holy Spirit as the Mutual Love," 196–98.

48. Augustine, *Trinity,* 5.3.12. Coffey contends that the title gift is appropriate for the Spirit in an economic sense, but not in the immanent Trinity "because it is of the essence of a gift that it be bestowed gratuitously, whereas all that happens in the immanent Trinity does so with a necessity of nature." He is not contending that the Father and the Son do not bestow the Spirit on each other, but only that the term gift is not applicable to the immanent Trinity, like it is to the economic Trinity. Coffey, "Holy Spirit as the Mutual Love," 197.

49. Augustine, *Trinity,* 5.3.13.

to the Father and the Son, he also argued that the Spirit is the mutual-love of the Father and the Son.[50]

Basing his conclusion on 1 John 4:8–16, in which John stated that God is love, he argued that while the whole Trinity is indeed love, the Holy Spirit is rightly called the love of the Trinity. The love of God is both the very nature of God and that which God gives to humanity. First John 4:7 states that believers should love one another because love is from God, while in v. 8, John declared that God himself is love. In giving humanity love, God gives humanity his very self. Love is both God and from God, but according to Augustine "the Father alone is God in such a way that he is not from God, and thus the love which is God in such a way that it is from God must be either the Son or the Holy Spirit."[51]

People are able to love because God has given himself to humanity in order to allow them to love. John 4:12 reveals that if believers love each other then God abides in them and his love is perfected or completed in them. It is not that they have a nonpersonal idea called love that abides in them, but it is God himself who abides in them and is brought to fullness and completion within them. His abiding is evidenced by the love that they show for each other. The reciprocity of love between believers is nothing other than the reciprocity of God himself between them.[52] In this way, believers are able to experience the fullness of God's communion with them. In v. 13, John revealed that believers can know God is abiding in them and they are abiding in God, in that he has given the believers his Holy Spirit. It is the presence of the Holy Spirit in the midst of the community, both individually and corporately, that was the sign and seal that they were abiding in God and that God's love was abiding in them. Since love is God's very nature, and the believers received confirmation of God's love abiding in them through the Spirit's abiding in them, Augustine concluded that the Spirit was the love of God indwelling and abiding within the believers and bringing their communion to completion.[53]

---

50. "What is meant is that while in that supremely simple nature substance is not one thing and charity another, but substance is charity and charity is substance, whether in the Father or in the Son or in the Spirit, yet all the same the Holy Spirit is distinctively named charity." Ibid., 15.5.29.

51. Ibid., 15.5.31.

52. Ibid. "So it is God the Holy Spirit proceeding from God who fires man to the love of God and neighbor when he has been given to him, and he himself is love."

53. Ibid.

Additionally, Augustine employed Rom 5:5 as further evidence for the mutual-love paradigm. Paul was encouraging his readers to endure in the face of suffering and persecution because God was using the situation to produce hope in their lives. If they held on to this hope, they would not be put to shame because God's love had been poured into their hearts through the Holy Spirit.[54] He is the guarantee of the Father's promises to his people, and therefore, his presence in the believers' lives guaranteed the hope upon which they rested. It is in the Spirit that God's love is poured into the believers' hearts, but God's love is nothing other than the Spirit who is poured out on all flesh. God's love and Spirit function in the same capacity, to induce hope in the lives of believers and to solidify the hope produced. When God pours out his love, he pours out nothing other than his own self, and this is done through the Spirit inasmuch as he is the mutual-love of the Father and the Son.

Although Douglas Moo does not comment upon the mutual-love paradigm in his commentary he does make the connection that Paul uses the same verb for "poured out" to refer to God's love in Rom 5:5 and the Spirit in Titus 3:6. He then entertains the idea that the subject of Rom 5:5 might be the Holy Spirit himself, but concludes that the love of God is the subject. However, God's love "is conveyed to our sensations by the Holy Spirit, who resides in every believer."[55] Even if, as Moo argues, the subject in the verse is God's love and not the Spirit, it is only in the Spirit that the love can be experienced by humanity, and therefore, the basic contention of the mutual-love paradigm in the economy is maintained. It is the love of the entire Trinity that is given to believers, but this is accomplished through the Spirit, who is the love of both the Father and the Son, the basis for the *communio* of the Three.[56]

While David Coffey accepts the mutual-love paradigm, he argues that Augustine failed to prove his thesis. He has therefore sought to strengthen Augustine's proposal by approaching the issue from a different direction. Coffey writes, "If it can properly be said that the Father and the Son are divine persons, then the bond between them can literally, and not just metaphorically, be said to be love, since love, and especially interpersonal love,

---

54. Ibid.

55. Moo, *Epistle to the Romans*, 304–5.

56. "The particularity of the Holy Spirit is evidently that he is what the Father and Son have in common. His particularity is being unity. The general name 'Holy Spirit' is the most appropriate way to express him in the paradox characteristic of him—mutuality itself." Ratzinger, "Holy Spirit as Communio," 326.

is the adequate expression in act, of a person." He further argues that there are only three biblical texts that directly mention the Holy Spirit and love: Rom 5:5, 15:30, and Gal 5:22. Romans 5:5 has already been treated, while Rom 15:30 speaks of a fraternal love created by the Spirit in the community, and Gal 5:22 lists love first as the fruit of the Spirit. Since the Bible does not explicitly make the connection between the Holy Spirit and love, if it is a legitimate deduction, it must be deduced from elsewhere.[57]

He argues that as the Trinity is revealed in Christ, not in clear words, but as a necessary deduction from his person, so too, the Spirit as the mutual-love of the Father and the Son is revealed in Jesus, not in the direct words of Scripture.[58] The first step in his argument is that the Holy Spirit is the Father's love for the Son. Jesus is conceived and empowered by the Spirit as the "beloved" Son of God. He is not just a servant who accomplishes a task, but is a Son who is loved by his Father. From the objective side, Jesus experienced God in the Spirit, as witnessed by both his conception and baptism, while "subjectively it is essentially an experience of God's fatherly love. God's Spirit, seen in OT terms only as creative and empowering, is seen in the NT, in the actual event of Christ, as the communication of God's love."[59] The Father's love is experienced by Jesus in the Spirit, and it is this experience of the Father's love that defines Jesus' relationship with him. Coffey concludes that the Spirit "stands essentially revealed as the love of God the Father for Jesus, a love that calls the latter into human existence, and so sanctifies him that he comes into being as His beloved Son."[60]

The second phase of the argument is designed to show the Spirit is the love of Jesus for the Father. From his conception, Jesus was bound to the Father in the Holy Spirit. At his baptism, it became publicly clear that he was the Spirit-endowed Messiah, and from that time forth, he went about his mission in the power of the Spirit. He did not fulfill his mission strictly out of a sense of obligation or duty, but out of a deep love for the Father, a love that was primarily the work of the Holy Spirit in him.[61]

Additionally, by combining Heb 9:14 with the accounts of the crucifixion where Jesus gave up his spirit, Coffey concludes that on the cross

57. Coffey, *Deus Trinitas*, 30–31.

58. Coffey, "Holy Spirit as the Mutual Love," 205. For a fuller defense of his position see Coffey, *Deus Trinitas*, 33–65.

59. Coffey, "Holy Spirit as the Mutual Love," 204.

60. Ibid., 205.

61. Ibid., 206.

Jesus' love for the Father reached perfection or completion, and that this was accomplished by the Spirit's power. Hebrews 9:14 declares that Christ offered himself to God through the eternal Spirit. There is some controversy over exactly how to understand the phrase "eternal Spirit," but F. F. Bruce presents a compelling argument when he links the passage under consideration with the Suffering Servant of Isa 42:1, where the Servant is first introduced, and God declares that he will place his Spirit upon him to endow him to accomplish his task. Jesus, as the Spirit-endowed Servant, finished his task upon the cross, and it is most reasonable to assume that he finished his mission in the Spirit's power, and therefore the phrase 'eternal Spirit' is a reference to the Holy Spirit.[62] Jesus' death on the cross was an expression of his love for the Father and this love was empowered by the Holy Spirit, and in that conclusion the Son's love for the Father is established as the Holy Spirit.

Finally, Coffey makes the connection between Jesus' love for his people and the pouring out of the Spirit upon those same people. When the Spirit is sent, he is so associated with Christ that he is described as Christ's Spirit or as the other *Paraclete*. The Spirit is "impregnated with the personality of Jesus."[63] It is in the Spirit that Christ's love is given to the church. While the New Testament does not explicitly state that the Holy Spirit is the mutual-love of the Father and the Son, Coffey writes, "One can only properly understand Jesus as the medium of God's love for us when we understand him first as its principal and active (therefore reciprocating) recipient. And, most importantly, it is only by laying hold of the missing link of Christ's love of God that we gain access to the mutual-love paradigm in its scriptural foundation."[64]

The Spirit as the mutual-love of the Father and the Son is a well-established axiom within Trinitarian theology. The axiom does not seek to prove that the Father and the Son do not also love, but only to explicate how the Spirit relates to the other two members of the Godhead in the immanent Trinity. As the Son proceeds from the Father by generation, and the Spirit proceeds from the Father through the Son by procession, he is the love that the Father and Son share together. In the economic Trinity it is in, by, and through the Holy Spirit that humanity is able to encounter and experience God's love. This statement holds true even if one rejects the mutual-love

---

62. Bruce, *Epistle to the Hebrews*, 217.

63. Coffey, "Holy Spirit as the Mutual Love," 212.

64. Ibid., 216.

paradigm, as is attested by Rom 5:5. Having established that humanity experiences God's love in, by, and through the Spirit, it is possible to advance to the discussion of the relationship between God's love and wrath.

The Spirit as God's Love and Wrath

A God without wrath, without displeasure at the corruption and bondage of his creation, is one without love for that same creation. It is because of his deep love for creation, and humanity in particular, that his wrath is aroused against the sin and rebellion that plagues it. As mentioned earlier, God's wrath is not to be equated with human wrath, as if the two were identical. There is a similarity between the two so that one is able to use the same word for both, but one must also be aware of the infinite qualitative distinction between God's and humanity's wrath.

God's holiness and love working in conjunction call forth his wrath. If he were not holy, then humanity's rebellion would not offend him. He would have no problem with those who choose to disobey him, since he would not have a standard to which he holds humanity accountable. Secondly, if he did not love his creation, then sin would not arouse his wrath because he would be indifferent to what his creation did. However, God is holy and God is love.[65] Therefore, when his creation turns its back on him and attempts to find its good in some place other than him, his wrath is aroused against the offense. Sin is not the breaking of an impersonal law passed by a distant legislator, but is instead the rejection of God himself, and this rejection is none other than the rejection of all that is good and right. When a person seeks to find completion and wholeness outside of God, he is seeking for that which is only found in him. By his very nature, God reaches out in love to the world to bring the world back into a proper relationship with himself so that it can find its completion. This reaching out in love, however, does not overlook the reality that humanity has gone its own way, has turned its back on its Creator, and has therefore violated his holiness.

Romans 6:23 declares that the "wages of sin is death." If one refuses to accept the only source of life available, then death is all that can result. From the foregoing discussion of God's love and holiness, it would seem that God is trapped in a dilemma regarding humanity. His holiness will not allow people off the hook for their sin, but his love will not abandon them

65. Lev 11:45; 1 John 4:8.

to the hook upon which they have impaled themselves. The answer to the dilemma is not found in deep philosophical speculation over his nature, but instead is found in the historical revelation of God on the cross. It is on the cross that his wrath and love meet, with love breaking through wrath to reveal that wrath is not an immanent attribute of God, but is called forth in reaction to humanity's rebellion.[66] God is love, but he displays wrath.

Human reason cannot determine whether God is love or wrath. It is only in the revelation that God gives of himself that a correct interpretation of creation can be made. It is only by faith in Christ that a person can know that God's love overcomes his wrath. On the cross, God's wrath and love meet, but in the meeting, God's love prevails over his wrath and provides a means whereby fallen humanity can return home. The truth of the previous statement is not attainable by human reason, for to human reason, the cross is nothing other than wrath and defeat. If the cross speaks to fallen humanity at all, it can only declare the absence of God. It is only through the eyes of faith that one can see the objective reality of God's nature. It is only through the eyes of faith that a person understands the cross as both wrath and love. It is only through the eyes of faith that one sees how God's love breaks through his wrath to redeem his creation.[67] The tension between God's love and wrath has been dealt with in numerous ways, from the facile assumption that he has no wrath, through the universalistic assumption that although he has wrath, it has a purificatory effect upon creation so that eventually wrath will cease as creation *in toto* returns to him, all the way to the more sophisticated, albeit equally as disastrous claim that his wrath is nothing more than the natural outworking of cause and effect in a moral universe.

The question remains how adequately to correlate God's love and wrath, how to explain that while God is love, he does, in reality, have wrath toward those elements within creation that stand in opposition to him. The path to reconciling his love and wrath will pass first through Martin Luther's assessment of the *opus proprium Dei* and the *opus alienum Dei*, and after explicating Luther's understanding between redemption and condemnation, the journey will quickly pass through a study of several modern theologians who have adopted Luther's axiom, often in modified form, to elucidate the relationship between love and wrath. Finally, the journey will end where it began, at Stanley Grenz, who will serve as the paradigm of those who equate God's love and wrath. From his equation of

66. Brunner, *Mediator*, 515–35.
67. Grislis, "Luther's Understanding," 284–86.

God's love-wrath and his acceptance of Augustine's mutual-love paradigm, it will be possible to say what Grenz has hinted at, but failed to say, about the relationship between the Holy Spirit and wrath.

Luther recognized the truth of the claim that sin strikes at the very person of God, because God is love and righteousness, and sin injures and insults righteousness.[68] Luther writes, "He (God) is not only justice but also love of justice; and whoever loves justice, receives it from Him. It would not be sin if it did not offend God."[69] Sin as an attack on God's very person necessitates a response in him that will not allow sin to stake a claim to legitimacy, since there is only one true God, and all others are mere idols. His jealousy to protect his status as God is not motivated from fear, but from love. To establish anything other than the one true God as God is to embrace the lesser over the greater. God is the greatest possible good for creation and when something lesser is chosen, God, in his love, must react in wrath against that choice. His wrath is "coextensive with his majesty; like God himself, it is eternal, omnipotent, and infinite."[70]

Althaus makes this claim from a statement of Luther's on Ps 90. Luther is arguing that in evangelism, one must approach the hardened, smug sinner with the reality of God's wrath, but for the person who has already been terrified, who no longer imagines that there is a safe place to hide from God, one needs to show God's grace and love, to show that "God is not an enraged demon, but the true God Himself, who is Lord of all things." From the understanding of God as infinite, two things are learned, one is that his grace and love is infinite toward those who fear and love him, while at the same time his wrath is infinite toward those who remain in their smug rejection of God. "For the effect is always commensurate with the magnitude of the efficient cause."[71]

Luther, however, did not understand God's wrath as an essential part of his nature, but instead argued that wrath is the subjective experience of the person who stands in opposition to him. Luther writes, "For faith leads you up and opens up the heart and will of God for you. There you see sheer, superabundant grace and love. . . . Anyone who regards Him as angry is not seeing Him correctly, but has pulled down a curtain and cover, more, a

---

68. For an overview of the various positions regarding Luther's understanding of God's wrath see ibid., 277–88.

69. Luther, *Selected Psalms III*, 14:316.

70. Althaus, *Theology of Martin Luther*, 169.

71. Luther, *Selected Psalms II*, 13:93.

dark cloud over his face. But in Scriptural language 'to see His face' means to recognize Him correctly as a gracious and faithful Father."[72]

He contended that God's "compassion is more abundant because it is part of God's nature, since wrath is truly God's alien work, in which He engages contrary to His nature, because He is forced into it by the wickedness of man."[73] This is not to say that his wrath is not real, but it is to say that his wrath is not the final reality.[74] Luther described God's wrath as experienced by humanity and God's redemptive nature of love as his alien and proper work, respectively. Luther employed the words of Isa 28:21 for his doctrine of the *opus alienum* and *proprium*. Isaiah 28:21 states, "For the LORD will rise up as on Mount Perazim; as in the Valley of Gibeon he will be roused; to do his deed—strange is his deed! And to work his work—alien is his work!" This work is a work of condemnation, not salvation. Luther, in explaining Isaiah, writes, "It is as if he were saying: Although He is the God of life and salvation and this is His proper work, yet, in order to accomplish this, He kills and destroys. These works are alien to Him, but through them He accomplishes His proper work. For He kills our will that His may be established in us. He subdues the flesh and its lusts that the spirit and its desires may come to life."[75]

There is a dialectic between wrath and grace, law and gospel, and the dividing line between the two is found in Christ. For those outside of Christ, God's wrath is a reality, but for those in Christ, his wrath is nothing other than his mercy, and his punishment is discipline, not condemnation.[76] In Christ, God has reconciled his wrath toward humanity; therefore, he is able both to justify sinners, and to remain just in the process.[77]

The transition from God's wrath to his love is not made through an intellectual enterprise, as if one need merely come to realize that God does not have any wrath at all, as if one needed only to think correctly about him, but is instead made through Jesus' death on the cross.[78] The fatal flaw of the moral influence paradigm of the atonement, and all such theories, is that it understands God's wrath as only a misunderstanding of God on

---

72. Ibid., 13:37.

73. Luther, *Lectures on Genesis*, 2:134.

74. McGrath, *Luther's Theology of the Cross*, 155.

75. Luther, *Lectures on Genesis*, 2:335.

76. Althaus, *Theology of Martin Luther*, 171.

77. Rom 3:26.

78. Driggers, "Development of the Moral Influence," 20–32.

humanity's part, with no objective basis for the reality in God. According to proponents of the moral influence paradigm, what humanity needs is not to be reconciled, but reeducated. There is no retributive need in God, either in his own nature or his law, which requires some form of sacrifice or propitiation to be made in order for him to forgive humanity. God is already reconciled with humanity through his love. What is needed is a means whereby humanity can be enlightened, educated, or persuaded of the love of God.

This is not what Luther was declaring, but instead that wrath is an objective reality for the person under it. Wrath, however, is not the final reality. The final reality is that God is love. For the person who refuses to accept this truth about God on God's terms, not the person's, then God's love is experienced as wrath and condemnation, God's *opus alienum*.

The wrath of God is only removed in Christ, and entry into the sphere of Christ's existence, into the body of Christ, is only gained by faith in Christ. This is a faith that encounters God's wrath, breaks through that wrath by Christ's absorption and defeat of it in the cross and resurrection, and subsequently stands in God's presence recognizing that he is indeed love, not wrath, in his essential being.

As shown earlier, many attempts have been made to relate God's love and wrath, often with damage being done to the biblical reality of his wrath. Let it be said again that in light of the fallenness of creation, God cannot truly love the world without at the same time having wrath toward the sinfulness in the world. If he did not react against the evil in the world that harms and destroys that which he loves, it would imply a defect in his love.[79] From this perspective, it is clear that his wrath is a result of his love for creation. In order to verify this claim, it will be necessary to demonstrate how his wrath is a reflection of his love, how in the midst of condemnation one can still proclaim that God is love.

If God's love is displayed in his wrath, does this suggest that he has two attributes that are battling within himself, so that he must bring his wrath under control in order to express his love, or does he turn his love and wrath on and off so that he loves at one time and is then wrathful at another? It is from the explication of Luther's work above that a resolution can be found. Emil Brunner writes, "God's anger is real and it cannot be denied or explained away. However, the wrath of God is not the ultimate reality; it is the divine reality that corresponds to sin. It is not the essential reality of

---

79. Lane, "Wrath of God," 160.

God. In Himself God is love."[80] The knowledge of God as loving can only be ascertained from a special revelation from God, and this is offered in Christ on the cross.[81] Numerous theologians from a wide spectrum of belief have understood God's love and wrath as two sides of the same coin. In order to make the coin analogy work concerning the nature of God, however, one needs to be clear that in the immanent Trinity there is only one side of the coin and that is love, while in the economic Trinity the one-sided coin of love is manifested as two-sided due to sin.

It might be helpful to highlight a selection of theologians who have adopted the postulate that God's wrath is the obverse of his love. Of course, not all the theologians mentioned use the idea with the same meaning, and thus, it will be necessary to clarify their presuppositions to understand fully what is meant by the relationship between love and wrath. The question hinges upon how the person understands the nature of wrath: Is it an objective aspect of God, or is it only a subjective experience of the person? As already demonstrated, Brunner adopts Luther's postulate about the love and wrath of God when he states, "God is present in this anger, it is actually *His* anger. For God is not mocked. That something has been interposed between God and man objectively, not merely subjectively in the consciousness of man, is thus not a pagan idea, but it is the view of the Christian Bible itself."[82] Brunner is clear that God's wrath objectively encounters humanity.

R. P. C. Hanson writes that "wrath is the converse, the underside, of God's love. It accompanies love, as darkness accompanies light, if you reject light you must have darkness."[83] In contradiction to Brunner, however, Hanson argues that "wrath is carefully treated as something ordained and controlled by God indeed, but distinct from him."[84] J. W. Wenham describes God's wrath as "the obverse of the love of God, it is love rejected."[85] God's wrath is not an objective reality imposed between himself and humanity, but instead is the absence of the experience of God's love. James Stewart declares, "God's wrath is God's grace. It is his grace smitten with dreadful

---

80. Brunner, *Mediator*, 519.

81. Ibid., 520.

82. Ibid., 518.

83. Hanson, *God*, 47.

84. Ibid., 46.

85. Wenham, *Goodness of God*, 69. While Wenham is not clear on the issue, it appears that he holds to the objective nature of God's wrath.

sorrow. It is His love in agony."[86] According to J. Arthur Baird, "Wrath is the antithesis of love. It is God's reaction to man's rebellion against his sovereignty. It is a broken fellowship. It is God's confirmation of a man's self-rejection. In effect, God's wrath is his rejected grace. As such, it is an indivisible part of his love."[87]

The above selection of theologians is given to show the widespread adoption of Luther's distinction between God's two works. As already demonstrated, another theologian who adopted Luther's distinction is Stanley Grenz. He maintained that love is the very essence of God. He is love apart from creation, and therefore, "God is love is the foundational ontological statement we can declare concerning the divine essence. God is foundationally the mutuality of the love relationship between the Father and the Son, and this personal love is the Holy Spirit."[88] With love as the foundation of God, it is the manner in which he interacts with his creation.[89]

While Grenz does not depreciate the holiness of God, he rejects the move of a theologian such as James Leo Garrett who elevates the holiness of God to the position of being a fundamental attribute on par with God's love. He argues that the intention of elevating God's holiness is to justify God's prerogative in condemning people to hell. God must be holy in order to accommodate the biblical evidence for condemnation. Grenz believes, however, that holiness, by its nature, is contained within the concept of love. Ultimately, the debate is academic, as both arguments arrive at the same location in relation to God's love and wrath.

True love will jealously defend the love relationship in which it exists. Thus, a husband is rightly jealous that his wife belongs to no other man. Love will not allow outside intruders into the relationship. From this assertion, one can understand that God is a "jealous, wrathful God. Those who would undermine the love God pours forth for the world experience his

---

86. Stewart, *Man in Christ*, 221. Stewart's conception of wrath does not match Brunner's. For Stewart, God's wrath is nothing more than humanity's self-punishment for not accepting the good. This is similar in conception to C. H. Dodd's thesis that wrath is simply the natural outworking of sin in a moral universe. God is not directly involved in the result.

87. Baird, *Justice of God*, 72. Baird makes reference to Stewart's conception of wrath as God's love in agony, but Baird does not hold to the distinction between God and wrath that Stewart maintains.

88. Grenz, *Theology for the Community of God*, 93.

89. Garrett, *Systematic Theology*, 2:239–46; Grenz, *Theology for the Community of God*, 94.

love in the form of wrath." From another angle, Grenz suggests that when people choose to reject the good and refuse to become that for which God intended them, "they remain the recipients of God's love, but experience that love in the form of wrath."[90] From this, Grenz concludes that hell is nothing other than the eternal experience of the rejection of God's love.

Combining the Mutual-Love and Love-Wrath Paradigms

It is now possible to combine the mutual-love and the love-wrath paradigms in order to explicate the Spirit's relationship to God's wrath. From the outset, it needs to be maintained that God's wrath is not the same thing as the final judgment. Paul clearly shows in Eph 2:3 that believers were at one time children of wrath. God's wrath stands in opposition to all that is opposed to him, and while this wrath has an eschatological perspective in that all temporality gains its bearing from the eschaton, it is not solely an eschatological phenomenon. God's wrath is revealed from heaven against all ungodliness. The reason for making this distinction becomes clear when one examines the issue of soteriology.

It is in the salvation event that a person passes from under God's wrath and comes into the final reality that is his love. If the Spirit is indeed the mutual-love of the Father and the Son, and God's wrath is the reverse side of his love, then in truth, when a person is transferred from the kingdom of darkness to the kingdom of light, when a person is saved, he moves from under God's wrath as experienced through the Holy Spirit into his love as experienced through the Holy Spirit. The Spirit does not change in the transfer, but the person's relationship to God as experienced by him in the Spirit is changed. Furthermore, it is in the Spirit's power that a person is able to accept Christ's work on the cross as the payment for his own sin. When a person accepts Christ's bearing of God's wrath on the cross he is transformed into a new creation; life springs into existence from death. This coming to life, this recognizing of God's love behind, beneath, and within his wrath, is accomplished by the very Spirit under whom the person experiences both the wrath, which is truly God's wrath, but not his final reality, and the love, which is truly God's love and is indeed the final reality of God. God is love, but has wrath toward sinful humanity. The Spirit is love, but has wrath toward sinful humanity, inasmuch as sinful humanity remains in its sin.

90. Grenz, *Theology for the Community of God*, 95.

"God is an eternal lover," and as such, God loves his creation eternally.[91] Those who reject that love relationship experience the "dark side" of God's love. Grenz writes, "Those who spurn or seek to destroy the holy love relationship God desires to enjoy with creation experience the divine love as protective jealousy or wrath. Because God is eternal, our experience of God's love—whether as fellowship or as wrath—is also eternal."[92] While Grenz gets this part of the equation correct, he fails to follow through on his own implications and ascribe the "dark side" of God's love to the bright side of his love. Both are experiences of the Spirit, who is the unifying love of God. Nevertheless, even if someone were to reject the mutual-love paradigm of Augustine, he would not by that remove the Spirit from participating in judgment, for Rom 5:5 states that the love of God is poured into people's hearts through the Holy Spirit. According to this verse, the Spirit is the person in whom people experience the love of the entire Godhead. Conversely, if God's wrath is the flip side of his love, then the flip side, it would stand to reason, is experienced in the Holy Spirit as well.

Conclusion

Stanley Grenz serves as a perfect representative of those unwilling to directly ascribe the judgmental aspects of God's nature to the Spirit. Grenz makes all the connections in his systematic work that are necessary to show that the Spirit is the channel for both God's love and wrath, but only follows through on explicitly stating that the Spirit is his love. Either he refuses to declare the Spirit as God's wrath or it never occurred to him to connect the dots he established. Either way, the Spirit's role in judgment is more clearly elucidated when one is able to see the unified nature both of the immanent Trinity's love as manifested and bonded in the Spirit and of God's love and wrath as it is encountered by both the redeemed and unredeemed. In the combination of the mutual-love paradigm and the love-wrath paradigm one is able to more clearly see the role of the Holy Spirit in judgment.

91. Grenz, *Theology for the Community of God*, 836.
92. Ibid.

7

The Spirit, the Cross, and the Lake of Fire

PEOPLE ARE IN A state of estrangement from God, from each other, and from themselves. One may deny this estrangement on sunny days when all is right with the world, but it comes crashing in when the storm clouds gather, the thunder rolls, and the reality of sin and death cling to the individual and the community like so much wet clothing. All is not right with the world; something has gone terribly wrong and stands in need of correction. How to achieve that correction, or how it is achieved, has been a staple of discussion for humanity since the Fall. How can humanity be reunited with God, each other, and themselves? How can the weight of guilt, shame, failure, and offense be removed so that relationship can be restored?

The writings of the Old and New Testaments concern themselves with answering the question of reconciliation and atonement.[1] The healing of the divide between God and man, between communities, individuals, and within one's own self is found in Jesus Christ. His life, death, and resurrection transform estrangement into fellowship and hatred into love and overcome rejection with acceptance.

---

1. "The English word 'atonement' traces its origin to the sixteenth century. The *New Oxford Dictionary* indicates that in the first instance it appeared as two separate words 'at onement,' but soon became a quasi-technical term." Bromiley, "Atone," 1:352. Green and Baker make the compelling argument that while the word atonement does not appear frequently in the New Testament; only twice in the NRSV and five times in the NIV, the concept of atonement is pervasive in the text. They furthermore adopt a working definition of atonement as "the saving significance of Jesus' death." While this definition is helpful, it limits the atonement to only the death of Jesus, thus leaving out both his life and his resurrection, two aspects that are crucial to a full understanding of atonement. Green and Baker, *Recovering the Scandal of the Cross*, 36.

The cross is the heart of history, the point from which all of history gains its ultimate bearing, for the cross reveals God's very nature.[2] For those who conceive of God as distant and disinterested, the cross cries out that he is intimately concerned with the way of the world. For those who conceive of him as full of wrath, looking for his next victim, the cross cries out that he is love and that he so loves the world that he sent his only Son. For those who conceive of him as a mild-mannered indulgent parent who is all too willing to let his children's misdeeds pass by with a mere wink of the eye and a knowing nod of the head, the cross cries out that he is holy and as such he cannot let the awful consequences of sin go unfulfilled. The cross unites God's holiness and his love in an at-one-ment that reveals to his creation that he is indeed both holiness and love simultaneously.[3] The cross is the final answer to the Psalmist's cry when he asks God if his anger will be with his people forever. The cross reveals that "righteousness and peace kiss each other."[4]

God pours out both his wrath and love upon Christ, so that those who accept Christ will not experience wrath, but only love. Those in Christ experience a reverent fear of God's holiness, but a fear that is conditioned by love. It is on the cross that the Father pours out his wrath upon the Son, where the Son becomes sin for humanity, where he takes the place of fallen humanity, and where he takes the punishment rightly due fallen humanity upon himself. It is from the midst of Jesus' suffering upon the cross, a suffering that transcends physical pain, that redemption is procured and atonement is accomplished. The price for that atonement was the death of the perfect sacrifice, the abandonment of the Son by the Father.

From a Binitarian to a Trinitarian Crucifixion

While the atonement is a Trinitarian event, for the most part, it has been presented within a binitarian framework.[5] The Son offers himself upon the

2. Stott, *Cross of Christ*, 204–26.

3. "The love of God is the motive for the saving work of Jesus Christ as the Son of God. Jesus did not die to purchase, obtain, or secure the love of God, but in dying for the salvation of human beings Jesus revealed or demonstrated the self-giving love of the Father." Garrett, *Systematic Theology*, 2:34. Conner argued that "the love of God manifest in the cross of Christ is holy love. It is love that is eternally opposed to sin, actively opposed to sin." Conner, *Gospel of Redemption*, 111.

4. Ps 85:10.

5. For Erickson, the Spirit is only mentioned in connection with the beginning of

cross and the Father pours out his wrath upon him, and in popular language turns his back upon the Son. From the abandonment, the Son cries out in anguish, questioning why his Father has forsaken him. Noticeably absent from the entire scene is the Spirit. This binitarian approach to Jesus' suffering has often caused the entire discussion of the atonement to take on a detached ethos in which the redemption offered on the cross has no real connection to people in the present.[6] It was an event that took place in the distant past, an event that gained redemption, but that has no ontological connection to the believer. The Spirit is often brought in only as a herald of the event, revealing to the believer what took place on the cross, with the Spirit himself not being a vital part of it.

While Anselm and Abelard are radically different in their understanding of the atonement, both of them are agreed that the atonement involves the Father, the Son, and humanity. This binitarian approach has plagued much of Western theology. It is surprising that the Spirit's role in the atonement has not been treated in more depth. One reason for this might be, as mentioned previously, the reluctance of people to associate the Spirit with judgment. Additionally, and more importantly, the Spirit does not explicitly show up during the crucifixion of Jesus. He is, however, not absent from the event. The lack of direct mention of the Spirit does not warrant the conclusion that he was not present, for Jesus' entire ministry was accomplished in the power of the Spirit.

Furthermore, Heb 9:14 states, "How much more will the blood of Christ, who through the eternal Spirit offered himself without blemish to God, purify our conscience from dead works to serve the living God." The phrase of "eternal Spirit" in this verse is unique to Hebrews and there have been those who have argued that the reference is not the Holy Spirit, but instead to the locale and quality of Christ's sacrifice.[7] The most probable understanding is that the writer is referring to the Holy Spirit. F. F. Bruce connects the idea back to Isa 42:1 and the bestowal of the Spirit upon the

---

the Christian life. Erickson, *Christian Theology*, 888. Grudem, likewise, does not connect the Spirit with the cross. Grudem, *Systematic Theology*, 568–607. Leon Morris in his monograph on the cross in the New Testament never connects the Spirit with Jesus' condemnation upon the cross. Morris, *Cross in the New Testament*. While these three theologians are given as examples, the list could be greatly expanded, as the Spirit is absent in the event of the cross in most theologies.

6. Clements, "Atonement and the Holy Spirit," 169–70.

7. Attridge, *Epistle to the Hebrews*.

Suffering Servant.[8] The Spirit and the blood of Christ are closely connected in this verse, thus giving credence to the thesis that the Spirit is present and active in the atonement.

The Spirit's work in the crucifixion is in desperate need of elucidation. Keith Clements has attempted such an entrance into the topic, but does not fully carry out the program, only presenting the Spirit as the bond between the Father and the Son that allows the Godhead to remain together, even in the midst of the Father turning his back upon the Son.[9] In his book *Fire and Blood*, Mark Stibbe seeks to demonstrate the intimate bond between the cross and the Spirit, moving further than Clements in the endeavor in that he understands the Spirit as empowering Jesus for affliction and suffering, even to the point of death. He does not understand, however, the Spirit as actualizing condemnation to the Son on the cross.[10]

Likewise, according to Moltmann, the Spirit is the "link joining the bond between the Father and the Son with their separation."[11] While Moltmann goes a good way toward a fuller presentation of the Spirit's work, he still presents the crucifixion in a binitarian manner. Jesus' suffering and death is explicated as an event between the Father and the Son. Moltmann writes:

> In the cross, Father and Son are most deeply separated in forsakenness and at the same time are most inwardly one in their surrender. What proceeds from this event between Father and Son is the Spirit which justifies the godless, fills the forsaken with love and even brings the dead alive, since even the fact that they are dead cannot exclude them from this event of the cross; the death in God also includes them.[12]

The Spirit only appears after the crucifixion and resurrection, proceeding from the binitarian event to justify and make alive. The Spirit's

8. Bruce, *Epistle to the Hebrews*, 205. For others who argue for Holy Spirit as the correct reference see Koester, *Hebrews*, 410; Lane, *Hebrews 9–13*, 230–40; Ellingworth, *Epistle to the Hebrews*, 456–57.

9. "The work of at-one-ment must therefore be ascribed to the Spirit's agency in maintaining oneness no less than to the Father who reconciles the world, and to the Son by whose obedience the world is reconciled. It is through the Spirit that the Father and Son remain ultimately at one despite the cross, and it is therefore in the Spirit that the world, with whom the Son has identified himself, has access to the Father." Clements, "Atonement and the Holy Spirit," 170.

10. Stibbe, *Fire and Blood*.

11. Moltmann, *Trinity and the Kingdom of God*, 82.

12. Moltmann, *Crucified God*, 244.

exclusion from the judgment of the Son upon the cross is unfortunate and fails to accomplish Moltmann's stated intention, which is to present a Trinitarian theology of the cross. While Moltmann, Stibbe, and Clements' insights are valuable and correct, they all fail to reveal fully the Spirit's work in conjunction with the Father's judgment of Jesus.

If the Spirit is the bond of love joining the Father and the Son, and furthermore, if God's love and wrath are correlated as in the theology of Luther, Brunner, and Grenz, then the obvious conclusion is that in the event in which God the Father pours out his wrath upon God the Son, the Spirit is both the bond of love that unites the two even in the separation, and conversely, the Spirit also applies to the Son the Father's wrath, which is nothing other than the wrath of all three persons together. The mistake is often made in elucidating the cross that it is only the Father who is angry at sin, while the truth of the matter is that Father, Son, and Spirit are all equally angry at humanity's rebellion. While the Son takes upon himself the sins of humanity that is not to imply that he is not angry with those sins. It is the holiness and love of all three persons that compels them to atone for the sins of humanity.

When the Spirit's work in judgment is properly explicated, it becomes apparent that the crucifixion is not a binitarian event, but indeed a Trinitarian event in all respects. The Spirit actualizes to the Son the Father's condemnation, as the Son vicariously assumes the consequences of humanity's sin and rebellion. If the Son is the judge judged in place of humanity, then the Spirit executes the judge's judgment.

The Spirit and Penal Substitution

"My God, my God, why have you forsaken me?"[13] Jesus' cry of dereliction from the cross poignantly captures the abandonment he felt as he became

13. Jesus' cry of dereliction in which he quotes Ps 22:1 should not be viewed as a cry of victory in which the entirety of the Psalm is in focus, as a cry of unbelief or despair, or a cry of abandonment in which Jesus only felt forsaken, but was not in actuality. Read, "Cry of Dereliction," 60–62; Lane, *Gospel According to Mark*, 572–73; Stott, *Cross of Christ*, 80–82. Morris offers a thorough critique of all the positions and comes to the conclusion that Jesus' cry was a reflection of the reality of his abandonment by the Father. Additionally, he rightly notes that this cry causes one to think deeply about its Trinitarian implications. One must be able to both maintain the abandonment of the Son with the unity of the Trinity that remains unbroken. While Morris does not ground his conclusion that the unity of the Trinity is maintained in the face of the abandonment, it will be argued that both the unity and the abandonment are works of the Spirit. Morris, *Cross in*

a curse and was forsaken by the Father. Paul relates in Gal 3:13 that Jesus is able to redeem sinners from the curse of the law by becoming a curse for them. Paul gains this idea from Deut 21:22–23 which states, "And if a man has committed a crime punishable by death and he is put to death, and you hang him on a tree, his body shall not remain all night on the tree, but you shall bury him the same day, for a hanged man is cursed by God. You shall not defile your land that the LORD your God is giving you for an inheritance." It is telling that Jesus became a curse for sinners, because in himself there was no cause for him to be cursed as he was sinless. Paul, probably early in his Christian walk, made the connection between Jesus' crucifixion and his being a curse. The scandal of the cross is found in that God's chosen one was hanged upon a tree, and by the very Scripture that Jesus endorsed he was declared cursed.

Jesus' death on the cross was not accidental, as if any death would have sufficed. The manner of his death was ordained by God, but also most likely consciously chosen by his adversaries to discredit his message. The great paradox is that in the attempt to discredit his message by having him crucified, his adversaries accomplished God's purpose of defeating the curse of the law by becoming a curse himself. It is the resurrection of Jesus that vindicates his declaration that he is the Son of God. It is for us that Christ became a curse. He stood in the place of sinners and took the full force of God's wrath upon himself, so that "in Christ Jesus the blessing of Abraham might come to the Gentiles."[14] The Son who had known no sin his entire life became sin and took upon himself the punishment due humanity. The beloved Son, with whom the Father was well pleased, became the cursed beloved.[15]

There are various theories that have been promulgated throughout church history as to the exact nature of the atonement and how it affects both God and humanity. Broadly speaking, there are three major models: Christ as victor over the forces of evil, the subjectivist Abelardian model, and the objectivist Anselmian model.[16] The first understands the atonement as primarily affecting the forces of evil that hold humanity captive, while the Abelardian approach is characterized by an emphasis upon God's love

the New Testament, 42–49.

14. George, Galatians, 237–43.

15. Baxter, "Cursed Beloved," 54–72.

16. Packer, "What Did the Cross Achieve," 19–21. The Christ as victor model was forcefully restated by Gustaf Aulén, while the other two models have been adopted by various theologians throughout history. Aulén, Christus Victor.

and the subjective impact of the atonement upon the person atoned. The Anselmian approach, on the other hand, is characterized by an emphasis upon God's holiness with the atonement having an objective impact upon the relationship between God and humanity. The Abelardian approach interprets the cross event in such a way as to allow a person to understand the true nature of his relationship to God, while the Anselmian approach sees the cross as affecting the very relationship between God and humanity.

Within evangelical theology, the Anselmian approach as represented by the penal substitution paradigm of the atonement has dominated, but with modifications to allow God's love to impact his holiness, so that the atonement is not presented as the holy, wrathful Father punishing an innocent, victimized Son.[17] Instead, in a proper understanding of the atonement the entire Godhead is active in reconciling the world to God. It is the combined work of the Father, Son, and Spirit that accomplishes atonement, an atonement that is offered because of God's love and that is necessary because of his holiness.

Penal substitution is at the heart of the atonement, and while other motifs are presented in the Scripture, this motif will serve as the one from which to understand the Spirit's role in the cross event. That is not to suggest that the other motifs exclude the Spirit's work. The Spirit is operative in each motif, but space restrictions prohibit each motif from being investigated. The other motifs speak more to the victory that is achieved by Christ, such as freedom from bondage, victory over the forces of darkness, ransom from sin, and the subjective impact that the atonement has upon the believer. The Spirit is intimately involved in each of these events. In the motifs of Christ as sacrifice, propitiation, and substitute, however, he is presented as bearing the consequences of humanity's sin, and as such it is this motif that can most clearly demonstrate the Spirit's work in the judgment of the Father upon the Son.[18]

---

17. Packer has presented a concise overview of penal substitution, as well as a thorough defense of the paradigm. Packer, "What Did the Cross Achieve," 3–45. Paige Patterson has stated that penal substitution is the "major and indispensable model for comprehending what God was doing in Christ." Patterson, "Reflections on the Atonement," 317. Likewise, Peter Jensen states, "The doctrine of Penal Substitution is inherent to evangelical religion; it is part of the logic of it." Jensen, "Good News of God's Wrath," 46. For a recent defense of penal substitution see Williams, "Penal Substitution," 71–86.

18. Packer, "What Did the Cross Achieve," 21. According to Packer, the other two motifs, Christ as Victor and the Abelardian motif, are both subsumed under the Anselmian model.

The penal substitution paradigm of the atonement states that on the cross Christ vicariously bore the sins of humanity and took upon himself the punishment that was due it in order to free it from its deserved punishment. According to Packer, "The notion which the phrase 'penal substitution' expresses is that Jesus Christ our Lord, moved by a love that was determined to do everything necessary to save us, endured and exhausted the destructive divine judgment for which we were otherwise inescapably destined, and so won us forgiveness, adoption, and glory."[19]

God's ability to offer forgiveness to humanity and remain a just God lies at the foundation of the penal substitutionary model. Paul wrote in Rom 3:23–26 that God has put forth Jesus as a propitiation in order that he might "be just and the justifier of the one who has faith in Jesus."[20] His holy love will not allow sin to remain unpunished. However, is not forgiveness such a simpler concept than that? Someone wrongs a person and the person wronged relinquishes the person from the consequences of his misdeed by forgiving him. God commands people to forgive each other, not just once or twice, but seventy times seven times.[21] If he commands humanity to forgive each other unconditionally, why then does he attach a condition to his forgiveness? Why is it that God demands some form of punishment for the sinner in order to forgive the sin? The answer to that question is found in the radical difference between humanity and divinity.

God's holy love dictates that atonement be accomplished in a way that is "fully consistent with his own character. It is not only that he must overthrow and disarm the devil in order to rescue his captives. It is not even only that he must satisfy his law, his honour, his justice or the moral order: it is that he must satisfy himself."[22] Within God there is not a disharmony between his love and wrath, even though it might appear this way experientially at times, but as previously shown the love and wrath of God are not at odds with each other; "indeed, the two are more than simultaneous, they are identical, or at least alternative expressions of the same reality."[23]

19. Ibid., 25.

20. God had passed over the former sins of humanity, but this could throw God's justice into question. The reason, however, for passing over the former sins, was because God had intended all along to display both his justice and his mercy in his Son upon the cross. The cross maintains both his love and justice. Mounce, *Romans*, 116–18; Morris, *Epistle to the Romans*, 184.

21. Matt 18:22.

22. Stott, *Cross of Christ*, 129.

23. Ibid., 131.

Because he is holy, he cannot allow sin to remain unpunished as if it was not a direct affront to his very being. Moreover, because he is love, he cannot leave his creation to suffer the destruction due it for its sin. The Father in love sends the Son "in the likeness of sinful flesh" in order to bear within himself the penalty that is due humanity because of his holiness. The Son, in love, obediently responds to his Father's sending. The Spirit, likewise in love, empowers the Son to accomplish his mission and is then sent by the Father and the Son to proclaim the atonement accomplished on the cross and to draw people into a salvific relationship with the Triune God. God satisfies his holy love on the cross, for it is the cross in all its horror, shame, and hatred that reveals both God's love for humanity and his utter revulsion at sin.

Moltmann, taking a cue from Goethe, speaks of the roses that have surrounded the cross, which have grown up over time in Christian tradition so that the harshness of the cross is masked by the gentleness of the roses. However, before Christians can understand the cross as victory they must see it in its historical reality as a sign of Jesus' defeat by the Romans and his being cursed by God. The cross throws all of Jesus' proclamations into question. Was he indeed the Son of God, and if so, why did he die upon a cross? Would God allow his beloved Son to die in such a manner? The resurrection redefines the cross from defeat to victory, but Good Friday comes before Easter Sunday and the order needs to be maintained. That is not to say that Easter Sunday does not retroactively provide the correct interpretation for Good Friday, but that Good Friday needs to be confronted in all its horror alongside of and in conjunction with the victory of Easter Sunday. Jesus, who knew no sin, was made to be sin and took humanity's punishment upon himself.[24]

As a substitute for humanity's sin, Jesus took upon himself the sin of humanity and became a curse. Galatians 5:17 relates that the Spirit and the flesh stand in opposition to each other. Furthermore, Rom 8:3–13 states that God sent his son in the likeness of sinful flesh so that the requirements of the law might be fulfilled in those who are in Christ. Additionally, it reveals that the mind-set on the flesh is hostile to God, and those who are in the flesh cannot please him. To set one's mind on the flesh is death, but to set one's mind on the Spirit is life and peace. Paul makes a distinct contrast between the flesh and the Spirit, between death and life.

24. Moltmann, *Crucified God*, 32–41.

When he says that Christ came in the likeness of sinful flesh, Paul is not suggesting that Jesus sinned, but that he took upon himself a human nature. When Christ was on the cross and became sin for humanity, the conflict between the Spirit and the flesh would of necessity have affected him. In Rom 8:13 Paul admonishes his readers to put to death the deeds of the body by the Spirit. It is the Spirit that accomplishes the death of the flesh by the person's participation in the suffering, death, and resurrection of Jesus. On the cross, the Spirit stood in opposition to sin as the Son suffered by being made sin and being cursed.

On the cross, Jesus endured the punishment due humanity, but what exactly did that entail? Was it only physical pain, or did the crucifixion reach deeper into the heart of the Savior? And what is the Spirit's relationship to his suffering? Wayne Grudem offers a convenient framework within which to tease out the work of the Spirit in the crucifixion in relationship to Jesus' suffering. He does not discuss the Spirit's work in the crucifixion himself, but offers four areas in which he suffered on the cross: (1) physical pain and death; (2) the pain of bearing sin; (3) abandonment; and (4) bearing God's wrath.[25]

The first aspect of Christ's suffering and the one with which most people relate is the physical torment he underwent: the flogging by the guards, the crown of thorns, and ultimately the cross itself. He was physically devastated in the crucifixion, and while his death was no different from countless other crucifixions, that does not reduce the sheer physical brutality of the event. But what role might the Spirit have played in the physical suffering of Christ?

It was the Spirit who came upon Jesus at his baptism, who empowered him throughout his ministry, and who ultimately led him to the cross in the fulfillment of the Father's will. Mark Stibbe remarks that Jesus' anointing by the Spirit at his baptism was also an anointing for affliction. He derives the connection by citing Mark 10:38, where James and John asked Jesus if they might occupy thrones on either side of him when he comes into his kingdom. In response, Jesus asked them if they could undergo the baptism with which he was going to be baptized. When the Spirit came upon Jesus at his baptism, "he was endowed with the power for martyrdom as well as miracles."[26] In a similar vein, Ferguson writes, "The Spirit's role in Jesus' ministry is now evident. He serves as the heavenly cartographer and divine

25. Grudem, *Systematic Theology*, 572–77.
26. Stibbe, *Fire and Blood*, 58–59.

strategist who maps out the battle terrain and directs the Warrior-King to the strategic point of conflict. He is Christ's adjutant-general in the holy war which is waged throughout the incarnation."[27]

As Jesus finished the Last Supper and made his way to the Garden of Gethsemane, he was still empowered by the Spirit. Furthermore, the Spirit gives physical life to people, and upon the removal of God's Spirit people die.[28] As the Son suffered physically upon the cross, the Spirit sustained his life until the time he uttered that it was finished and he died. Jesus' life was his to lay down and to take up again, but his was a life that was conceived and sustained by the Spirit.

From his conception to his crucifixion the Spirit was with him, moving him forward from baptism to temptation, from temptation to his ministry of proclamation and healing, and from proclamation to his encounter with the religious authorities and ultimately to his death. In the Spirit's power, Jesus preached liberty to the captives, a liberty that could only be gained by way of the cross. There is no indication in Scripture that the Spirit, in some gnostic-like manner, departed Jesus before the crucifixion. He was with him throughout the physical torment he underwent. There is also no indication in Scripture that physical suffering is the Spirit's work. Jesus' physical death, however, is directly related to the withdrawal of the Spirit's life-giving function. In order for Jesus to die physically, the Spirit's sustaining and preserving power must have been removed from his body.[29]

The second aspect of suffering is the pain of bearing, or of becoming, sin. Second Corinthians 5:21 states, "For our sake he made him to be sin who knew no sin, so that in him we might become the righteousness of God." This verse does not support the idea that Jesus became a sinner on the cross, but instead highlights the contrast between the sinless Jesus, he who knew no sin, and the sinful world. The sin of the world was placed upon Jesus so that he took the full weight of sin's punishment upon himself. God's revulsion at sin was aimed at Christ as he became the embodiment of sin upon the cross. Jesus was made to be sin in our place so that believers could become the righteousness of God, not in and of themselves, but only in Christ.[30]

27. Ferguson, *Holy Spirit*, 50.

28. Grudem, *Systematic Theology*, 636. For a fuller treatment of the Spirit's role in creation and life see Pinnock, *Flame of Love*, 49–77 and Ferguson, *Holy Spirit*, 19–22.

29. For an explanation of Job 34:14–15 on which this statement is predicated see Reyburn, *Handbook on the Book of Job*, 631–32.

30. Thrall, *Second Epistle to the Corinthians*, 439–44; Garland, *2 Corinthians*, 300–302; Barnett, *Second Epistle to the Corinthians*, 312–14; Hughes, *Paul's Second Epistle to*

Upon the cross, Jesus endured the terrible psychological weight of the sin of the world. He experienced the guilt that sin produces. Sin's nature is to ruin fellowship, to break relationships. Sin establishes a barrier between the sinner and all others.[31] Each sin that is committed puts another brick in the wall of separation. The Spirit is not absent in this sense of estrangement and guilt, but is intimately present as the means whereby sin causes these reactions in a person. He is the "Spirit of righteousness and justice who speaks in the *guilty conscience* of the people who commit violence."[32] It is the Spirit's presence that accounts for humanity's sense of "separation from all that is right in the universe, an awareness of something that in a very deep sense ought not to be."[33] When the Father laid the sins of humanity upon Christ, the revulsion within the Son was created not only by his holiness, but also by the Spirit that remained upon him. The very name Holy Spirit reveals the contrast that was established upon the cross. The Son became sin and as such God's holiness must stand in opposition to him. The destabilizing effect that the Spirit has upon this world's rebellion was operative upon Christ while he was on the cross resulting in the psychological suffering he underwent.

The third area of suffering experienced by Jesus was the sense of abandonment. While he loved his followers until the end, his followers deserted him. The rejection of his closest friends must have been painful, but the abandonment of the Father was a far deeper suffering. From the depths of his being, he cried out, "*Eloi, Eloi, lama sabachthani*." In popular terms, the Father turned his back upon the Son because he could not look upon the sin laid upon him.[34] In this forsakenness, Jesus was left alone on the cross to bear the full weight of judgment. At this point, the Spirit is the bond that held the Trinity together.

the Corinthians, 211–16.

31. Erickson contends that sin "results in the inability to love. Since other people stand in our way, representing competition and a threat to us." Erickson, *Christian Theology*, 636. Grenz understands sin as destroying God's intended community between the person, those around him and God himself. Grenz, *Theology for the Community of God*, 207–08.

32. Moltmann, *Spirit of Life*, 142–43.

33. Grudem, *Systematic Theology*, 573. Grudem does not make the connection between the believer's revulsion to evil and the Holy Spirit. He does not directly suggest as Moltmann does that it is the Spirit who causes this sense of revulsion, but taking Grudem's theology as a whole, it is likely that he would endorse this idea.

34. Isa 59:2 states, "But your iniquities have made a separation between you and your God, and your sins have hidden his face from you so that he does not hear."

An extended quote from Clements will show how he comes right up to the point of recognizing the Spirit's dual role in the abandonment of Jesus, but then fails to make the final step. Clements states,

> At the start of Jesus' ministry, the heavens open and the Spirit descends upon him. At the end, the heavens remain closed. Nothing except death itself comes to release Jesus from the writhing agony under the dark sky. The Spirit is there to the end; even to the cry of dereliction . . . He remained true to his Father, while remaining true to the human predicament of alienation. As throughout his ministry, he remained at one with his Father in perfect freedom of will, in the Spirit. Now, paradoxically, the oneness could only be experienced as an abyss of separation. At this point we can only infer the activity of the Spirit at its most profound, in maintaining the bond of love between the Father who gives up his Son, and the Son who has been given up.[35]

While that is assuredly correct, it fails to capture another element of the Spirit's work, his actualizing of the Father's judgment given to the Son, in which the Son comes under his own judgment. When Jesus experienced the abandonment of the Father, it was executed by and in the Spirit as the one who actualizes God's interaction with humanity. The abandonment of the Father was experienced by Jesus in the Spirit, while at the same time, underneath and in concert with the abandonment the Spirit held the Father and Son together in unity.

The final suffering Jesus underwent, one closely tied to abandonment, is the bearing of God's wrath. Not only did the Father turn away in a sense from the Son, but the Son also experienced the Father's wrath as it pertains to sinful humanity. While the Son's abandonment might be viewed as a passive act on the Father's part, the pouring out of wrath actively displays God's displeasure with sin. Romans 3:25 states that God presented Jesus as a propitiation for sin. Likewise, the idea of Jesus as the propitiation for sin is found in Heb 2:17, and 1 John 2:2 and 4:10. The idea behind propitiation is that an offering is made that turns aside God's wrath.[36] On the cross, the Son encountered the "dark side" of God's love, his *opus alienum*. This alien work of God is an

---

35. Clements, "Atonement and the Holy Spirit," 170.

36. Morris, *Cross in the New Testament*, 144–213. While this definition has been endlessly debated, within evangelical circles the conclusions of Morris have been almost universally accepted. For a few examples see Grudem, *Systematic Theology*, 574–76; Erickson, *Christian Theology*, 809–11; Garrett, *Systematic Theology*, 2:11–14; Ladd, *Theology of the New Testament*, 429–31.

active one in which he pours out his displeasure at sin upon Christ. Isaiah 53 describes how the Messiah will be stricken and smitten by God for the iniquities of humanity. It was God's will to crush Jesus, thus bringing him to grief and through that horrendous event to free humanity from bondage and to reconcile God's wayward creatures back to himself.

As already established, the Spirit actualizes God's love to humanity, and when humanity rejects that love it experiences and lives under his wrath, his rejected love. Jesus, as humanity's substitute experienced God's wrath on the cross as 2 Cor 5:21 states, "He made him to be sin who knew no sin, so that in him we might become the righteousness of God." God's wrath at the rebellion of his creation was borne by the Son. This wrath had been stored up since the Fall, awaiting the coming of the Messiah upon whom it would be poured out. God was able to forgive the sins of those who lived before Christ because he was storing up his wrath at their disobedience in order to satisfy his justice against his Son. As already stated, the Son was not a helpless victim in this event, but was equally outraged at humanity's sin and equally loved the creation so that he was a willing participant in the reconciliation of fallen humanity.

On the cross, Jesus experienced God's wrath as actualized by the Spirit. The mystery of the Trinity is fully on display in the cross. The Father who loves the Son from all eternity pours out his wrath against humanity upon the God-man Jesus Christ. The Son who has loved his Father from all eternity accepts the punishment due humanity from the Father. The Spirit who is the eternal bond of love between the Father and the Son actualizes God's wrath to the Son. Jesus experiences this wrath on the cross as God's holy revulsion to sin, as his *opus alienum,* his strange work, in which he destroys in order to rebuild, kills in order to make alive.

The Father does not cease to love the Son in the crucifixion, but his love is, as it were, masked by his wrath, and both his love and his wrath are nothing other than the Spirit. One must not conceive of God's love and wrath as entities that exist outside of him or as attributes that exist inside him, but are somehow different from him. "God is love." Moreover, because he is love, and because humanity experiences that love through the Spirit, when a person experiences God's wrath, which is his spurned love, that experience is also mediated by the Holy Spirit. Consequently, when Jesus experienced the Father's wrath upon the cross and cried out the lament of dereliction from the depths of his being, the Son was not separated from the Father and the Spirit ontologically, but rather experientially. The Son experienced the Father's wrath, while at the same time the ontological bond of love remained in place. The Spirit indeed held the Father and the Son together on the cross, but he also simultaneously actualized God's wrath to the Son.

In the case of the cross, the judgment was condemning. Three days later, however, in the power of the Holy Spirit the Father judged Jesus in the resurrection. This time the judgment resulted in glorification. It was by the Spirit's power that Jesus was resurrected from the grave.[37] The grave could not hold the righteous Son of God, but instead, Jesus overcame death and sin by his resurrection from both. He had paid sin its due wage, so the Father raised the Son by the Spirit's power and thereby vindicated all that the Son had proclaimed before his death. If he had remained in the grave and if all he had experienced was God's condemnatorial judgment, then his entire ministry would have been invalidated. Jesus' message of salvation and the Kingdom of God was none other than Jesus himself, so if he was not raised from the dead, then his message became false and of all people Christians are the most to be pitied. Jesus' death is the basis for atonement and his resurrection is the vindication of his message and the ground of hope for the believer. Jesus underwent both judgments of God, condemnation and glorification, with both of the Father's judgments being actualized in the Son by the Spirit.

The Relationship of the Spirit to the Lake of Fire

Calvin, in his commentary on Isa 30:27–33 asked a deep theological question: whether perdition is a place the Spirit places people or if the Spirit is the place of perdition. A. H. Strong concludes that the spatial location of hell is not as important as its relational aspect. The Bible does not give a detailed roadmap of hell, and therefore one should not be sought. Strong writes, "Here we are to remember, as in the final state of the righteous, that the decisive and controlling element is not the outward, but the inward. If hell is a place, it is only that the outward may correspond to the inward. If there be outward torments, it is only because there will be first, though subordinate, accompaniments of the inward state of the soul."[38]

---

37. Rom 1:4, 8:11; 1 Pet 3:18.

38. Strong, *Systematic Theology*, 3:1034. For an overview of the debate between whether the descriptions of hell in the Bible should be understood as literal or metaphorical see the arguments by Walvoord and Crockett in Crockett et al., *Four Views on Hell*.

The current era in which the belief in hell as a literal geographical location in the center of the earth has been abandoned amplifies the problem, while the renewed understanding that the Bible does not teach the redeemed will live in some celestial dwelling, but that they will in fact live on a renewed earth, a geographical location, attenuates the complexity.[39] The question, which naturally arises, is where are those who have been consigned to perdition? Are they located in some penal colony in the far reaches of the New Heaven and Earth? Second Peter 3:10–13 mitigates against such an understanding. A logical answer is that when the unredeemed encounter God's wrath as actualized by the Spirit they are annihilated. While this option solves the problems nicely, in that no location for the unredeemed is necessary, it does not appear to be aligned with the biblical data.[40]

A person's relationship to God and other people is either blessedness or perdition; all depends upon one's relationship to Christ in the Spirit. This relational bond creates tensions that are often implied but never discussed. Hell cannot be complete separation from God, for there is no existence apart from him, and if a person ceases to exist then he cannot logically be described as separated from God. In order to be separated there must be something from which one is separated. The power of God must be present in hell to maintain the existence of those people who have chosen to reject God's love and hence experience his wrath. The Spirit maintains existence in the present time, and there is no biblical data that would suggest some other agent will carry out the maintenance of people in hell. Hell is, therefore, not primarily a physical location, but a relational position, with the Holy Spirit actualizing the relationship of the unredeemed to God. From this can be drawn the radical conclusion that hell is nothing other than a person's rejection of Jesus Christ and the resulting experience of God as

---

39. The literature on hell is legion. The current debate raging within evangelical circles is annihilationism, and as such most of the energy being spent is in that arena. For an overview of the current issues surrounding the doctrine of hell see Dixon, *Other Side of the Good News*; Crockett, *Four Views on Hell*; Fudge and Peterson, *Two Views of Hell*; Buis, *Doctrine of Eternal Punishment*. For an overview of the location of the redeemed upon the earth see Wright, *Resurrection of the Son of God*.

40. The scope of the current project does not allow complete answers to be offered to these questions. The focus on the Holy Spirit in judgment, however, is maintained under each option. If the unredeemed are annihilated, this takes place in the Spirit, and if they are to undergo eternal conscious punishment then they must be maintained in existence by the Spirit.

manifested by the Holy Spirit. In Luther's words, "He (God) is everywhere, in death, in hell, in the midst of our foes, yes, also in their hearts."[41]

In order to prove the above thesis, which is admittedly speculative, an initial inquiry into the relationship between God and those in hell, as presented by representative evangelical theologians, will be undertaken to establish that those in hell, while separate from the presence of God, cannot be separate from his continued conservation of them in existence. Secondly, the theological conclusion of God's presence in hell will be placed upon a scriptural foundation. Finally, the description of hell as God's wrath and the connection previously established between his wrath/love and the Holy Spirit will be combined to demonstrate the Spirit's work in those people who are in hell.

While hell has often been described in popular terms as separation from God, and on an unsophisticated level that description can be maintained as valid, when one approaches the issue of God's relationship to a person in hell, two theological constructs forbid the idea that God is completely absent from hell.[42] First, if God's omnipresence is maintained, then he must of necessity be in hell in some capacity, or one will have to redefine what is meant by omnipresence.[43] God cannot both be everywhere at every time and concurrently not in hell. Additionally, the theological construct of God's preservation of his creation also argues for his presence in hell. Now at this point, it might be helpful to distinguish between the various understandings of God's presence, for the Bible reveals that his presence does not have the same affect in all circumstances.

The two broad categories of God's presence are his extensive/general presence and his intensive/special presence. His general presence refers to his presence throughout creation that allows creation to both exist and to

41. Luther, *Lectures on the Minor Prophets*, 19:68.

42. In *The Problem of Pain*, C. S. Lewis described hell as God leaving man alone. Lewis, *Problem of Pain*, 116. Erickson is mistaken in his reliance upon C. S. Lewis. The reality is that God cannot leave man alone, for God's love will not allow that. Hell is man's experience of God outside of Christ. Erickson, *Christian Theology*, 1240.

43. Grudem states, "God is present in different ways in different places, or that God acts differently in different places in his creation. Sometimes God is present to punish." Grudem, *Systematic Theology*, 175. Likewise, W. T. Conner wrote, "The omnipresence of God does not mean that God is present everywhere in the same sense or with reference to the same end or purpose. He is not present in the rock and in the reason of Plato in the same sense. He is not present in the sinful life of Nero and the holy life of Jesus in the same sense. He is not present in hell or in heaven in the same sense or with reference to the same function or end." Conner, *Christian Doctrine*, 84–85.

continue in existence. "There is indeed no place where God is completely absent. Human beings, even in their desperation, can never ultimately flee from the presence of God."[44] God's general presence can refer to his sustaining, blessing, or even punishing activity.[45] Amos 9:1–4 depicts God seeking out those whom he intends to punish as they attempt to hide from him in Sheol, on the summit of Mount Carmel, on the ocean's floor, or even in captivity.

God's special presence refers to his gracious and beneficent presence that is mediated through a salvific relationship with Christ. Admittedly, in this life, those who are not believers experience the benefits of God's grace and goodness, but in hell, those benefits are removed and all that person encounters is his general presence as sustaining and punishing. It is the special or intensive presence of God from which a person in hell is separated, not his presence in general.

God's preservation of his creation, which is directly tied to his omnipresence, also excludes the proposition that hell is complete separation from God. Creation is not self-sustaining, but is at all times held together by God. If at any moment he removed his preserving power from hell, it would sink back into nonexistence. Therefore, in light of both his omnipresence and his preservation of creation, one cannot accept the popular description of hell as separation from God without first qualifying exactly what that separation entails.

If a person cannot escape God's presence, then he cannot escape the Holy Spirit who is the active presence of God in creation. The world was created at the command of the Father through the Son in the power of the Spirit. According to Pannenberg, "The presence of God with his creatures wherever they are has first the form of the creative presence of his Spirit by which he calls them into existence and upholds them in it."[46] As the Son creates, he does so in conjunction with the Spirit who actualizes his work. The Spirit is hovering over the waters in Gen 1:2, waiting to bring order out of chaos. Likewise, it is the Spirit that gives life to Adam. In addition to the Spirit conveying God's creative presence, he also conveys God's punishing presence. Psalm 139:7–12 is a cry from David that there is no place he can go from God's Spirit, from his presence.[47] The inability to escape

44. Garrett, *Systematic Theology*, 1:200.

45. Grudem, *Systematic Theology*, 175.

46. Pannenberg, *Systematic Theology*, 1:414.

47. Kraus, *Psalms 60–150*, 515.

"God's presence by his Spirit means that God is present even with those who turn from him, though it might seem to those who do so that he is absent from them. The presence of the Holy Spirit of God will mean judgment for them."[48]

Paul, in his second letter to the Thessalonians, offers comfort and encouragement by showing the church that when Christ returned he would repay those who had been persecuting them. In 2 Thess 1:9 he wrote, "They will suffer the punishment of eternal destruction, away from the presence of the Lord and from the glory of His might."

While the ESV, NASB, and NIV all translate this verse so that the person is excluded from the Lord's presence and power, the verse can also be interpreted so that the "from" should be taken as causal and not spatial, with the meaning being that the presence (literally face) and power of the Lord brings about the eternal destruction of those opposed to God. Both Psalm 34:16 and Jer 4:26 show that God's face is set in opposition to evil and brings about destruction. A similar idea is also expressed in 2 Thess 2:8 in which Jesus will destroy the lawless one by the breath of his mouth and the appearance of his coming.

Malhere concludes that the translation of the ESV and NASB is correct, but that the translation offered above is probable. He also highlights two other interpretations that have been offered. The first is that "from" should be understood temporally, so that the destruction takes place immediately after the Lord returns. The second interpretation is that "from" should be understood so that the face of the Lord is the source of the destruction. This interpretation is similar to the one offered above.[49]

Ellingworth and Nida argue that in order for the passive expression "separated from" to be intelligible, it needs to be shown who does the separating and from what the person is separated.[50] Gene Green argues that the correct translation is that the presence of the Lord is the source from which the destruction comes. He cites Num 16:46, Judg 5:5, Pss 34:16 and 96:13, Jer 4:6, Ezek 38:20, Rev 6:16 and 20:11 as verses in which the Lord's presence is associated with judgment. "The destruction they will suffer will be *from the majesty of his power*. This *majesty* is the visible 'glory' of God and is synonymous with his presence (Rom 1:23; Jude 24)."[51] Edward Fudge

48. Pannenberg, *Systematic Theology*, 1:414.

49. Malhere, *Letters to the Thessalonians*, 402–03.

50. Ellingworth and Nida, *Translator's Handbook*, 149.

51. Green, *Letters to the Thessalonians*, 292–93.

correctly argues that both interpretations can be accepted. Those opposed to God are both excluded from his presence and excluded by his presence. The statement from Paul is a quote from Isa 2:10, 19, and 21 in which the enemies are described three times as fleeing from God when he appears. "They flee because of dread of the Lord, but also away from His approaching terror."[52] Fudge's dual translation makes sense in connection with the Spirit's dual role in judgment, in that he both excludes people from God's presence, while at the same time being the means whereby the exclusion is maintained.

The most recognized verse in the Bible is John 3:16. It tells of God's great love for the world, a love so great that the Father sent his only Son in order to save the world so that no one who believes in the Son will perish. At the end of the third chapter of John is a verse that is not quite so popular, that sits in the shadow of God's love cast from v. 16. John 3:36 reiterates that those who believe in the Son will not perish, but have eternal life; however, it does not end there, instead moving on to those who refuse to believe, to those who prefer darkness over light. Those who will not obey the Son will not see life, but instead the wrath of God remains on them. According to John 3:18 the final judgment is manifested presently in both those who believe and disbelieve. The one who does not believe in the Son is condemned already. As stated earlier, this present judgment gains its bearing and validity from the eschatological judgment, but it is nonetheless a present judgment upon the unbeliever.

Romans 1:18 records that God's wrath is currently being revealed from heaven against all those who suppress the truth in unrighteous. While it is true that those who stand in opposition to God are storing up wrath for themselves in the day of his righteous judgment, that future wrath is also presently exhibited and operative against them. At the final judgment, when the verdict has been read and all those not found in the Book of Life are cast into hell, God's wrath will still abide upon them.

As already shown, the Holy Spirit actualizes God's wrath to humanity in the present time and he will also continue to actualize his wrath to those who refused to accept his love in this life. The rejection of God's love is the condition for his wrath—a wrath that abides, a wrath that excludes the person from God's beneficial presence and leaves him encountering God outside of Christ. The only way to avoid the wrathful God is to flee from God to God, to flee from wrath to love, to accept the sacrifice of Christ, the

52. Fudge, *Fire that Consumes*, 246–47.

one who drank the dregs of the cup of the wine of God's fierce wrath so that humanity does not have to drink that cup. For those who refuse Christ, who reject God's reconciling love, they themselves must drink the cup of God's wrath. For those who reject Christ and the love he offers in the Spirit, they must encounter the Spirit as God's rejected love, as his wrath.

Conclusion

All the persons in the Trinity are involved in all the works of the Godhead, but as stated earlier, it is appropriate to highlight the individual work of each member in order to elucidate the Trinitarian structure of God's unified work. The Holy Spirit's work has been greatly neglected in the area of salvation, especially in the atonement and the judgment that the Son undertook on behalf of humanity. This neglect stems from an unwillingness to ascribe a condemnatorial role to the Spirit, and has thus led to an atonement in which only the Father and the Son are involved. The Spirit's role has for the most part begun at the point where salvation is offered to a person, and then the Spirit is only operative within those who believe. For the person who rejects God's offer of salvation the Spirit plays little, if any role.

The present chapter has sought to correct this theological lacuna by showing how the Spirit is related to condemnation, first in relation to Christ on the cross as humanity's substitute and then for those people who refuse to accept his vicarious atonement. Initially, it was shown that the Holy Spirit is the mutual-love of the Father and the Son. From this understanding of the Spirit as love, it was further shown how God's love and wrath are intimately connected. The conclusion was then reached that the Holy Spirit actualizes God's wrath to fallen creation.

On the cross, Christ experienced God's wrath as he endured the judgment that was rightly due to sinners. In this event, the Holy Spirit was both the bond of love that maintained the unity within the Trinity, and he also applied God's judgment to the Son as evidenced by Jesus' cry of dereliction. From Jesus' experience of judgment on the cross, the logical connection between those who reject Christ and the Holy Spirit was established. Hell is not separation from God, but is instead being in a relationship of rejection of God's love, which thus places a person under God's abiding wrath that is actualized by the Spirit.

Conclusion

GOD'S GOOD CREATION IS not right. Things are not the way they are supposed to be and because of that there must be a judgment upon those parts of creation that are not in harmony with God. Since the Fall humanity has tried to stake out creation as its own, to claim ownership to what only God has a right. In order to redeem this fallen world God must judge those elements within it that stand in opposition to him. While the idea of judgment is often unpleasant, even for those who long for the vindication and liberation that judgment will bring, it is a necessity in light of both God's holiness and his love. He cannot abandon his very good creation to the effects of sin and rebellion, for his love compels him to enter into the fallenness of creation in order to restore that which was lost, to bring his creation back to a state of "very good."

Unfortunately, the idea of judgment has become taboo in the current cultural climate. People have become unwilling to discuss how God intends to eradicate evil from his creation. Many cannot countenance a barbarous god who delights in the suffering of his creation. They have misunderstood biblical judgment and replaced it with a warped image because they have neglected to condition God's judgment with his love. Others have adopted a postmodern mind-set that refuses to judge anyone at any time. While this view is prevalent in theory, it is often shattered upon the reality of evil and the need to condemn those elements within the culture that are destructive. Some have rejected the idea of a divine being to which all people are accountable and have therefore removed the need for an ultimate judgment; while others have argued that we are evolving ever closer to God and that the final judgment is over those parts of humanity that were useful at one time but no longer serve a purpose. All of the reasons for avoiding judgment fail to deal with the reality of a holy God that is presented in the Bible. It is therefore imperative in this time in which judgment is kept under wraps that Christians proclaim that God is holy and that he is coming to rescue his creation that has fallen into darkness. There is hope for a brighter day because he loves his creation and will not allow evil to have the final say.

Because God is supreme in every sense he stands alone in the process of judging creation. He makes the laws for the world. The laws however, are not arbitrary, but are direct reflections of God's nature. Additionally, he seeks out injustice in the world in order to restore justice. He is active in his judgment as he liberates those who are oppressed. The United States governmental system, with its division of powers, can serve in an illustrative manner to show how God executes all three branches of power. He is the legislator, the enforcer of laws, and the judge who passes sentence. All judgment has been given to the Son by the Father, and the Son executes his judgment in the power of the Spirit.

The Bible utilizes numerous symbols for judgment, and four of the most prominent are fire, God's breath, his arm/hand, and his wrath. Each symbol of judgment serves in both a condemning and a redeeming capacity. Fire is both salvific and destructive depending upon the person's relationship to it. The same is true for God's breath and his hand/arm. God's wrath cannot be separated from his love for it is his love that necessitates his wrath. God is love, but he has wrath toward the evil in the world precisely because he loves the world.

In judgment God reveals his character. He shows both his holiness and his love. Judgment is also a vindication of God's rightful ownership of creation. Humanity in its arrogance and pride has attempted to establish itself as the rightful owner of creation. God cannot allow this rebellion to stand because ultimately it brings destruction to his creation. Instead, he enters into creation to judge those elements that are incongruous with his nature, and in so doing he purifies that which has been contaminated. He restores it to its original condition of being very good. Of course, to purify creation he must remove those elements that refuse to be purified, that stand in defiant opposition to his claim upon creation, and, in this case judgment is not purificatory but condemnatory. Nevertheless, as God judges his entire creation he does so in love. The judgment of God is a lament!

God's judgment is a triune work in which the Father gives all judgment into the hands of the Son. The Son then executes judgment in the

Spirit's power. It was shown in the second chapter how the Bible supports the thesis that the Spirit actualizes the judgment of the Father given to the Son. This was accomplished by highlighting those passages in the book of Judges where the Spirit empowered men to liberate Israel through military campaigns. It was also demonstrated from the book of Acts that the Spirit executed the judgment upon Ananias, Sapphira, and Elymas.

To further support the above thesis, the Messiah's role of bringing justice to creation was correlated with his anointing by the Spirit to carry out his task. Isaiah repeatedly mentioned the coming Messiah who would be anointed by the Spirit to proclaim both the favorable year of the Lord and the day of his fierce vengeance. It is by a Spirit of judgment and burning that God will purge his creation of all evil. Jesus told his disciples that the Holy Spirit would convict the world of sin, righteousness, and judgment. He would continue the work that Jesus had been doing while he was on the earth. Finally, the opposition that Paul established between the flesh and the Spirit, in which believers are commanded to put to death the deeds of the flesh by the Spirit, reveals that it is by the Spirit that the old nature is judged and destroyed.

A correlation was established between the symbols of judgment presented in the second chapter and the Holy Spirit. First, the relationship between the Holy Spirit and fire was established. From this connection, in which the Holy Spirit is described as fire, it was shown that there was a further connection between the Holy Spirit as fire and the fires of judgment. John the Baptist proclaimed that Jesus would baptize in the Holy Spirit and fire. This single baptism involves all people, both those who are redeemed and those who are condemned. All will be baptized in the Holy Spirit and fire, which, it was argued, was a single agent, with the outcome of that baptism depending upon the person's relationship to Jesus. The Holy Spirit actualizes the holy fire of God's presence and this fire purifies and purges, redeems and destroys.

In a similar manner, God's breath also stands as a symbol for both judgment and the Holy Spirit. The Holy Spirit is symbolized as God's breath in the insufflation in John 20:22, in the God-breathed nature of Scripture, and in Ezekiel's vision of the valley of dry bones. With the Spirit established as God's breath, a link with numerous passages that connect his breath with condemnatorial judgment was shown. God's breath withers the grass of the field, purges evil from creation, and removes life from people. The tendency to translate *ruach* in those passages that deal with condemnation as "breath" was shown to be driven by a presupposition that the Spirit is not involved in judgment, when instead a better translation would have been "Spirit" in many cases.

Like fire and God's breath, his finger/hand/arm symbolize his judgment upon creation. Furthermore, it was shown that all three symbols are used in reference to the Holy Spirit and his work in actualizing the judgment of the Son. Jesus cast out demons by the finger of God, and in that act of liberation, the oppressing demon was condemned.

The Holy Spirit is the mutual-love of the Father and the Son. He is also the outgoing love of the Trinity to creation. He is the point of spiritual contact between God and humanity. Because he is the bond of love, he is also the point of contact for the actualizing of God's wrath toward humanity. God's wrath is predicated upon his love; it is the converse of his love. God displays wrath to those parts of creation that stand against his love and his desire to restore his very good creation. This person experiences wrath as the absence of the benefits of God, as his displeasure. Just as the love of God is poured into people's hearts by the Holy Spirit, so too is God's wrath poured out upon people by the Holy Spirit.

Before the wrong impression is given that God is a sadist, it must be made clear that God endured his own wrath in order to offer humanity a means whereby they can pass from under his wrath to stand justified in his love. The Father sent the Son in the power of the Spirit to redeem creation on the cross. In the humiliation of the Son, God is able to be both just and the justifier of those who come to him in Christ. On the cross, Jesus endured God's wrath as actualized by the Spirit as the entire Trinity worked to bring redemption to fallen humanity. The atonement offered in Christ is truly a work of all three persons of the Godhead. The elucidation of the Spirit's role serves to highlight further the great lengths to which God has gone at great price to himself to demonstrate his love for his people.

As much as God pours out his love, however, there are those who will refuse to accept it. Instead, they will defiantly maintain their rights to rule their own life. They will continue to claim ownership of that which is not theirs. In the final judgment those people who refuse to accept God must of necessity face the judgment due their rebellion. In popular terms hell has been described as separation from God, but it was shown that while this phrase can be useful it must be qualified in that nothing can exist apart from God's sustaining presence. It is the Holy Spirit, as the sustaining power of the Godhead, who actualizes the judgment of condemnation upon those who refuse to accept God's rightful place in their life. When one refuses the light, all that is left is the darkness.

The thesis of this work was that the Holy Spirit executes the judgment, both redemptive and condemnatory, of the Father given to the Son. While the thesis was proven, there is still room for further work to be done. Both judgment and pneumatology are enormous doctrines, and this work has only scratched the surface of the implications involved in connecting the two doctrines together. Hopefully the scratches offered by this work will be picked up by others who will cut each scratch deeper and wider as they attempt to broaden our understanding of God. The Triune God has entered into judgment with his fallen creation. The Father has given the task of judging the world to the Son and has empowered him by the Holy Spirit, who actualizes his judgment to creation.

Bibliography

Alden, Robert L. *Job*. The New American Commentary 11. Nashville: Broadman & Holman, 1993.

Alexander, Joseph A. *Commentary on Isaiah*. Grand Rapids: Kregel, 1996.

Allen, Leslie C. *Ezekiel 1–19*. Word Biblical Commentary 28. Dallas: Word Books, 1994.

———. *Ezekiel 20–48*. Word Biblical Commentary 29. Dallas: Word Books, 1990.

Aloisi, John. "The Paraclete's Ministry of Conviction: Another Look at John 16:8–11." *Journal of the Evangelical Theological Society* 47 (2004) 55–69.

Aloysia, M. "The God of Wrath?" *Catholic Biblical Quarterly* 8 (1946) 407–15.

Althaus, Paul. *The Theology of Martin Luther*. Translated by Robert C. Schultz. Philadelphia: Fortress, 1966.

Ambrose. *Exposition of the Holy Gospel According to Saint Luke: With Fragments on the Prophecy of Isaias*. Translated by Theodosia Tomkinson. Etna, CA: Center for Traditionalist Orthodox Studies, 1998.

Arndt, William F. "The Wrath of God and the Grace of God in Lutheran Theology." *Concordia Theological Monthly* 23 (1952) 569–82.

Attridge, Harold W. *The Epistle to the Hebrews: A Commentary on the Epistle to the Hebrews*. Edited by Helmut Koester. Hermeneia—a Critical and Historical Commentary on the Bible. Philadelphia: Fortress, 1989.

Augustine, Saint, Bishop of Hippo. "On the Holy Trinity." Translated by Arthur West Haddan. In vol. 3 of *A Select Library of the Nicene and Post-Nicene Fathers of the Christian Church*, edited by Philip Schaff, 2–228. Grand Rapids: Eerdmans, 1978.

———. *Tractates on the Gospel of John 55–111*. Translated by John W. Rettig. The Fathers of the Church: A New Translation 90. Washington, DC: Catholic University of America, 1995.

———. *The Trinity*. Translated by Edmund Hill. Edited by John E. Rotelle. The Works of Saint Augustine 5. Brooklyn: New City, 1991.

Aulén, Gustaf. *Christus Victor: An Historical Study of the Three Main Types of the Idea of the Atonement*. Translated by A. G. Hebert. London: SPCK, 1970.

———. *The Faith of the Christian Church*. Translated by Eric H. Wahlstrom. Philadelphia: Fortress, 1973.

Aune, David. *Revelation*. Word Biblical Commentary 52. Dallas: Word Books, 1997.

BIBLIOGRAPHY

Badcock, Gary D. *Light of Truth and Fire of Love: A Theology of the Holy Spirit*. Grand Rapids: Eerdmans, 1997.

Baird, J. Arthur. *The Justice of God in the Teaching of Jesus*. Philadelphia: Westminster, 1963.

Baloian, Bruce Edward. *Anger in the Old Testament*. New York: Peter Lang, 1992.

Barnett, Paul. *The Second Epistle to the Corinthians*. The New International Commentary on the New Testament. Grand Rapids: Eerdmans, 1997.

Barrett, C. K. *The Holy Spirit and the Gospel Tradition*. London: SPCK, 1966.

Barth, Karl. *The Doctrine of Reconciliation*. Translated by Geoffrey W. Bromiley. Vol. 4, part 1, *Church Dogmatics*, edited by G. W. Bromiley and T. F. Torrance. Edinburgh: T & T Clark, 1956.

———. *The Epistle to the Romans*. Translated by Edwyn Clement Hoskyns. 6th ed. London: Oxford University Press, 1933.

Barth, Markus. *Ephesians*. 1st ed. Garden City, NY: Doubleday, 1974.

Basil, Saint, Bishop of Caesarea. *On the Holy Spirit*. Translated by David Anderson. Crestwood, NY: St. Vladimir's Seminary Press, 1980.

Baxter, Christina. "The Cursed Beloved: A Reconsideration of Penal Substitution." In *Atonement Today*, edited by John Goldingay, 54–72. London: SPCK, 1995.

Beale, G. K. *The Book of Revelation: A Commentary on the Greek Text*. Grand Rapids: Eerdmans, 1999.

Beasley–Murray, George Raymond. *Baptism in the New Testament*. London: Macmillan, 1962.

———. *John*. Word Biblical Commentary 36. Waco, TX: Word Books, 1987.

Bell, Rob. *Love Wins: A Book About Heaven, Hell, and the Fate of Every Person Who Ever Lived*. New York: HarperOne, 2011.

Benson, Alphonsus. *The Spirit of God in the Didactic Books of the Old Testament*. Washington: Catholic University of America Press, 1949.

Bergen, Robert D. *1, 2 Samuel*. The New American Commentary 7. Nashville: Broadman & Holman, 1996.

Berkhof, Hendrikus. *Christian Faith: An Introduction to the Study of the Faith*. Translated by Sierd Woudstra. Grand Rapids: Eerdmans, 1979.

———. *The Doctrine of the Holy Spirit*. Richmond: John Knox, 1964.

Berkhof, Louis. *Systematic Theology*. 4th ed. Grand Rapids: Eerdmans, 1949.

———. *Vicarious Atonement through Christ*. Grand Rapids: Eerdmans, 1936.

Bernstein, Alan E. *The Formation of Hell: Death and Retribution in the Ancient and Early Christian Worlds*. Ithaca: Cornell University Press, 1993.

Best, Ernest. *A Commentary on the First and Second Epistles to the Thessalonians*. New York: Harper & Row, 1972.

———. *Ephesians: A Shorter Commentary*. London: T & T Clark, 2003.

———. "Spirit–Baptism." *Novum Testamentum* 4 (1960) 236–43.

Betz, Hans Dieter. *Galatians: A Commentary on Paul's Letter to the Churches in Galatia*. Hermeneia—a Critical and Historical Commentary on the Bible. Philadelphia: Fortress, 1979.

Blenkinsopp, Joseph. *Isaiah 1–39: A New Translation with Introduction and Commentary*. Anchor Bible 19. New York: Doubleday, 2000.

———. *Isaiah 56–66: A New Translation with Introduction and Commentary*. Anchor Bible 19b. New York: Doubleday, 2003.

Block, Daniel Isaac. *The Book of Ezekiel*. The New International Commentary on the Old Testament. Grand Rapids: Eerdmans, 1997.

———. "Empowered by the Spirit of God: The Holy Spirit in the Historiographic Writings of the Old Testament." *Southern Baptist Journal of Theology* 1 (1997) 42–61.

———. *Judges, Ruth*. The New American Commentary 6. Nashville: Broadman & Holman, 1999.

———. "The Prophet of the Spirit: The Use of Ruach in the Book of Ezekiel." *Journal of the Evangelical Theological Society* 32 (1989) 27–49.

Bloesch, Donald G. *The Last Things: Resurrection, Judgment, Glory*. Downers Grove, IL: InterVarsity, 2004.

Blomberg, Craig. *Matthew*. New American Commentary 22. Nashville: Broadman & Holman, 1992.

Böcher, Otto. "γέεννα." In vol. 2 of *Exegetical Dictionary of the New Testament*, edited by Horace Balz and Gerhard Schneider, 239–40. Grand Rapids: Eerdmans, 1990.

Bock, Darrell L. *Luke 1:1—9:50*. Baker Exegetical Commentary on the New Testament. Grand Rapids: Baker, 1994.

———. *Luke: 9:51—24:5*. Baker Exegetical Commentary on the New Testament, Grand Rapids: Baker, 1996.

Borchert, Gerald L. *John 12–21*. The New American Commentary 25b. Nashville: Broadman & Holman, 2002.

Boulnois, Marie Odile. "Le Souffle Et L'esprit: Exegèses Patristiques De L'insufflation Originelle De Gn 2, 7 En Lien Avec Celle De Jn 20, 22." *Recherches Augustiniennes* 24 (1989) 3–37.

Brandon, S. G. F. *The Judgment of the Dead: An Historical and Comparative Study of the Idea of a Post-Mortem Judgment in the Major Religions*. London: Weidenfeld & Nicolson, 1967.

Briggs, Charles A. *The Messiah of the Gospels*. New York: Scribner's, 1894.

Bromiley, Geoffrey William. "Atone." In vol. 1 of *The International Standard Bible Encyclopedia*, edited by Geoffrey William Bromiley, 352. Grand Rapids: Eerdmans, 1979.

Brown, Raymond Edward. *The Gospel According to John*. Garden City, NY: Doubleday, 1966.

———. *The Gospel According to John (XIII–XXI)*. Anchor Bible 29a. New York: Doubleday, 1970.

Brownlee, William H. *Ezekiel 1–19*. Word Biblical Commentary 28. Dallas: Word Books, 1986.

Bruce, A. B. *Matthew*. Grand Rapids: Eerdmans, 1967.

Bruce, F. F. *The Epistle to the Galatians: A Commentary on the Greek Text*. New International Greek New Testament Commentary. Grand Rapids: Eerdmans, 1982.

———. *The Epistle to the Hebrews: The English Text with Introduction, Exposition, and Notes*. New International Commentary on the New Testament. Grand Rapids: Eerdmans, 1964.

Brueggemann, Walter. *1 & 2 Kings*. Smyth & Helwys Bible Commentary. Macon, GA: Smyth & Helwys, 2000.

———. *First and Second Samuel*. Interpretation: A Bible Commentary for Teaching and Preaching. Louisville: John Knox, 1990.

———. *Isaiah*. Westminster Bible Companion. 2 vols. 1st ed. Louisville: Westminster John Knox, 1998.

Brunner, Emil. *The Christian Doctrine of God*. Vol. 1, *Dogmatics*. Translated by Olive Wyon. Philadelphia: Westminster, 1946.

———. *Eternal Hope*. Translated by Harold Knight. London: Lutterworth, 1954.

———. *Man in Revolt: A Christian Anthropology*. Translated by Olive Wyon. Philadelphia: Westminster, 1947.

———. *The Mediator: A Study of the Central Doctrine of the Christian Faith*. Translated by Olive Wyon. London: Lutterworth, 1934.

Buis, Harry. *The Doctrine of Eternal Punishment*. Grand Rapids: Baker, 1957.

Bulgakov, Sergius Nikolaevich. *The Comforter*. Translated by Boris Jakim. Grand Rapids: Eerdmans, 2004.

Bultmann, Rudolf Karl. *The Gospel of John: A Commentary*. Translated by G. R. Beasley-Murray. Edited by R. W. N. Hoare and J. K. Riches. Philadelphia: Westminster, 1971.

———. *The History of the Synoptic Tradition*. Translated by John Marsh. Rev. ed. Oxford: Basil Blackwell, 1968.

Burgess, Stanley. *The Holy Spirit: Medieval Roman Catholic and Reformation Traditions*. Peabody, MA: Hendrickson, 1997.

———. *The Spirit and the Church: Antiquity*. Peabody, MA: Hendrickson, 1984.

Burrow, Rufus, Jr. "The Love, Justice, and Wrath of God." *Encounter* 59 (1998) 379–407.

Calvin, John. *Acts of the Council of Trent with the Antidote*. Translated by Henry Beveridge. Vol. 3. Grand Rapids: Eerdmans, 1958.

———. *Commentaries on the Book of the Prophet Daniel*. Translated by Thomas Myers. Vol. 1. Grand Rapids: Eerdmans, 1948.

———. *Commentary on the Book of Psalms*. Translated by James Anderson. Vol. 1. Grand Rapids: Eerdmans, 1949.

———. *Commentary on the Epistles of Paul the Apostle to the Corinthians*. Translated by William Pringle. Vol. 1. Grand Rapids: Eerdmans, 1957.

———. *Commentaries on the Epistles to Timothy, Titus, and Philemon*. Translated by William Pringle. Grand Rapids: Eerdmans, 1948.

———. *Commentary on the Prophet Isaiah*. Translated by William Pringle. 4 vols. Edinburgh: Calvin Translation Society, 1850–1948.

———. *Commentary Upon the Acts of the Apostles*. Translated by Christopher Fetherstone and Henry Beveridge. Grand Rapids: Eerdmans, 1949.

———. *Zechariah and Malachi*. Translated by John Owen. Commentaries on the Twelve Minor Prophets 5. Grand Rapids: Eerdmans, 1950.

Cambier, J. M. "Le Jugement De Tous Hommes Par Dieu Seul, Selon La Verite, Dans Rom 2:1–3." *Zeitschrift für Die Neutstamentliche Wissenschaft und Die Kunde Alteren Kirche* 67 (1976) 187–213.

Campbell, Alastair V. "The Anger of a Loving God." *Modern Churchman* 25 (1983) 2–11.

Capon, Robert Farrar. *The Parables of Judgment*. Grand Rapids: Eerdmans, 1989.

Carroll, B. H., J. W. Crowder, and J. B. Cranfill. *The Day of the Lord*. Nashville: Broadman & Holman, 1936.

Carson, D. A. *The Difficult Doctrine of the Love of God*. Wheaton, IL: Crossways, 2000.

———. "The Function of the Paraclete in John 16:7–11." *Journal of Biblical Literature* 98 (1979) 547–66.

———. "God Is Love." *Bibliotheca Sacra* 156 (1999) 131–42.

———. "God's Love and God's Sovereignty." *Bibliotheca Sacra* 156 (1999) 259–71.

———. "God's Love and God's Wrath." *Bibliotheca Sacra* 156 (1999) 387–98.

———. *The Gospel According to John*. Grand Rapids: InterVarsity, 1991.

————. "On Distorting the Love of God." *Bibliotheca Sacra* 156 (1999) 3–12.

Cave, Sydney. *The Doctrine of the Work of Christ*. London: University of London Press, 1937.

Charles, R. H. *Eschatology: The Doctrine of a Future Life in Israel, Judaism and Christianity*. New York: Schocken, 1963.

Childs, Brevard S. *Exodus: A Commentary*. The Old Testament Library. London: SCM, 1974.

Chrysostom, John. *The Homilies of S. John Chrysostom, Archbishop of Constantinople, on the Gospel of St. Matthew*. Translated by George Prevost. Library of Fathers of the Holy Catholic Church 1. Oxford: John Henry Parker, 1843.

Clements, Keith W. "Atonement and the Holy Spirit." *The Expository Times* 95 (1984) 168–71.

Clines, David J. A. *Job 1–20*. Word Biblical Commentary 17. Dallas: Word Books, 1989.

Coffey, David. *Deus Trinitas: The Doctrine of the Triune God*. New York: Oxford University Press, 1999.

————. "The Holy Spirit as the Mutual Love of the Father and the Son." *Theological Studies* 51 (1990) 193–229.

Cole, Graham. *He Who Gives Life: The Doctrine of the Holy Spirit*. Wheaton, IL: Crossway, 2007.

Collins, John Joseph. *Daniel*. Hermenia: A Critical and Historical Commentary on the Bible. Minneapolis: Fortress, 1993.

Collins, John Joseph, Bernard McGinn, and Stephen J. Stein. *Apocalypticism in Western History and Culture*. Vol. 3, *Encyclopedia of Apocalypticism*. New York: Continuum, 1998.

Compere, Robert L. Jr. "The Biblical Doctrine of the Wrath of God in Contemporary Theology." MA thesis, Southwestern Baptist Theological Seminary, 1957.

Cone, James. *A Black Theology of Liberation*. New York: Lippincott, 1970.

Congar, Yves. *I Believe in the Holy Spirit*. Translated by David Smith. Milestones in Catholic Theology. New York: Crossroad, 1997.

————. *The Word and the Spirit*. Translated by David Smith. San Francisco: Harper & Row, 1986.

Conner, Walter Thomas. *Christian Doctrine*. Nashville: Broadman, 1937.

————. *The Gospel of Redemption*. Nashville: Broadman, 1945.

————. *The Work of the Holy Spirit: A Treatment of the Biblical Doctrine of the Divine Spirit*. Nashville: Broadman, 1949.

Cooper, Lamar Eugene. *Ezekiel*. The New American Commentary 17. Nashville: Broadman & Holman, 1994.

Couroyer, B. "Le 'Doigt de Dieu' (Exode 8:15)." *Revue Biblique* 63 (1956) 481–95.

Cranfield, C. E. B. *The Gospel According to Saint Mark*. Cambridge Greek New Testament Commentary. Cambridge: University Press, 1963.

————. "Romans 1.18." *Scottish Journal of Theology* 21 (1968) 330–35.

Crockett, William V., et al. *Four Views on Hell*. Grand Rapids: Zondervan, 1992.

————. "Wrath that Endures Forever." *Journal of the Evangelical Theological Society* 34 (1991) 195–202.

Cullmann, Oscar. *Christ and Time: The Primitive Christian Conception of Time and History*. Translated by Floyd V. Filson. Philadelphia: Westminster, 1964.

Cunningham, David S. *These Three Are One: The Practice of Trinitarian Theology*. Challenges in Contemporary Theology. Malden, MA: Blackwell, 1998.

Cyril, Saint, Patriarch of Alexandria. *Matthew 1–13*. Edited by Manlio Simonetti. Ancient Christian Commentary on Scripture. Downers Grove, IL: InterVarsity, 2001.

Davies, D. R. *Divine Judgment in Human History*. London: Sheldon, 1943.

Davies, W. D., and Dale C. Allison. *A Critical and Exegetical Commentary on the Gospel According to Saint Matthew*. The International Critical Commentary. Edinburgh: T & T Clark, 1988.

Davis, Stephen T. "Universalism, Hell, and the Fate of the Ignorant." *Modern Theology* 6 (1990) 173–86.

Delitzsch, Franz Julius. *Biblical Commentary on the Prophecies of Isaiah*. Translated by James Denney. London: Hodder and Stoughton, 1891.

Devor, Richard Campbell. *The Concept of Judgment in the Epistles of Paul*. Ann Harbor: University Microfilms International, 1959.

Dhorme, E. *A Commentary on the Book of Job*. Translated by Harold Knight. London: Nelson, 1967.

Dixon, Larry. *The Other Side of the Good News*. Wheaton, IL: Victor, 1992.

Dodd, C. H. *The Epistle of Paul to the Romans*. New York: Long & Smith, 1932.

Dostoyevsky, Fyodor. *The Brothers Karamazov*. Translated by Constance Garnett. New York: Random House, 1948.

Downer, Arthur Cleveland. *The Mission and Ministration of the Holy Spirit*. Edinburgh: T & T Clark, 1909.

Driggers, Samuel Wyatt. "Development of the Moral Influence of the Atonement." MA thesis, Southwestern Baptist Theological Seminary, 1934.

Dumbrell, William J. "Spirit and Kingdom of God in the Old Testament." *Reformed Theological Review* 33 (1974) 1–10.

Dunn, James D. G. *The Acts of the Apostles*. 1st US ed. Narrative Commentaries. Valley Forge: Trinity Press International, 1996.

———. *Baptism in the Holy Spirit: A Re-examination of the New Testament Teaching on the Gift of the Spirit in Relation to Pentecostalism Today*. Studies in Biblical Theology. Naperville, IL: A. R. Allenson, 1970.

———. "Birth of a Metaphor: Baptized in the Spirit." *Expository Times* 89 (1978) 134–38.

———. *The Epistle to the Galatians*. Black's New Testament Commentaries. London: Hendrickson, 1993.

———. *Jesus Remembered*. Christianity in the Making 1. Grand Rapids: Eerdmans, 2003.

———. *Jesus and the Spirit: A Study of the Religious and Charismatic Experience of Jesus and the First Christians as Reflected in the New Testament*. Philadelphia: Westminster, 1975.

———. "Matthew 12:28/Luke 11:20—a Word of Jesus?" In *Eschatology and the New Testament: Essays in Honor of George Raymond Beasley-Murray*, edited by W. Hulitt Gloer, 29–49. Peabody, MA: Hendrickson, 1988.

———. "Spirit-and-Fire Baptism." *Novum Testamentum* 14 (1972) 81–92.

Durham, John. *Exodus*. Word Biblical Commentary 3. Waco, TX: Word Books, 1987.

Eichrodt, Walther. *Ezekiel: A Commentary*. Translated by Cosslett Quin. The Old Testament Library. Philadelphia: Westminster, 1970.

———. *Theology of the Old Testament*. Translated by J. A. Baker. Philadelphia: Westminster, 1961.

Eisler, Robert. *The Messiah Jesus and John the Baptist According to Flavius Josephus' Recently Rediscovered "Capture of Jerusalem" and Other Jewish and Christian Sources*. Translated by Alexander Haggerty Krappe. London: Metheun, 1931.

Ellingworth, Paul. *The Epistle to the Hebrews: A Commentary on the Greek Text*. The New International Greek Testament Commentary. Grand Rapids: Eerdmans, 1993.

Ellingworth, Paul, and Eugene A. Nida. *A Translator's Handbook on Paul's Letters to the Thessalonians*. Help for Translators. New York: United Bible Societies, 1976.

Ellis, E. Earle, ed. *The Gospel of Luke*. New Century Bible. London: Nelson, 1967.

Erickson, Millard J. *Christian Theology*. 2nd ed. Grand Rapids: Baker, 1998.

———. *God in Three Persons: A Contemporary Interpretation of the Trinity*. Grand Rapids: Baker, 1995.

———. *Making Sense of the Trinity: 3 Crucial Questions*. Grand Rapids: Baker, 2000.

Erlandsson, Seth. "The Wrath of ΥΗΨΗ." *Tyndale Bulletin* 23 (1972) 111–16.

Farrar, Frederic William. *Mercy and Judgment: A Few Last Words on Christian Eschatology, with Reference to Dr. Pusey's "What Is of Faith?"* New York: Dutton, 1881.

Fee, Gordon D. *The First Epistle to the Corinthians*. New International Commentary on the New Testament. Grand Rapids: Eerdmans, 1987.

———. *God's Empowering Presence: The Holy Spirit in the Letters of Paul*. Peabody, MA: Hendrickson, 1994.

Ferguson, Sinclair B. *The Holy Spirit*. Contours in Christian Theology. Downers Grove: InterVarsity, 1996.

Fernando, Ajith. *Crucial Questions About Hell*. Wheaton, IL: Crossway, 1991.

Feuerbach, Ludwig. *The Essence of Christianity*. Translated by George Eliot. New York: Harper and Brothers, 1957.

Finamore, Steve. "The Gospel and the Wrath of God in Romans 1." In *Understanding, Studying and Reading: New Testament Essays in Honour of John Ashton*, edited by Christopher Rowland and Crispin H. T. Fletcher-Louis, 137–55. Journal for the Study of the New Testament Supplemental Series 153. Sheffield, England: Sheffield Academic Press, 1998.

Fishbane, Michael A. "Sin and Judgment in the Prophecies of Ezekiel." *Interpretation* 38 (1984) 131–50.

Fitzmeyer, Joseph. *The Gospel According to Luke*. Anchor Bible 28a. Garden City, NY: Doubleday, 1985.

———. *The Gospel According to Luke*. Anchor Bible 28b. Garden City, NY: Doubleday, 1981.

Flowers, H. J. "ἐν πνευματι ἀγίῳ καὶ πυρί." *The Expository Times* 64 (1953) 155–56.

Fortman, Edmund J. *The Triune God: A Historical Study of the Doctrine of the Trinity*. Philadelphia: Westminster, 1972.

Fredricks, Gary. "Rethinking the Role of the Holy Spirit in the Lives of Old Testament Believers." *Trinity Journal* 9 (1988) 81–104.

Fretheim, Terence E. "Theological Reflections on the Wrath of God in the Old Testament." *Horizons in Biblical Theology* 24 (2002) 1–26.

Fudge, Edward William. "The Final End of the Wicked." *Journal of the Evangelical Theological Society* 27 (1984) 325–34.

———. *The Fire that Consumes: A Biblical and Historical Study of Final Punishment*. Houston: Providential, 1982.

Fudge, Edward William, and Robert A. Peterson. *Two Views of Hell: A Biblical & Theological Dialogue*. Downers Grove, IL: InterVarsity, 2000.

Fulgentius, Saint, Bishop of Ruspa. *Selected Works: Fulgentius*. Translated by Robert Eno. Fathers of the Church: A New Translation 95. Washington, DC: Catholic University of America Press, 1997.

Garland, David E. *2 Corinthians*. The New American Commentary 29. Nashville: Broadman & Holman, 1999.

Garrett, James Leo, Jr. *Systematic Theology: Biblical, Historical, and Evangelical*. Vol. 1. 2nd ed. Grand Rapids: Eerdmans, 2000.

————. *Systematic Theology: Biblical, Historical, and Evangelical*. Vol. 2. Grand Rapids: Eerdmans, 1995.

Geldenhuys, Norval. *Commentary on the Gospel of Luke*. Grand Rapids: Eerdmans, 1988.

George, Augustin. *Etudes Sur L'oeuvre De Luc*. Paris: Gabalda, 1978.

George, Timothy. *Galatians*. The New American Commentary 30. Nashville: Broadman & Holman, 1994.

Giblin, Charles Homer. *The Threat to Faith: An Exegetical and Theological Reexamination of 2 Thessalonians* 2. Anelecta Biblica. Rome: Pontifical Biblical Institute, 1967.

Ginsberg, H. L. "The Arm of YHWH in Isaiah 51–63 and the Text of Isa 53:10–11." *Journal of Biblical Literature* 77 (1958) 152–56.

Godet, Friedrich Louis. *Commentary on 1 Corinthians*. Grand Rapids: Kregel, 1977.

Goldingay, John E. *Daniel*. Word Biblical Commentary 30. Dallas: Word Books, 1989.

Goodrick, Edward W. "Let's Put 2 Timothy 3:16 Back in the Bible." *Journal of the Evangelical Theological Society* 25 (1982) 479–87.

Green, Gene L. *The Letters to the Thessalonians*. Pillar New Testament Commentary. Grand Rapids: Eerdmans, 2002.

Green, Joel B. *The Gospel of Luke*. The New International Commentary of the New Testament. Grand Rapids: Eerdmans, 1997.

Green, Joel B., and Mark D. Baker. *Recovering the Scandal of the Cross: Atonement in New Testament & Contemporary Contexts*. Downers Grove, IL: InterVarsity, 2000.

Grenz, Stanley. "The Holy Spirit: Divine Love Guiding Us Home." *Ex Auditu* 12 (1996) 1–13.

————. *Theology for the Community of God*. Nashville: Broadman & Holman, 1994.

Griffiths, John Gwyn. *The Divine Verdict: A Study of Divine Judgment in the Ancient Religions*. Studies in the History of Religions 52. New York: E. J. Brill, 1991.

Grislis, Egil. "Luther's Understanding of the Wrath of God." *Journal of Religion* 41 (1961) 277–92.

Grudem, Wayne A. *Systematic Theology: An Introduction to Biblical Theology*. Grand Rapids: Zondervan, 1994.

Gundry, Robert. *Matthew: A Commentary on His Handbook for a Mixed Church under Persecution*. Grand Rapids: Eerdmans, 1994.

Gunton, Colin E. *The Promise of Trinitarian Theology*. 2nd ed. London: T & T Clark, 2003.

Habel, Norman C. *The Book of Job: A Commentary*. The Old Testament Library. Philadelphia: Westminster, 1985.

Haenchen, Ernst. *The Acts of the Apostles: A Commentary*. Translated by Bernard Noble and Gerald Shinn. Philadelphia: Westminster, 1971.

Hamerton-Kelly, Robert G. "A Note on Matthew 12:28 par Luke 11:20." *New Testament Studies* 11 (1965) 167–69.

Haney, Herbert M. *The Wrath of God in the Former Prophets*. 1st ed. New York: Vantage, 1960.

Hanson, Anthony Tyrell. *The Wrath of the Lamb*. London: SPCK, 1957.

Hanson, R. P. C. *The Attractiveness of God: Essays in Christian Doctrine*. Richmond, VA: John Knox, 1973.

————. *God: Creator, Saviour, Spirit*. Naperville, IL: SCM, 1960.

Harrelson, Walter. "Famine in the Perspective of Biblical Judgments and Promises." *Soundings* 59 (1976) 84–99.

———. "A Meditation on the Wrath of God: Psalm 90." In *Scripture in History & Theology: Essays in Honor of J. Coert Rylaarsdam*, edited by Arthur L. Merrill and Thomas W. Overholt, 181–92. Pittsburgh: Pickwick, 1977.

Hartley, John E. *The Book of Job*. The New International Commentary on the Old Testament. Grand Rapids: Eerdmans, 1988.

Hendriksen, William. *Exposition of the Gospel According to Matthew*. New Testament Commentary. Grand Rapids: Baker, 1977.

———. *Exposition of the Pastoral Epistles*. New Testament Commentary. Grand Rapids: Baker, 1957.

Herntrich, Volkmar. "Κρίνω." Translated by Geoffrey W. Bromiley. In vol. 3 of *Theological Dictionary of the New Testament*, edited by Gerhard Friedrich, 921–41. Grand Rapids: William B. Eerdmans, 1965.

Heschel, Abraham Joshua. *The Prophets*. 1st ed. New York: Harper & Row, 1962.

Hildebrandt, Wilf. *An Old Testament Theology of the Spirit of God*. Peabody, MA: Hendrickson, 1995.

Hodge, Charles. *Systematic Theology*. vol. 1. New York: Scribner's, 1909.

Hoekema, Anthony A. *The Bible and the Future*. Grand Rapids: Eerdmans, 1979.

Hoeksema, Herman. *Reformed Dogmatics*. Grand Rapids: Reformed Free Publishing, 1966.

Hoffmeier, James K. "The Arm of God Versus the Arm of Pharaoh in the Exodus Narratives." *Biblica* 67 (1986) 378–87.

House, H. Wayne. "Biblical Inspiration in 2 Timothy 3:16." *Bibliotheca Sacra* 137 (1980) 54–63.

Hoyt, Samuel L. "The Judgment Seat of Christ in Theological Perspective." *Bibliotheca Sacra* 137 (1980) 32–40.

———. "The Negative Aspects of the Christian's Judgment." *Bibliotheca Sacra* 137 (1980) 125–32.

Hughes, Philip Edgcumbe. *Paul's Second Epistle to the Corinthians: The English Text with Introduction, Exposition and Notes*. The New International Commentary on the New Testament. Grand Rapids: Eerdmans, 1962.

Irenaeus, Saint, Bishop of Lyon. *The Apostolic Fathers: Justin Martyr, Irenaeus*. Vol. 1, *The Ante-Nicene Fathers: Translations of the Writings of the Fathers Down to A.D. 325*. Grand Rapids: Eerdmans, 1981.

Isaacs, Marie E. *The Concept of Spirit: A Study of Pneuma in Hellenistic Judaism and Its Bearing on the New Testament*. Edited by Michael J. Walsh. Heythrop Monographs. London: Heythrop College, 1976.

Jensen, Joseph. *Isaiah 1–39*. Old Testament Message 8. Wilmington, NC: M. Glazier, 1984.

Jensen, Peter. "The Good News of God's Wrath: At the Heart of the Universe, There Is a Just and Gracious God." *Christianity Today* 48 (2004) 45–47.

Jenson, Robert W. *The Triune God*. Vol. 1, *Systematic Theology*. Oxford: Oxford University Press, 1997.

———. *The Works of God*. Vol. 2, *Systematic Theology*. Oxford: Oxford University Press, 1999.

Jeremias, Joachim. "γέεννα." Translated by Geoffrey W. Bromiley. In vol. 1 of *Theological Dictionary of the New Testament*, edited by Gerhard Friedrich, 657–58. Grand Rapids: Eerdmans, 1964.

Jerome. *Isaiah 1–39*. Edited by Steven A. McKinion. Ancient Christian Commentary on Scripture 10. Downers Grove, IL: InterVarsity, 2004.

Johnson, Luke Timothy. *The Acts of the Apostles*. Sacra Pagina 5. Collegeville, MN: Liturgical Press, 1992.

Johnston, George. "The Doctrine of the Holy Spirit in the New Testament." *Scottish Journal of Theology* 1 (1948) 47–55.

Johnstone, William. *1 and 2 Chronicles*. Edited by David J. A. Clines and Philip R. Davies. Journal for the Study of the Old Testament: Supplement Series 253. Sheffield: Sheffield Academic Press, 1997.

Kaiser, Otto. *Isaiah 1–12: A Commentary*. Translated by John Bowden. 2nd ed. Philadelphia: Westminster, 1983.

———. *Isaiah 13–39: A Commentary*. Translated by R. A. Wilson. Philadelphia: Westminster, 1974.

Kapelrud, Arvid S. "God as Destroyer in the Preaching of Amos and in the Ancient Near East." *Journal of Biblical Literature* 71 (1952) 33–38.

Kärkkäinen, Veli–Matti. *Pneumatology: The Holy Spirit in Ecumenical, International, and Contextual Perspective*. Grand Rapids: Baker Academic, 2002.

Keener, Craig S. *The Gospel of John: A Commentary*. Peabody, MA: Hendrickson, 2003.

———. *Matthew*. The IVP New Testament Commentary. Downers Grove, IL: InterVarsity, 1997.

Keil, Carl Friedrich, and Franz Julius Delitzsch. *Biblical Commentary on the Prophecies of Ezekiel*. Grand Rapids: Eerdmans, 1950.

———. *Isaiah*. Translated by James Perry Martin. Biblical Commentary on the Old Testament 7. Grand Rapids: Eerdmans, 1978.

———. *Joshua, Judges, Ruth*. Translated by James Perry Martin. Biblical Commentary on the Old Testament 4. Grand Rapids: Eerdmans, 1950.

Kelly, J. N. D. *Early Christian Doctrines*. Rev. ed. San Francisco: Harper & Row, 1978.

Kelly, R. A. "Righteousness." In vol. 4 of *The International Standard Bible Encyclopedia*, edited by Geoffrey W. Bromiley, 2591–93. Grand Rapids: Eerdmans, 1988.

Kienzler, Jonathan. *The Fiery Holy Spirit: The Spirit's Relationship with Judgment in Luke–Acts*. Journal of Pentecostal Theology Supplement Series 44. Dorset: Deo, 2015.

Kistemaker, Simon. *Exposition of the Epistle to the Hebrews*. New Testament Commentary. Grand Rapids: Baker, 1984.

Klassen, William. "Vengeance in the Apocalypse of John." *The Catholic Biblical Quarterly* 28 (1966) 300–311.

Klein, Ralph W. *1 Samuel*. Word Biblical Commentary 10. Waco, TX: Word Books, 1983.

Klingbeil, Gerald A. "The Finger of God in the Old Testament." *Zeitschrift für die Alttestamentliche Wissenschaft* 112 (2000) 409–15.

Knight, G. A. F. *A Biblical Approach to the Doctrine of the Trinity*. Edited by T. F. Torrance and J. K. S. Reid. Scottish Journal of Theology, Occasional Paper 1. Edinburgh: Oliver and Boyd, 1953.

Koch, Klaus. "Is There a Doctrine of Retribution in the Old Testament?" Translated by Thomas H. Trapp. In *Theodicy in the Old Testament*, edited by James L. Crenshaw, 57–87. Issues in Religion and Theology 4. Philadelphia: Fortress, 1983.

———. *Revelation*. New Testament Commentary. Grand Rapids: Baker, 1953.

Koester, Craig R. *Hebrews: A New Translation with Introduction and Commentary*. 1st ed. Anchor Bible 36. New York: Doubleday, 2001.

Kraeling, Carl H. *John the Baptist*. New York: Scribner's, 1951.

Kraus, Hans-Joachim. *Psalms 1–59: A Continental Commentary.* Translated by Hilton C. Oswald. 1st Fortress ed. Minneapolis: Fortress, 1993.

———. *Psalms 60–150: A Commentary.* Translated by Hilton C. Oswald. Minneapolis: Augsburg, 1989.

Kuyper, Abraham. *The Work of the Holy Spirit.* Translated by Henri De Vries. New York: Funk & Wagnalls, 1900.

Lacoque, Andre. *The Book of Daniel.* Translated by David Pellauer. Atlanta: John Knox, 1979.

Ladd, George Eldon. *A Commentary on the Revelation of John.* Grand Rapids: Eerdmans, 1972.

———. *A Theology of the New Testament.* Grand Rapids: Eerdmans, 1974.

La Due, William J. *The Trinity Guide to the Trinity.* Harrisburg, PA: Trinity Press, 2003.

Lampe, G. W. H. "The Holy Spirit in the Writings of St. Luke." In *Studies in the Gospels: Essays in Memory of R. H. Lightfoot*, edited by D. E. Nineham, 159–200. Oxford: Blackwell, 1955.

———. *The Seal of the Spirit: A Study in the Doctrine of Baptism and Confirmation in the New Testament and the Fathers.* 2nd ed. London: SPCK, 1967.

Lane, Tony. "The Wrath of God as an Aspect of the Love of God." In *Nothing Greater, Nothing Better: Theological Essays on the Love of God*, edited by Kevin J. Vanhoozer, 138–67. Grand Rapids: Eerdmans, 2001.

Lane, William L. *The Gospel According to Mark: The English Text with Introduction, Exposition, and Notes.* The New International Commentary on the New Testament. Grand Rapids: Eerdmans, 1974.

———. *Hebrews 9–13.* Word Biblical Commentary 47b. Dallas: Word Books, 1991.

Lang, Friedrich. "πυρ." Translated by Geoffrey W. Bromiley. In vol. 6 of *Theological Dictionary of the New Testament*, edited by Gerhard Friedrich, 928–52. Grand Rapids: Eerdmans, 1968.

Latvus, Kari. *God, Anger and Ideology.* Edited by David J. A. Clines and Phillip R. Davies. Sheffield Journal for the Study of the Old Testament Supplemental Series. England: Sheffield Academic Press, 1998.

Lenski, R. C. H. *Interpretation of the Gospel of Luke.* Minneapolis: Augsburg, 1961.

———. *The Interpretation of Saint Matthew.* Minneapolis: Augsburg, 1943.

Letham, Robert. *The Holy Trinity: In Scripture, History, Theology, and Worship.* Phillipsburg, NJ: P & R, 2004.

Lewis, C. S. *Mere Christianity.* New York: Simon & Schuster, 1996.

———. *The Problem of Pain.* New York: Macmillan, 1957.

Lincoln, Andrew. *Ephesians.* Word Biblical Commentary 42. Dallas: Word Books, 1990.

Lind, Millard C. *Yahweh Is a Warrior: The Theology of Warfare in Ancient Israel.* Scottsdale, AZ: Herald, 1980.

Lischer, Richard. "Embarrassed by God's Wrath." *Dialog* 33 (1994) 259–62.

Locke, Jason W. "The Wrath of God in the Book of Isaiah." *Restoration Quarterly* 35 (1993) 221–33.

Lockyer, Herbert. *The Breath of God.* Cleveland: Union Gospel, 1949.

Lohse, Bernhard. *Martin Luther's Theology: Its Historical and Systematic Development.* Translated by Roy A. Harrisville. Minneapolis: Fortress, 1999.

Longenecker, Richard N. *Galatians.* Word Biblical Commentary 41. Dallas: Word Books, 1990.

Luther, Martin. *Lectures on Genesis: Chapters 6–14*. Vol. 2, *Luther's Works*. Translated by George V. Schick. Saint Louis: Concordia, 1960.

———. *Lectures on the Minor Prophets 2: Jonah and Habakkuk*. Vol. 19, *Luther's Works*. Translated by Charles D. Froehlich. Saint Louis: Concordia, 1974.

———. *Selected Psalms II*. Vol. 13, *Luther's Works*. Translated by Paul M. Bretscher. Saint Louis: Concordia, 1956.

———. *Selected Psalms III*. Vol. 14, *Luther's Works*. Translated by Jaroslav Pelikan. Saint Louis: Concordia, 1958.

———. *Sermon on the Mount and the Magnificat*. Vol. 21, *Luther's Works*. Translated by Jaroslav Pelikan. Saint Louis: Concordia, 1956.

Luyster, Robert. "Wind and Water: Cosmogonic Symbolism in the Old Testament." *Zeitschrift für die Alttestamentliche Wissenschaft* 93 (1981) 1–10.

Ma, Wonsuk. *Until the Spirit Comes: The Spirit of God in the Book of Isaiah*. Journal for the Study of the Old Testament Supplement Series. Sheffield: Sheffield Academic Press, 1999.

MacGregor, George Hogarth Carnaby. "Concept of the Wrath of God in the New Testament." *New Testament Studies* 7 (1961) 101–9.

Mafico, Temba L. "Judge, Judging." In vol. 3 of *The Anchor Bible Dictionary*, edited by David Noel Freedman, 1104–6. New York: Doubleday, 1992.

Malhere, Abraham J. *The Letters to the Thessalonians: A New Translation with Introduction and Commentary*. Anchor Bible 32b. New York: Doubleday, 2000.

Manson, Thomas Walter. *The Sayings of Jesus: As Recorded in the Gospels According to St. Matthew and St. Luke*. 1st American ed. London: SCM, 1949.

de Margerie, Bertrand. *The Christian Trinity in History*. Translated by Edmund J. Fortman. Still River: St. Bede's, 1982.

Marguerat, Daniel. "La Mort D'ananias Et Saphira (Ac 5:1–11) Dans La Stratégie Narrative De Luc." *New Testament Studies* 39 (1993) 209–26.

Marsh, F. E. *Emblems of the Holy Spirit*. Grand Rapids: Kregel, 1963.

Marshall, I. Howard. *The Gospel of Luke: A Commentary on the Greek Text*. The New International Greek New Testament Commentary. Exeter, UK: Paternoster, 1978.

———. "Meaning of the Verb 'to Baptize.'" *Evangelical Quarterly* 45 (1973) 130–40.

Martin, D. Michael. *1, 2 Thessalonians*. The New American Commentary 33. Nashville: Broadman & Holman, 1995.

Martin, James Perry. *The Last Judgment: In Protestant Theology from Orthodoxy to Ritschl*. Grand Rapids: Eerdmans, 1963.

Martyn, J. Louis. *Galatians: A New Translation with Introduction and Commentary*. The Anchor Bible 33a. New York: Doubleday, 1997.

Mason, Steven. "Fire, Water and Spirit: John the Baptist and the Tyranny of Canon." *Studies in Religion* 21 (1992) 163–80.

Matthews, Kenneth A. *Genesis 1—11:26*. The New American Commentary 1a. Nashville: Broadman and Holman, 1996.

Matthews, Victor Harold. *Judges and Ruth*. New Cambridge Bible Commentary. Cambridge: Cambridge University Press, 2004.

McDonald, H. D. *The Atonement of the Death of Christ: In Faith, Revelation, and History*. Grand Rapids: Baker, 1985.

McDonnell, Kilian, and George T. Montague. *Christian Initiation and Baptism in the Holy Spirit: Evidence from the First Eight Centuries*. Collegeville, MN: Liturgical Press, 1991.

McGinn, Bernard. "The Last Judgment in Christian Tradition." In *Apocalypticism in Western History and Culture*. Vol. 2, *The Encyclopedia of Apocalypticism*, ed. Bernard McGinn, John J. Collins, and Stephen J. Stein, 361–401. New York: Continuum, 1999.

McGrath, Alister. *Luther's Theology of the Cross: Martin Luther's Theological Breakthrough*. Oxford: Blackwell, 1985.

McGuiggan, Jim. *Celebrating the Wrath of God: Reflections on the Agony and the Ecstasy of His Relentless Love*. 1st ed. Colorado Springs: Waterbrook, 2001.

Meador, Marion Frank. "The Motif of God as Judge in the Old Testament." Ph.D. diss., Southwestern Baptist Theological Seminary, 1986.

Meier, John P. *A Marginal Jew*. Vol 2, *Mentor, Message, and Miracles*. The Anchor Bible Reference Library 2. New York: Doubleday, 1994.

Micka, Ermin Francis. *The Problem of Divine Anger in Arnobius and Lactantius*. Washington, DC: Catholic University of America Press, 1943.

Miller, Patrick D. *The Divine Warrior in Early Israel*. Cambridge: Harvard University Press, 1973.

———. *Sin and Judgment in the Prophets: A Stylistic and Theological Analysis*. Society of Biblical Literature Monograph Series. Chico, CA: Scholars Press, 1982.

Min, Anselm Kyongsuk. "The Dialectic of Divine Love: Pannenberg's Hegelian Trinitarianism." *International Journal of Systematic Theology* 6 (2004) 252–69.

Mitchell, T. C. "The Old Testament Usage of Nešama." *Vetus Testamentum* 11 (1961) 177–87.

Moltmann, Jürgen. *The Coming of God: Christian Eschatology*. Translated by Margaret Kohl. 1st Fortress ed. Minneapolis: Fortress, 1996.

———. *The Crucified God: The Cross of Christ as the Foundation and Criticism of Christian Theology*. Translated by R. A. Wilson and John Bowden. 1st Fortress ed. Minneapolis: Fortress, 1993.

———. *The Source of Life: The Holy Spirit and the Theology of Life*. Translated by Margaret Kohl. 1st Fortress ed. Minneapolis: Fortress, 1997.

———. *The Spirit of Life: A Universal Affirmation*. Translated by Margaret Kohl. Minneapolis: Fortress, 1993.

———. *The Trinity and the Kingdom of God*. Translated by Margaret Kohl. Minneapolis: Fortress, 1993.

Montague, George T. *The Holy Spirit: Growth of a Biblical Tradition*. New York: Paulist, 1976.

Moo, Douglas. *The Epistle to the Romans*. The New International Commentary on the New Testament. Grand Rapids: Eerdmans, 1996.

Moody, Dale. *Spirit of the Living God: The Biblical Concepts Interpreted in Context*. Philadelphia: Westminster, 1968.

Morris, Leon. *The Apostolic Preaching of the Cross*. London: Tyndale, 1965.

———. *The Biblical Doctrine of Judgment*. 1st ed. Grand Rapids: Eerdmans, 1960.

———. *The Cross in the New Testament*. Grand Rapids: Eerdmans, 1965.

———. *The Epistle to the Romans*. The Pillar New Testament Commentary. Grand Rapids: Eerdmans, 1988.

———. *The First and Second Epistles to the Thessalonians*. Rev. ed. The New International Commentary on the New Testament. Grand Rapids: Eerdmans, 1991.

———. *The Gospel According to John*. Rev. ed. The New International Commentary on the New Testament. Grand Rapids: Eerdmans, 1995.

———. *The Gospel According to Matthew*. The Pillar New Testament Commentary. Grand Rapids: Eerdmans, 1992.

———. "The Wrath of God." *Expository Times* 63 (1952) 142–45.

Motyer, J. A. *The Prophecy of Isaiah: An Introduction & Commentary*. Downers Grove, IL: InterVarsity, 1993.

Mounce, Robert H. *The Book of Revelation*. Rev. ed. The New International Commentary on the New Testament. Grand Rapids: Eerdmans, 1998.

———. *Romans*. The New American Commentary 27. Nashville: Broadman & Holman, 1995.

Mounce, William D. *Pastoral Epistles*. Word Biblical Commentary. Nashville: Thomas Nelson, 2000.

Myers, Jacob Martin, trans. *1 Chronicles*. 1st ed. The Anchor Bible 12. Garden City, NY: Doubleday, 1965.

Neve, Lloyd R. *The Spirit of God in the Old Testament*. Tokyo: Seibunsha, 1972.

Niebuhr, H. Richard. *The Kingdom of God in America*. Middletown: Wesleyan University Press, 1988.

Nielsen, Kirsten. *Yahweh as Prosecutor and Judge: An Investigation of the Prophetic Lawsuit (Rib–Pattern)*. Translated by Frederick Cryer. Journal for the Study of the Old Testament. Sheffield, England: JSOT, 1978.

Nietzsche, Friedrich. *The Gay Science*. Translated by Walter Kaufmann. New York: Vintage Books, 1974.

Nolland, John. *Luke*. Word Biblical Commentary 35. Dallas: Word Books, 1989.

———. *Luke 9:21—18:34*. Word Biblical Commentary 35b. Dallas: Word Books, 1993.

———. *Matthew*. The New International Greek New Testament Commentary. Grand Rapids: Eerdmans, 2005.

Nysse, Richard. "The Dark Side of God: Considerations for Preaching and Teaching." *Word & World* 17 (1997) 437–46.

Oakes, Robert A. "The Wrath of God." *International Journal for Philosophy of Religion* 27 (1990) 129–40.

O'Brien, Peter Thomas. *The Letter to the Ephesians*. The Pillar New Testament Commentary. Grand Rapids: Eerdmans, 1999.

Oden, Thomas C. *Life in the Spirit*. Systematic Theology 3. San Francisco: Harper San Francisco, 1992.

O'Donovan, Oliver. *The Desire of the Nations: Rediscovering the Roots of Political Theology*. New York: Cambridge University Press, 1996.

Origen. *Homilies on Luke. Fragments on Luke*. Translated by Jospeh T. Lienhard. The Fathers of the Church 94. Washington, DC: Catholic University of America Press, 1996.

———. *On First Principles: Being Koetschau's Text of the De Principiis Translated into English, Together with an Introduction and Notes*. Gloucester: Peter Smith, 1973.

Orr, William, and James Arthur Walther. *1 Corinthians: A New Translation*. 1st ed. The Anchor Bible 32. Garden City, NY: Doubleday, 1976.

Osborn, Eric Francis. *Irenaeus of Lyons*. Cambridge: Cambridge University Press, 2001.

Osborne, Grant R. *Revelation*. Baker Exegetical Commentary on the New Testament. Grand Rapids: Baker Academic, 2002.

Oswalt, John. *The Book of Isaiah: Chapters 1–39*. The New International Commentary on the Old Testament. Grand Rapids: Eerdmans, 1986.

————. *The Book of Isaiah: Chapters 40–66*. The New International Commentary of the Old Testament. Grand Rapids: Eerdmans, 1998.

O'Toole, Robert F. "'You did Not Lie to Us (Human Beings) but to God' (Acts 5, 4c)." *Biblica* 76 (1995) 182–209.

Owen, John. *The Holy Spirit: His Gifts and Power*. Grand Rapids: Kregel, 1954.

Packer, James I. "What Did the Cross Achieve: The Logic of Penal Substitution." *Tyndale Bulletin* 25 (1974) 3–45.

Pannenberg, Wolfhart. *Systematic Theology*. Translated by Geoffrey W. Bromiley. Vol. 1. Grand Rapids: Eerdmans, 1991.

————. *Systematic Theology*. Translated by Geoffrey W. Bromiley. Vol. 3. Grand Rapids: Eerdmans, 1993.

————. *What Is Man? Contemporary Anthropology in Theological Perspective*. Translated by Duane A. Priebe. Philadelphia: Fortress, 1970.

Patterson, Paige. "Reflections on the Atonement." *Criswell Theological Review* 3 (1989) 307–20.

Patzia, Arthur Gerald. "Did John the Baptist Preach a Baptism of Fire and the Holy Spirit?" *The Evangelical Quarterly* 40 (1968) 21–27.

Paulson, Steven D. "The Wrath of God." *Dialog* 33 (1994) 245–51.

Peterson, Eugene. "Why Did Uzzah Die? Why Did David Dance?: 2 Sam 6–7." *Crux* 31 (1995) 3–8.

Phillips, Gary. "Religious Pluralism in a Postmodern World." In *The Challenge of Postmodernism: An Evangelical Engagement*, edited by David Dockery, 131–43. Grand Rapids: Baker, 1995.

Pinnock, Clark H. *Flame of Love: A Theology of the Holy Spirit*. Downers Grove, IL: InterVarsity, 1996.

Pinnock, Clark H., and Robert C. Brow. *Unbounded Love: A Good News Theology for the 21st Century*. Downers Grove, IL: InterVarsity, 1994.

Pittenger, W. Norman. *The Holy Spirit*. Philadelphia: United Church, 1974.

Poetker, Katrina. "The Wrath of Yahweh." *Direction* 16 (1987) 55–61.

Polhill, John B. *Acts*. The New American Commentary 26. Nashville: Broadman & Holman, 1992.

Raabe, Paul R. *Obadiah: A New Translation with Introduction and Commentary*. The Anchor Bible 24d. New York: Doubleday, 1996.

————. "The Particularizing of Universal Judgment in Prophetic Discourse." *The Catholic Biblical Quarterly* 64 (2003) 652–74.

Rahner, Karl. *The Trinity*. Translated by Jospeh Donceel. Milestones in Catholic Theology. New York: Crossroad, 2005.

Rashdall, Hastings. *The Idea of Atonement in Christian Theology*. London: Macmillan, 1920.

Ratzinger, Joseph. "The Holy Spirit as Communio: Concerning the Relationship of Pneumatology and Spirituality in Augustine." *Communio* 25 (1998) 324–39.

Read, David H. C. "Cry of Dereliction." *Expository Times* 68 (1957) 260–62.

Reyburn, William David. *A Handbook on the Book of Job*. UBS Handbook Series. New York: United Bible Societies, 1992.

Richardson, Kurt A. *James*. New American Commentary 36. Nashville: Broadman & Holman, 1997.

Ridderbos, Herman N. *The Gospel According to John: A Theological Commentary*. Grand Rapids: Eerdmans, 1997.

———. *Matthew*. Translated by Ray Togtman. Bible Student's Commentary. Grand Rapids: Zondervan, 1987.

Ridderbos, J. *Isaiah*. Translated by John Vriend. Grand Rapids: Regency Reference Library, 1985.

Rissi, M. "κρίνω." In vol. 2 of *Exegetical Dictionary of the New Testament*, edited by Horace Balz and Gerhard Schneider, 317–21. Grand Rapids: Eerdmans, 1981.

Robbins, Jerry K. "God's Wrath: A Process Exposition." *Dialog* 33 (1994) 252–58.

Robinson, W. "The Judgment of God." *The Scottish Journal of Theology* 4 (1951) 136–47.

Rodd, Cyril S. "Spirit or Finger." *Expository Times* 72 (1961) 157–58.

Roetzel, Calvin J. *Judgement in the Community: A Study of the Relationship between Eschatology and Ecclesiology in Paul*. Leiden, Netherlands: Brill, 1972.

Rosato, Philip J. *The Spirit as Lord: The Pneumatology of Karl Barth*. Edinburgh: T & T Clark, 1981.

Schleiermacher, Friedrich. *The Christian Faith*. Translated by H. R. Mackintosh and James Stuart Stewart. Edinburgh: T & T Clark, 1928.

———. *Servant of the Word: Selected Sermons of Friedrich Schleiermacher*. Translated by Dawn De Vries. Fortress Texts in Modern Theology. Philadelphia: Fortress, 1987.

Schnackenburg, Rudolf. *Ephesians: A Commentary*. Translated by Helon Heron. Edinburgh: T & T Clark, 1991.

———. *The Gospel According to St. John*. Translated by David Smith and G. A. Kon. Herder's Theological Commentary on the New Testament 3. New York: Crossroad, 1982.

———. *The Gospel of Matthew*. Translated by Robert R. Barr. Grand Rapids: Eerdmans, 2002.

Schneider, Tammi. *Judges*. Berit Olam. Collegeville, MN: Liturgical Press, 2000.

Schneider, W. "Judgment, Judge, Deliver, Judgment Seat." In *The New International Dictionary of New Testament Theology*, edited by Colin Brown, 362–67. Grand Rapids: Zondervan, 1977.

Schoemaker, William Ross. "The Use of Rûah in the Old Testament, and of Pneuma in the New Testament." *Journal of Biblical Literature* 23 (1904) 13–67.

Schwarz, Hans. *Eschatology*. Grand Rapids: Eerdmans, 2000.

———. "Twelfth Locus: Eschatology." In *Christian Dogmatics*, edited by Carl E. Braaten and Robert W. Jenson, 471–588. Philadelphia: Fortress, 1984.

Schweizer, Eduard. *The Holy Spirit*. Philadelphia: Fortress, 1980.

———. "With the Holy Ghost and Fire." *The Expository Times* 65 (1953) 29.

Scobie, Charles Hugh Hope. *John the Baptist*. Philadelphia: Fortress, 1964.

Smeaton, George. *The Doctrine of the Holy Spirit*. London: Banner of Truth, 1958.

Snaith, Norman H. *The Distinctive Ideas of the Old Testament*. London: Epworth, 1962.

Snodgrass, Klyne. "The Holy Spirit." *Ex Auditu* 12 (1996) 1–165.

Stahlin, Gustav. "ὀργη." Translated by Geoffrey W. Bromiley. In vol. 5 of *Theological Dictionary of the New Testament*, edited by Gerhard Friedrich, 382–447. Grand Rapids: Eerdmans, 1967.

Stein, Robert H. *Luke*. New American Commentary. Nashville: Broadman & Holman, 1992.

Stewart, James Stuart. *A Man in Christ: The Vital Elements of St. Paul's Religion*. New York: Harper, 1963.

Stibbe, Mark. *Fire and Blood: The Work of the Spirit, the Work of the Cross*. London: Monarch, 2001.

Stott, John R. W. *The Cross of Christ*. Downers Grove, IL: InterVarsity, 1986.

Strong, Augustus Hopkins. *Systematic Theology*. Vol. 3. Philadelphia: Judson, 1909.

Stronstad, Roger. "Unity and Diversity: New Testament Perspectives on the Holy Spirit." *Paraclete* 23 (1989) 15–28.

Swete, Henry Barclay. *The Holy Spirit in the New Testament: A Study of Primitive Christian Teaching*. London: Macmillan, 1910.

Swetnam, James. "Bestowal of the Spirit in the Fourth Gospel." *Biblica* 74 (1993) 556–76.

Talbert, Charles H. *Reading Luke: A Literary and Theological Commentary on the Third Gospel*. New York: Crossroad, 1982.

Tannehill, Robert C. *Luke*. Abingdon New Testament Commentaries. Nashville: Abingdon, 1996.

Tasker, R. V. G. *The Biblical Doctrine of the Wrath of God*. London: Tyndale, 1951.

Taylor, Joan E. *The Immerser: John the Baptist within Second Temple Judaism*. Grand Rapids: Eerdmans, 1997.

Taylor, Vincent. *The Gospel According to St. Mark*. New York: St. Martin's, 1966.

Taylor, Willard H. "Baptism with the Holy Spirit: Promise of Grace or Judgment?" *Wesleyan Theological Journal* 12 (1977) 16–25.

Tennant, Frederick. *The Origin and Propagation of Sin*. Cambridge: Cambridge University Press, 1902.

Thielicke, Helmut. *Prolegomena: The Relation of Theology to Modern Thought Forms*. Translated and edited by Geoffrey W. Bromiley. Vol. 1, *The Evangelical Faith*. Grand Rapids: Eerdmans, 1974.

———. *Theology of the Spirit*. Translated and edited by Geoffrey W. Bromiley. Vol. 3, *The Evangelical Faith*. Grand Rapids: Eerdmans, 1974.

Thompson, J. A. *1, 2 Chronicles*. The New American Commentary 9. Nashville: Broadman & Holman, 1994.

Thompson, John. *The Holy Spirit in the Theology of Karl Barth*. Princeton Theological Monograph Series. Allison Park, PA: Pickwick, 1991.

———. *Modern Trinitarian Perspectives*. New York: Oxford University Press, 1994.

Thrall, Margaret. *The Second Epistle to the Corinthians*. The International Critical Commentary. Edinburgh: T & T Clark, 1994.

Tillich, Paul. *Systematic Theology*. Vol. 1. Chicago: University of Chicago Press, 1951.

Torrey, R. A. *The Person and Work of the Holy Spirit as Revealed in the Scriptures and in Personal Experience*. New York: Fleming H. Revell, 1910.

Travis, Stephen H. *Christ and the Judgment of God: Divine Retribution in the New Testament*. Foundations for Faith. Southampton: Marshall, Morgan, and Scott, 1986.

———. *Christian Hope and the Future*. Downers Grove, IL: InterVarsity, 1980.

———. "Judgment." In *The IVP Dictionary of the New Testament*, edited by Daniel G. Reid, 624–33. Downers Grove, IL: InterVarsity, 2004.

———. *The Jesus Hope*. Downers Grove, IL: InterVarsity, 1974.

Tur-Sinai, Naphtali H. *The Book of Job: A New Commentary*. Jerusalem: Kiryath Sepher, 1957.

Van Cangh, Jean-Marie. "Par L'esprit De Dieu—Par Le Doigt De Dieu: Mt 12:28 Par Lc 11:20." In *Logia*, edited by J. Delobel, 337–42. Leuven: Leuven University Press, 1982.

van der Horst, Peter W. "'The Finger of God.' Miscellaneous Notes on Luke 11:20 and Its *Umwelt*." In *Sayings of Jesus: Canonical and Non-Canonical: Essays in Honour of Tjitze Baarda Leiden*, edited by William Lawrence Petersen, Johan S. Vos, and Henk J. de Jonge, 89–104. New York: Brill, 1997.

Vanhoozer, Kevin J. *Nothing Greater, Nothing Better: Theological Essays on the Love of God.* Grand Rapids: Eerdmans, 2001.

Van Iersel, B. M. F. "He Will Baptize You with Holy Spirit (Mark 1, 8)." In *Text and Testimony: Essays on New Testament and Apocryphal Literature in Honour of A. F. J. Klijn*, edited by T. Baarda, 132–41. Kampen, Netherlands: Uitgeversmaatschappij J. H. Kok, 1988.

van Rossum, Joost. "The "Johannine Pentecost": John 20:22 in Modern Exegesis and in Orthodox Theology." *St Vladimir's Theological Quarterly* 35 (1991) 149–67.

Vos, Geerhardus. *The Pauline Eschatology.* Grand Rapids: Eerdmans, 1952.

Wall, Robert W. "The Finger of God: Deuteronomy 9:10 and Luke 11:20." *New Testament Studies* 33 (1987) 144–50.

Walvoord, John F. *The Holy Spirit: A Comprehensive Study of the Person and Work of the Holy Spirit.* Wheaton, IL: Van Kampen, 1954.

Ware, Bruce A. *Father, Son, and Holy Spirit: Relationships, Roles, and Relevance.* Wheaton, IL: Crossway, 2005.

Warfield, Benjamin Breckinridge. *The Inspiration and Authority of the Bible.* Philadelphia: Presbyterian and Reformed, 1948.

Webb, Robert. "The Activity of John the Baptist's Expected Figure at the Threshing Floor (Matthew 3.12=Luke 3.17)." *Journal for the Study of the New Testament* 43 (1991) 103–11.

———. *John the Baptizer and Prophet: A Socio-Historical Study.* Sheffield, England: JSOT, 1991.

Weber, Otto. *Foundations of Dogmatics.* Translated by Darrell L. Guder. Vol. 1. Grand Rapids: Eerdmans, 1981.

Weinfeld, Moshe. *Deuteronomy 1–11: A New Translation with Introduction and Commentary.* 1st ed. The Anchor Bible 5. New York: Doubleday, 1991.

Welch, Claude. *In This Name: The Doctrine of the Trinity in Contemporary Theology.* New York: Scribner, 1952.

Welker, Michael. *God the Spirit.* Translated by John F. Hoffmeyer. 1st English-language ed. Minneapolis: Fortress, 1994.

Wenham, John William. *The Goodness of God.* London: InterVarsity, 1974.

Westall, M. R. "Scope of the Term 'Spirit of God' in the Old Testament." *Indian Journal of Theology* 26 (1977) 29–43.

Westermann, Claus. *Isaiah 40–66: A Commentary.* Translated by David M. G. Stalker. The Old Testament Library. Philadelphia: Westminster, 1969.

Wildberger, Hans. *Isaiah 1–12: A Continental Commentary.* Translated by Thomas H. Trapp. Minneapolis: Fortress, 1996.

———. *Isaiah 28–39: A Continental Commentary.* Translated by Thomas H. Trapp. Minneapolis: Fortress, 2002.

Williams, Gary J. "Penal Substitution: A Response to Recent Criticisms." *Journal of the Evangelical Theological Society* 50 (2007) 71–86.

Williams, Janet. "Judging Judgment: An Apophatic Approach." *Theology Today* 58 (2002) 541–53.

———. "Speaking Judgment: An Investigation into Some Theological Resources." *Theology Today* 59 (2002) 206–25.

Williams, Victor H. *Judges and Ruth.* Cambridge: Cambridge University Press, 2004.

Willis, John T. *Isaiah.* The Living Word Commentary on the Old Testament 12. Austin: Sweet, 1980.

Witherington, Ben, III. *The Acts of the Apostles: A Socio-Rhetorical Commentary*. Grand Rapids: Eerdmans, 1998.

———. *The Gospel of Mark: A Socio-Rhetorical Commentary*. Grand Rapids: Eerdmans, 2001.

Woods, Edward J. *The "Finger of God" and Pneumatology in Luke–Acts*. Journal for the Study of the New Testament Supplement Series 205. Sheffield, England: Sheffield Academic, 2001.

Wright, N. T. *The Crown and the Cross: Meditations on the Cross and the Life of the Spirit*. Grand Rapids: Eerdmans, 1992.

———. *The New Testament and the People of God*. Minneapolis: Fortress, 1992.

———. *The Resurrection of the Son of God*. Minneapolis: Fortress, 2003.

Yarnell, Malcolm B. *God the Trinity: Biblical Portraits*. Nashville: B & H Academic, 2016.

Yates, J. E. "Luke's Pneumatology and Lk. 11, 20." In *Studia Evangelica*. Vol. 2, *Papers Presented to the Second International Congress on New Testament Studies Held at Christ Church, Oxford, 1961. Part 1: The New Testament Scriptures*, edited by F. L. Cross, 295–99. Berlin: Akademie–Verlag, 1964.

———. *The Spirit and the Kingdom*. London: SPCK, 1963.

Yinger, Kent L. *Paul, Judaism, and Judgment According to Deeds*. Society for New Testament Studies Monograph Series 105. Cambridge: Cambridge University Press, 1999.

Young, Edward J. *The Book of Isaiah: The English Text, with Introduction, Exposition, and Notes*. 3 vols. The New International Commentary on the Old Testament. Grand Rapids: Eerdmans, 1965–1972.

Zenger, Erich. *A God of Vengeance?: Understanding the Psalms of Divine Wrath*. 1st ed. Louisville: Westminster John Knox, 1996.

Zimmerli, Walther. *Ezekiel: A Commentary on the Book of the Prophet Ezekiel*. Vol. 1, *Chapters 1–24*. Translated by James D. Martin. Hermeneia—a Critical and Historical Commentary on the Bible. Philadelphia: Fortress, 1979.

———. *Ezekiel: A Commentary on the Book of the Prophet Ezekiel*. Vol. 2, *Chapters 25–48*. Translated by James D. Martin. Hermeneia—a Critical and Historical Commentary on the Bible. Philadelphia: Fortress, 1983.